THE EVERYTHING® CROSSWORD & PUZZLE BOOK VOLUME II

Dear Reader,

To me, solving a puzzle is like reading a good story. At the core is a conflict that grabs our attention and needs to be resolved. In the beginning, everything is in chaos as we try to understand what is going on. In the middle, the plot unfolds and we start to figure out how the problem can be tackled. As we sprint to the finish line, the satisfying "aha!" moments wash over us. By the end, chaos has once more been turned into order!

Like the best stories, puzzles can transport us away from the real world. Everything is logical (or nearly so) in the perfect world of puzzles, where creative intelligence rules. When we return to reality, we're hopefully a little more relaxed with a brain that is perhaps a bit sharper.

Every story has a character, and in these puzzles you get to play the hero. That's what I love about puzzles; they demand our active participation. Have fun!

Charles Timmerman

Welcome to the EVERYTHING® Series!

These handy, accessible books give you all you need to tackle a difficult project, gain a new hobby, comprehend a fascinating topic, prepare for an exam, or even brush up on something you learned back in school but have since forgotten.

You can choose to read an *Everything*® book from cover to cover or just pick out the information you want from our four useful boxes: e-questions, e-facts, e-alerts, and e-ssentials. We give you everything you need to know on the subject, but throw in a lot of fun stuff along the way, too.

We now have more than 400 *Everything*® books in print, spanning such wide-ranging categories as weddings, pregnancy, cooking, music instruction, foreign language, crafts, pets, New Age, and so much more. When you're done reading them all, you can finally say you know *Everything*®!

PUBLISHER Karen Cooper

DIRECTOR OF ACQUISITIONS AND INNOVATION Paula Munier

MANAGING EDITOR, EVERYTHING® SERIES Lisa Laing

COPY CHIEF Casey Ebert

ACQUISITIONS EDITOR Lisa Laing

EDITORIAL ASSISTANT Hillary Thompson

EVERYTHING® SERIES COVER DESIGNER Erin Alexander

LAYOUT DESIGNERS Colleen Cunningham, Elisabeth Lariviere, Ashley Vierra, Denise Wallace

THE EVERYTHING® CROSSWORD & PUZZLE BOOK VOLUME II

More than 350 mind-boggling puzzles
for endless gaming fun!

Charles Timmerman
Founder of Funster.com

Adams Media
New York London Toronto Sydney New Delhi

Dedicated to Suzanne and Calla.

An Everything® Series Book.
Everything® and everything.com® are registered trademarks of Simon & Schuster, Inc.

Published by Adams Media, an imprint of Simon & Schuster, Inc.
100 Technology Center Drive, Stoughton, MA 02072 U.S.A.
www.adamsmedia.com

ISBN 10: 1-60550-047-X
ISBN 13: 978-1-60550-047-8

Printed in the United States of America.

J I H G F E D C B A

Contents

Introduction / xi

Chapter 1: Quotagrams / 1

Chapter 2: Dropouts / 19

Chapter 3: Fill-ins / 37

Chapter 4: Groupies / 55

Chapter 5: Word Search / 73

Chapter 6: Lost and Found / 91

Chapter 7: Providers / 109

Chapter 8: Words Within Words / 127

Chapter 9: Crosswords / 141

Chapter 10: Diagramless / 159

Chapter 11: Double Scrambles / 177

Chapter 12: Sudoku / 191

Chapter 13: Cryptoquotes / 209

Answers / 225

THE EVERYTHING® CROSSWORD & PUZZLE BOOK

VOLUME II

Acknowledgments

I would like to thank each and every one of the more than half a million people who have visited my website, *www.funster.com*, to play word games and puzzles. You have shown me how much fun word puzzles can be, and how addictive they can become!

For her expert help and guidance over the years, I owe a huge debt of gratitude to my agent Jacky Sach.

It is a pleasure to acknowledge the folks at Adams Media who made this book possible. I particularly want to thank my editor Lisa Laing for so skillfully managing the many projects we have worked on together.

Introduction

PEOPLE HAVE BEEN AMUSING themselves with puzzles since probably before recorded history. We enjoy puzzles because they are a form of play. And as every child instinctively knows, play is important business. It provides a way to experiment and explore our world in a safe environment. Puzzles let us play again, and that is something we too often leave behind as we grow older.

Playing with words must have started shortly after language itself was developed. Riddles are perhaps the oldest type of word puzzle and found in nearly every culture throughout history. They were important in religion and philosophy as a means for sages to express their wisdom and to test others. Here is a riddle that, according to Greek legend, was posed by the Sphinx to Oedipus: "What walks on four legs in the morning, two legs at noon, and three in the evening?" Oedipus correctly answered (metaphorically), "A man who crawls as a child, walks upright in his prime, and uses a cane in old age." This bit of ingenuity saved Oedipus's life and he went on to become king of Thebes. Such is the power of word play!

Shortly after humans started writing, they started using secret codes. Julius Caesar devised a simple code where he moved each letter three places up in the alphabet, so A became D, B became E, etc. Evidently this was effective for Caesar, but the cryptoquotes in this book will present more of a challenge. One of the first uses of cryptograms for amusement purposes was in the Middle Ages by monks who had enough spare time for such intellectual frivolity.

Palindromes are another form of ancient word trickery. Palindromes are words that read the same backward or forward. Famous examples include "Madam, in Eden I'm Adam" and "A man, a plan, a canal—Panama!" Reportedly, palindromes were once considered magical because it was believed that the devil could not tamper with them due to the confusing repetition of letters.

Acrostics are a kind of word play that has been popular since before the time of Christ. In an acrostic the first letters of each line spells out another message, a word two-for-one. The Bible has a type of acrostic in which each stanza begins with the next letter in the Hebrew alphabet. With letters running both across and down, some say that acrostics were a precursor to crossword puzzles.

The crossword puzzle is a relatively recent invention. The first one was put together in 1913 by Arthur Wynne, who created a "word-cross" puzzle for the *New York World* newspaper. Though it was diamond shaped, it had all the features of crossword puzzles that we know and love today. His diamond included the entries "FUN" and "HARD" (for the clue "What this puzzle is"); an accurate response from crossword solvers then and now!

Sudoku is the newest phenomenon in the puzzle world and vies with crosswords for popularity. Invented by an Indianapolis architect named Howard Garns, sudoku was originally called Number Place. It first appeared in 1979 in *Dell Pencil Puzzles and Word Games*. The puzzle became a hit in Japan, where it was named sudoku (which means "only single numbers allowed"). Sudoku didn't explode in popularity until late 2004, when a London newspaper started carrying the puzzle. By 2005 the sudoku frenzy quickly spread to nearly all parts of the globe, including back home to the United States.

The material in this book builds on this rich history of puzzles. You will find familiar friends like crosswords, word search, and cryptoquotes. There are also new faces like sudoku, quotagrams, and dropouts. Some of the puzzles, like groupies, lost and found, and diagramless, are variations of other puzzles. Though you may have a favorite type of puzzle, this book will provide you with a healthy smorgasbord of challenges.

Chapter 1
Quotagrams

Answer the clues and then put the letters into the corresponding parts of the grid. Some clues might have multiple word answers. Work back and forth between the clues and the grid until you figure out the quote in the grid.

Robert Frost

A. Sundial indicator

38 32 103 54 16 74

B. Assets minus liabilities

45 37 109 31 82 69 88 63

C. Snow remover tool

49 67 23 79 30 72

D. Ship-to-shore board

87 35 53 46 99 29 93 57 96

E. Parka feature

84 89 100 12

F. Kitschy lawn figure

73 3 50 40 85 60 107 27

G. Biker's protection

77 41 11 17 64 83

H. Swap

66 10 91 22 97

I. Nutty ice cream flavor

18 44 90 62 78 55 43 105 33

J. Cheesy Mexican snacks

106 52 15 75 65 102

K. Bee product

70 76 81 98 104

L. Believer's confidence

24 56 108 58 34

M. Skull-and-crossbones substance

28 48 13 20 39 86

N. Pizzeria fixture

19 36 21 94

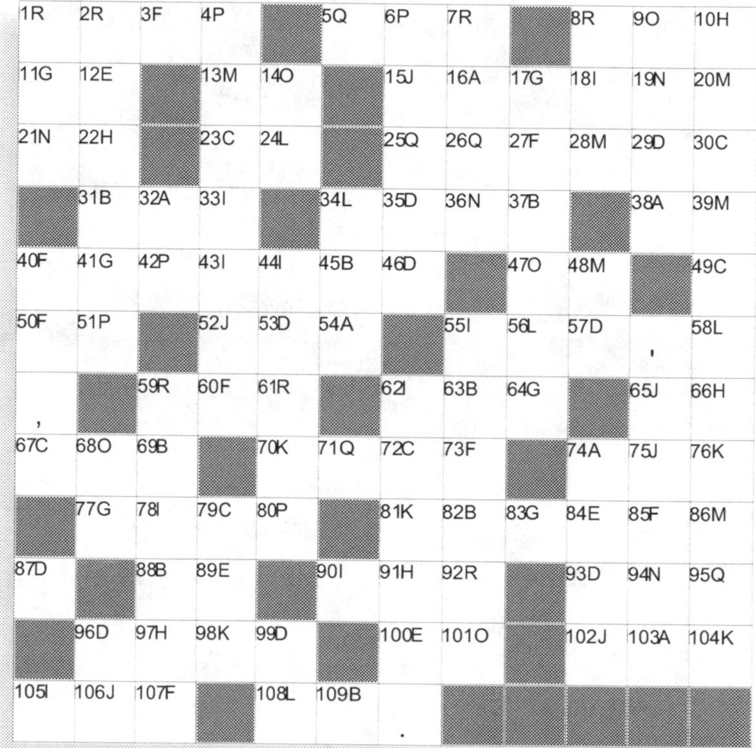

1R	2R	3F	4P		5Q	6P	7R		8R	9O	10H
11G	12E		13M	14O		15J	16A	17G	18I	19N	20M
21N	22H		23C	24L		25Q	26Q	27F	28M	29D	30C
	31B	32A	33I		34L	35D	36N	37B		38A	39M
40F	41G	42P	43I	44I	45B	46D		47O	48M		49C
50F	51P		52J	53D	54A		55I	56L	57D	'	58L
,		59R	60F	61R		62I	63B	64G		65J	66H
67C	68O	69B		70K	71Q	72C	73F		74A	75J	76K
	77G	78I	79C	80P		81K	82B	83G	84E	85F	86M
87D		88B	89E		90I	91H	92R		93D	94N	95Q
	96D	97H	98K	99D		100E	101O		102J	103A	104K
105I	106J	107F		108L	109B	.					

O. Rock

14 47 9 101 68

P. Whopping

6 80 4 42 51

Q. Recorded

5 71 25 26 95

R. Progress

1 7 59 61 8 2 92

Solution on page 226

Dwight Eisenhower

1R	2P	3Q	4G	5K	6P	■	7N	8B	9M	10N	11J
■	12K	13R	14A	■	15B	16P	17O	18R	19R	20H	21P
■	22B	23A	■	24J	25O	26M	27K	28I	29Q	30F	31E
32G	,	■	33F	34A	35G	36Q	■	37Q	38A	39L	40L
41R	42A	43D	,	■	44J	45A	46R	47K	48G	49I	50P
51I	,	■	52E	53A	54M	55H	56R	57N	58N	59G	60B
61F	62L	63K	64Q	■	65D	66R	67G	■	68D	69O	70M
71I	72A	73H	74G	75B	76M	77H	78L	■	79C	80E	81J
■	82F	83H	84E	85I	86J	87O	88K	■	89F	90C	91J
92Q	■	93D	94C	95D	■	96H	97D	■	98L	99H	100F
■	101L	102L	103J	104B	■	105I	106C	■	107E	108I	109K
110D	111C	112N	113E	■	114M	115M	116P	117B	118Q	.	■

A. Proclaim

45 34 14 53 38 23 42 72

B. Bonneville maker

15 8 104 75 22 60 117

C. Yard enclosure

106 90 111 79 94

D. Love story

110 97 93 65 95 68 43

E. Call off

31 80 84 52 107 113

F. Nonstick coating

61 100 82 89 33 30

G. Wash room

35 74 4 48 67 59 32

H. Emu's large cousin

77 55 96 73 83 20 99

I. Mail fee

71 105 51 108 85 28 49

J. Turn over a ___ ___

81 24 103 86 11 91 44

K. Food store

5 47 63 12 109 27 88

L. Far removed

101 62 39 98 102 78 40

M. Trailblazer

114 76 70 54 115 26 9

N. Joltless joe

57 58 10 112 7

O. Weaving machine

87 69 17 25

P. Defeat thoroughly, whip

21 6 16 116 50 2

Q. Received pleasure from

118 64 37 3 36 29 92

R. Kick off

56 66 46 18 41 13 1 19

Solution on page 226

Steve Martin

A. Big Bird's street

19 8 93 36 9 100

B. Hardliners for war

77 97 73 80 40

C. Whitish cloudy appearance

51 21 96 49 10

D. Cue

4 48 29 28 69 47

E. Dog treat

56 27 68 58 105 78 85

F. Kleenex

13 102 32 37 60 94

G. Harbor helper

84 18 34 14 75 59 45

H. Poor loser's reaction

81 31 83 66 70 26 53 82 65 38

I. "Balderdash!"

87 92 79 98 67 30 46 24

J. Motionless

61 55 86 35 44

K. Europe's "boot"

6 76 11 5 108

L. Nairobi's nation

7 39 90 72 41

M. Moolah

42 89 43 88 74

N. Moved like a pendulum

99 23 71 91 95

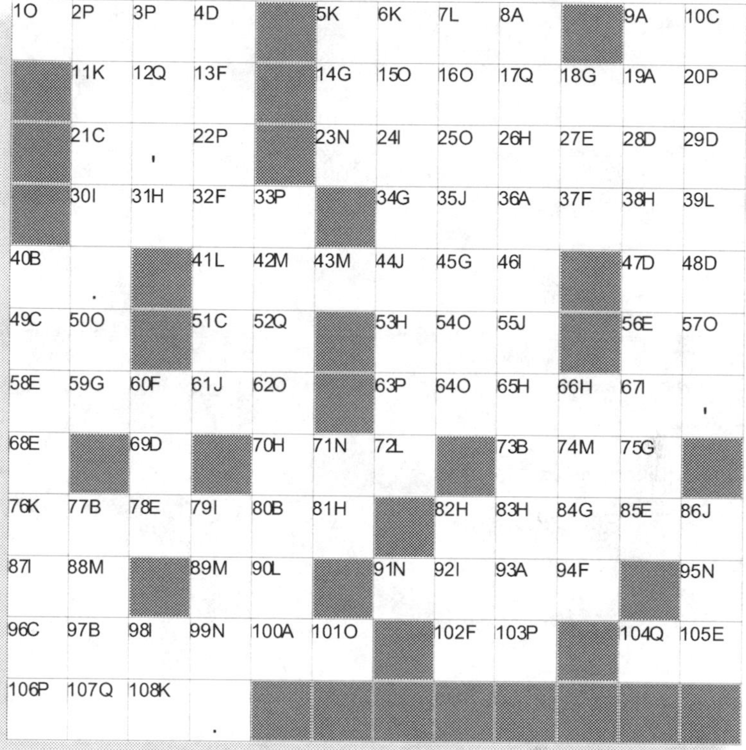

1O	2P	3P	4D		5K	6K	7L	8A		9A	10C
	11K	12Q	13F		14G	15O	16O	17Q	18G	19A	20P
	21C	'	22P		23N	24I	25O	26H	27E	28D	29D
	30I	31H	32F	33P		34G	35J	36A	37F	38H	39L
40B	.		41L	42M	43M	44J	45G	46I		47D	48D
49C	50O		51C	52Q		53H	54O	55J		56E	57O
58E	59G	60F	61J	62O		63P	64O	65H	66H	67I	'
68E		69D		70H	71N	72L		73B	74M	75G	
76K	77B	78E	79I	80B	81H		82H	83H	84G	85E	86J
87I	88M		89M	90L		91N	92I	93A	94F		95N
96C	97B	98I	99N	100A	101O		102F	103P		104Q	105E
106P	107Q	108K	.								

O. Rich dessert

54 64 15 50 101 62 16 25 1 57

P. Dregs

103 20 3 2 22 33 106 63

Q. Imagination that may be tickled

104 17 107 12 52

Solution on page 226

Albert Camus

1R	2T	3Q		4T	5Q	6T	7S		8Q	9P	10K
11S	12L		13R	14R		15T	16O	17F	18P	19B	
20D	21N		22J	23S	24I		25L	26J	27P	28G	29F
30P	31G	32M		33R	34A		35K	36Q	37T	38T	39E
40O		41D	42B	43J		44F	45F	46S	47S		48B
49S	50C	51L	52H	53A	54I	55Q	56R		57E	58B	59D
60K	61A	62I	63J	64G		65M	66G			67I	68F
69N		70H	71A	72N	73O		74E	75C	76A	77H	78C
	79Q	80L	81H	82K		83M	84G		85P	86E	87J
	88K	89I	90D		91A	92F	93E	94D	95M	96I	97K
	98N	99E	100I		101Q	102B	103L		104S	105M	106K
107L	108O	109O	110J		111B	112N		113K	114C	115S	116O

A. String instrument

___ ___ ___ ___ ___ ___
76 61 34 91 71 53

B. "___ and a bottle of rum"

___ ___ ___ ___ ___ ___
19 42 102 111 48 58

C. Ready for picking

___ ___ ___ ___
78 114 50 75

D. Bowie's weapon

___ ___ ___ ___ ___
94 59 20 41 90

E. Caterpillar's place

___ ___ ___ ___ ___ ___
57 86 39 99 93 74

F. Actress Goldberg

___ ___ ___ ___ ___ ___
44 45 92 68 17 29

G. Things

___ ___ ___ ___ ___
64 28 31 66 84

H. Vista

___ ___ ___ ___
81 52 77 70

I. Baby's room

___ ___ ___ ___ ___ ___ ___
96 24 100 62 54 89 67

J. Dannon product

___ ___ ___ ___ ___ ___
22 26 110 87 43 63

K. Casino city

___ ___ ___ ___ ___ ___ ___ ___
113 106 35 10 82 97 88 60

L. Royal son

___ ___ ___ ___ ___ ___
51 12 80 107 25 103

M. "Old MacDonald" refrain

___ ___ ___ ___ ___
32 83 105 95 65

N. Light down or fuzz

___ ___ ___ ___ ___
98 72 69 21 112

O. Fill the lungs

___ ___ ___ ___ ___ ___
108 109 40 16 73 116

P. Small change

___ ___ ___ ___ ___
18 9 30 27 85

Q. Fork, spoon, or knife

___ ___ ___ ___ ___ ___ ___
3 101 36 8 55 5 79

R. "Heavens to ___!"

___ ___ ___ ___ ___
13 14 33 56 1

S. Pop singer named for an entree

___ ___ ___ ___ ___ ___ ___ ___
104 11 46 47 7 23 49 115

T. Soup can painter

___ ___ ___ ___ ___ ___
4 37 38 15 2 6

Solution on page 226

Stanley Kubrick

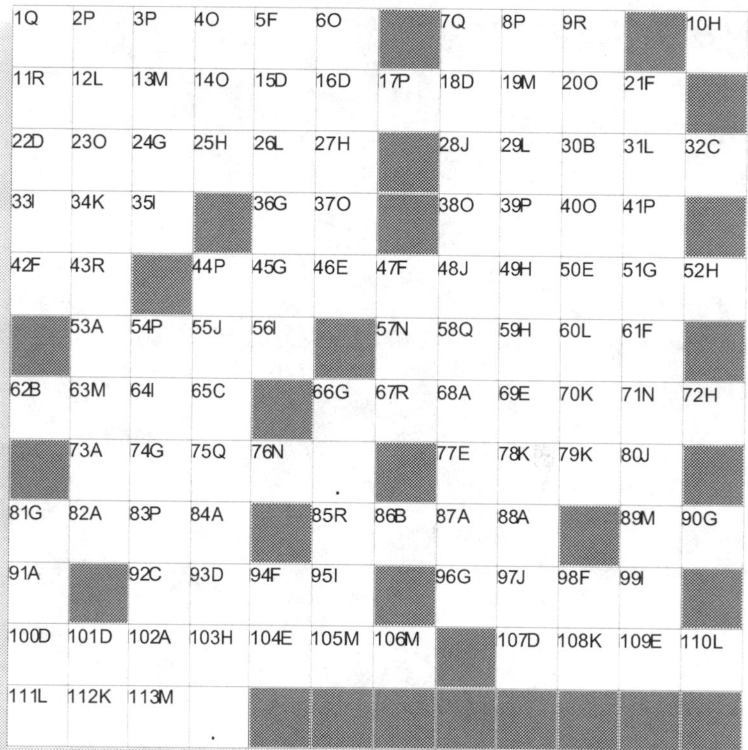

1Q	2P	3P	4O	5F	6O		7Q	8P	9R		10H
11R	12L	13M	14O	15D	16D	17P	18D	19M	20O	21F	
22D	23O	24G	25H	26L	27H		28J	29L	30B	31L	32C
33I	34K	35I		36G	37O		38O	39P	40O	41P	
42F	43R		44P	45G	46E	47F	48J	49H	50E	51G	52H
	53A	54P	55J	56I		57N	58Q	59H	60L	61F	
62B	63M	64I	65C		66G	67R	68A	69E	70K	71N	72H
	73A	74G	75Q	76N			77E	78K	79K	80J	
81G	82A	83P	84A		85R	86B	87A	88A		89M	90G
91A		92C	93D	94F	95I		96G	97J	98F	99I	
100D	101D	102A	103H	104E	105M	106M		107D	108K	109E	110L
111L	112K	113M									

A. Bait shop crawler

84 82 68 91 73 53 87 102 88

B. Give it a shot

62 86 30

C. "___ me?"

92 32 65

D. A to Z

22 101 18 93 100 107 16 15

E. Particular bit of info

50 69 77 104 46 109

F. Soup cracker

61 94 5 21 42 47 98

G. Cruise quarters

36 81 66 96 51 90 74 45 24

H. California national park

72 25 52 59 10 49 27 103

I. Fourscore

64 33 35 56 95 99

J. Pleasure boat

80 28 48 97 55

K. Paradise

78 79 70 112 108 34

L. Testimony giver

60 110 31 29 111 26 12

M. Rural wagon outing

63 89 106 19 13 105 113

N. Netflix mailing

76 57 71

O. Oryx, bushbuck, or addax

40 14 38 20 23 37 4 6

P. Salad heart ingredient

8 17 41 54 44 39 3 83 2

Q. Paper holder

7 75 58 1

R. Fire igniter

85 67 11 9 43

Solution on pages 226–227

Mary Calderone

1M	■	2N	3R	4J	5H	6Q	■	7D	8L	9R	10Q
■	11Q	12R	13D	14Q	■	15M	16Q	17Q	18I	19Q	■
20E	21O	22N	■	23R	24A	■	25L	26Q	27O	28G	■
29F	30P	31H	32R	■	33B	34G	■	35A	36F	37O	38A
39L	40A	■	41A	42F	■	43K	44D	45C	46D	47D	■
48G	49N	50I	■	51E	52I	53B	54Q	55P	56L	■	57G
58A	■	59B	60B	61E	■	62H	63A	64M	65L	66C	■
67L	68E	69E	■	70K	71E	■	72D	73F	74A	75L	76H
■	77E	78G	79J	■	80P	81E	82L	83J	■	84I	85P
■	86L	87I	88K	■	89H	90C	91C	92L	■	93H	94I
■	95B	96J	97J	98K	99N	■	100K	101O	102R	103M	104C
105O	.	■	■	■	■	■	■	■	■	■	■

A. It's burned on the road

40 41 24 63 35 38 58 74

B. Kind of fairy

59 53 33 95 60

C. Pasture

91 90 45 104 66

D. Sire

7 13 72 44 47 46

E. Rose Bowl city

51 20 71 81 69 61 68 77

F. Broadway offering

42 73 36 29

G. Wand wielder

34 48 57 78 28

H. Coward's color

31 76 5 89 93 62

I. Young cow

87 50 84 94 52 18

J. Senate's counterpart

96 97 4 83 79

K. Kindergarten adhesive

100 70 98 43 88

L. Basic

8 65 56 25 92 39 86 67 75 82

M. Stumble

15 64 1 103

N. Genealogy chart

2 49 99 22

O. At no time

27 101 37 105 21

P. Touch down

55 30 85 80

Q. Mind reading

14 19 10 17 54 26 11 16 6

R. Raspy

12 102 23 3 32 9

Solution on page 227

Barbara De Angelis

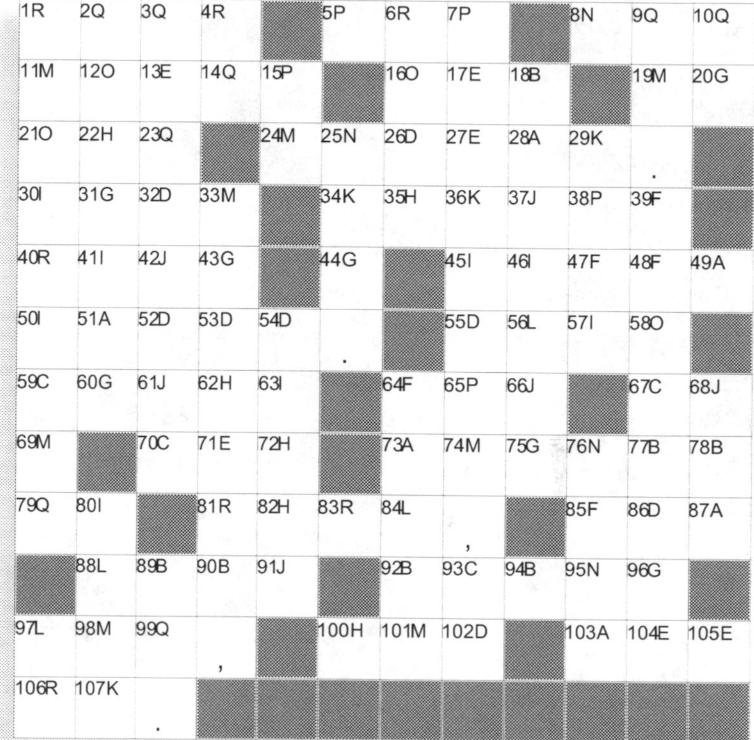

1R	2Q	3Q	4R		5P	6R	7P		8N	9Q	10Q
11M	12O	13E	14Q	15P		16O	17E	18B		19M	20G
21O	22H	23Q		24M	25N	26D	27E	28A	29K	.	
30I	31G	32D	33M		34K	35H	36K	37J	38P	39F	
40R	41I	42J	43G		44G		45I	46I	47F	48F	49A
50I	51A	52D	53D	54D	.		55D	56L	57I	58O	
59C	60G	61J	62H	63I		64F	65P	66J		67C	68J
69M		70C	71E	72H		73A	74M	75G	76N	77B	78B
79Q	80I		81R	82H	83R	84L	,		85F	86D	87A
	88L	89B	90B	91J		92B	93C	94B	95N	96G	
97L	98M	99Q	,		100H	101M	102D		103A	104E	105E
106R	107K	.									

A. University conferral

___ ___ ___ ___ ___ ___
87 49 103 73 51 28

B. Big hairdo

___ ___ ___ ___ ___ ___ ___
92 18 90 89 77 78 94

C. New Year's Day game

___ ___ ___ ___
59 67 70 93

D. Court judgment

___ ___ ___ ___ ___ ___ ___ ___
26 102 86 55 32 52 53 54

E. Prosper

___ ___ ___ ___ ___ ___
27 71 17 104 105 13

F. Personnel

___ ___ ___ ___ ___
39 64 85 47 48

G. First daughter of the '90s

___ ___ ___ ___ ___ ___ ___
75 31 20 60 96 43 44

H. Inexpensive inn

___ ___ ___ ___ ___ ___
82 72 62 100 22 35

I. Catastrophe

___ ___ ___ ___ ___ ___ ___ ___
45 46 63 41 80 30 57 50

J. Confederate enemy

___ ___ ___ ___ ___ ___
91 37 68 42 61 66

K. Sketch

___ ___ ___ ___
29 107 34 36

L. Legendary story

___ ___ ___ ___
84 97 88 56

M. Winter melon

___ ___ ___ ___ ___ ___ ___ ___
101 98 19 69 33 11 74 24

N. Rice wine

___ ___ ___ ___
95 25 8 76

O. Dark blue

___ ___ ___ ___
12 16 21 58

P. Disreputable

___ ___ ___ ___ ___
15 65 5 7 38

Q. Keepsake

___ ___ ___ ___ ___ ___ ___ ___
14 2 99 3 79 10 9 23

R. Periodic table item

___ ___ ___ ___ ___ ___ ___
106 1 83 40 4 6 81

Solution on page 227

Austin Dacey

1K	2S	3S	4N		5F	6L	7I		8A	9F	10B
11Q	12H	13A	14J	15O	16I	.		17R	18F	19E	20G
	21H	22Q	23A	24B		25A	26E	27A		28E	29S
30H	31B		32S	33C	34J	35D	36E	37B		38C	39Q
40G	41R	42I	43K	.		44H	45J	46M		47N	48Q
	49M	50L		51G	52M	53N	54D		55O	56B	57C
58F	59M	60N		61C	62N	63E	64P		65L	66C	67C
68D		69Q	70B	71D		72F	73L	74I	75S	76J	
77D	78I	79K	80P	81C	82G		83G	84M		85B	86G
87C	88E	89F	90B	91I		92G	93K	94R		95K	96A
97L	98O	99B		100F	101P	102D		103H	104H		105A
106P	107G	108J	109M	110R	111R	.					

A. Nonbeliever

25 13 96 27 8 105 23

B. Infield position

24 99 90 56 37 85 31 70 10

C. Follow too closely

38 57 33 67 81 87 61 66

D. Snapper, perhaps

102 71 54 77 68 35

E. Bewhiskered marine creature

28 63 88 26 19 36

F. "I Write the Songs" singer

9 5 100 58 89 18 72

G. Steps to the next floor

82 83 92 40 20 86 107 51

H. "Casablanca" star

44 104 21 30 12 103

I. Scale reading

91 7 74 42 78 16

J. Yuk it up

108 14 45 34 76

K. Big Band music

43 95 79 93 1

L. Polo or tee

50 73 97 6 65

M. Skin moisturizer

109 84 46 49 52 59

N. Japanese dish

60 53 4 62 47

O. Peacock network

15 55 98

P. Burg or hamlet

64 101 106 80

Q. One's early years

69 11 22 48 39

R. Feathery and soft, as fabric

94 110 111 41 17

S. Amsterdam natives

32 2 3 75 29

Solution on page 227

Mahatma Gandhi

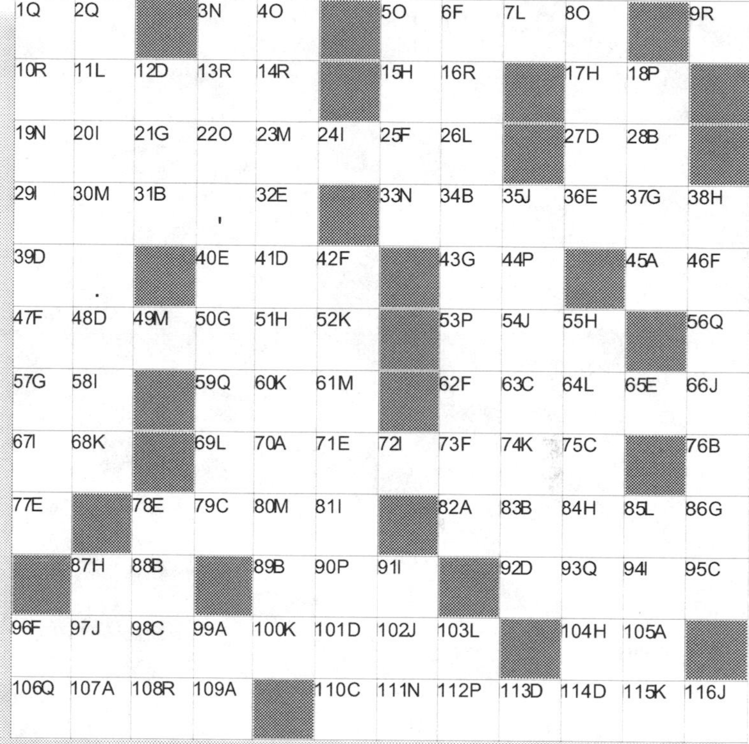

1Q	2Q		3N	4O		5O	6F	7L	8O		9R
10R	11L	12D	13R	14R		15H	16R		17H	18P	
19N	20I	21G	22O	23M	24I	25F	26L		27D	28B	
29I	30M	31B		32E		33N	34B	35J	36E	37G	38H
39D			40E	41D	42F		43G	44P		45A	46F
47F	48D	49M	50G	51H	52K		53P	54J	55H		56Q
57G	58I		59Q	60K	61M		62F	63C	64L	65E	66J
67I	68K		69L	70A	71E	72I	73F	74K	75C		76B
77E		78E	79C	80M	81I		82A	83B	84H	85L	86G
	87H	88B		89B	90P	91I		92D	93Q	94I	95C
96F	97J	98C	99A	100K	101D	102J	103L		104H	105A	
106Q	107A	108R	109A		110C	111N	112P	113D	114D	115K	116J

A. Flying toy disk

105 107 70 99 45 82 109

B. Benedict Arnold's crime

89 34 31 76 88 28 83

C. San Joaquin Valley town

75 110 63 98 95 79

D. Water pistol

39 92 12 113 48 27 114 41 101

E. Diplomat's post

36 71 40 65 32 77 78

F. Mail to a star

47 6 117 25 46 96 42 73 62

G. Right-angle degrees

57 21 37 50 43 86

H. Following orders

104 17 84 38 87 55 51 15

I. Fries or slaw

72 94 24 58 29 81 67 91 20

J. Valiant

54 97 66 116 35 102

K. Police officer's badge

68 60 115 100 74 52

L. Sneaker

64 26 85 7 69 11 103

M. Confederacy's foe

80 30 49 61 23

N. Colonial drum partner

33 3 19 111

O. Baby blues

5 8 22 4

P. Monopoly purchase

90 44 53 18 112

Q. Get the better of

56 93 106 59 1 2

R. "Stop!"

9 10 16 108 13 14

Solution on page 227

Martin Luther King Jr.

1A	2L	3J	■	4Q	5O	6L	7O	8M	9G	10Q	11B
■	12M	13C	14N	15Q	16J	17N	18K	■	19B	20H	■
21O	■	22L	23P	24A	■	25E	26O	■	27F	28P	29Q
■	30I	31B	32M	33A	34Q	■	35F	36P	■	37F	38O
39M	40Q	41M	42J	■	43O	44P	■	45I	46I	47E	48O
49J	50I	51B	■	52O	53H	■	54C	55L	56D	57G	58L
59I	60B	,	■	61P	62D	63J	■	64G	65H	66G	67O
68N	■	69J	70M	■	71P	72K	73D	74M	75Q	76B	■
77F	78H	■	79M	80H	81C	82A	83B	■	84I	85E	■
86J	87D	88C	89E	90G	91F	92D	93A	94A	■	95A	96M
97G	■	98N	99I	100K	101J	102C	103K	104F	105A	106I	107L
108P	.	■	■	■	■	■	■	■	■	■	■

A. Adolescent

1 105 82 24 95 93 94 33

B. Party person

31 19 83 60 11 51 76

C. Coffee lightener

54 102 13 88 81

D. Earthling

87 62 56 73 92

E. Flick

85 25 89 47

F. Without a beard

37 35 77 104 91 27

G. Defective

57 90 9 64 66 97

H. Liquor quantity

20 80 53 78 65

I. It's another day

50 84 45 99 106 59 46 30

J. Christmas roaster

86 69 3 42 63 49 16 101

K. Memo

100 103 72 18

L. Peanut butter choice

107 22 58 55 6 2

M. Constitution change

39 12 70 74 41 8 32 96 79

N. Give a hoot

98 14 17 68

O. Game for one

26 52 5 43 38 21 7 67 48

P. Protein source

71 28 108 61 36 23 44

Q. Pupil

15 29 4 75 34 40 10

Solution on page 228

Mark Twain

A. Language of China

___ ___ ___ ___ ___ ___ ___ ___
100 96 64 107 99 85 94 110

B. Bronze medalist's place

___ ___ ___ ___ ___
113 90 86 88 111

C. Largest city in Iowa

___ ___ ___ ___ ___ ___ ___ ___ ___
67 68 79 51 69 43 49 106 95

D. Corridor

___ ___ ___ ___
72 40 77 76

E. Use a loom

___ ___ ___ ___ ___
6 24 101 11 81

F. Take to court

___ ___ ___
47 75 91

G. Mr. Fixit

___ ___ ___ ___ ___ ___ ___ ___ ___
92 78 52 102 46 114 105 109 44

H. Metropolis

___ ___ ___ ___
103 50 16 108

I. Large

___ ___ ___
57 66 116

J. Nitrous ___ (laughing gas)

___ ___ ___ ___ ___
104 82 56 74 10

K. Doohickey

___ ___ ___ ___ ___ ___
45 112 97 31 26 23

L. Yell

___ ___ ___ ___ ___
65 39 53 37 61

M. Pester

___ ___ ___ ___ ___
48 30 22 87 119

N. Nun

___ ___ ___ ___ ___ ___
55 21 36 28 35 98

O. Fill with air

___ ___ ___ ___ ___ ___ ___
63 20 70 32 115 41 73

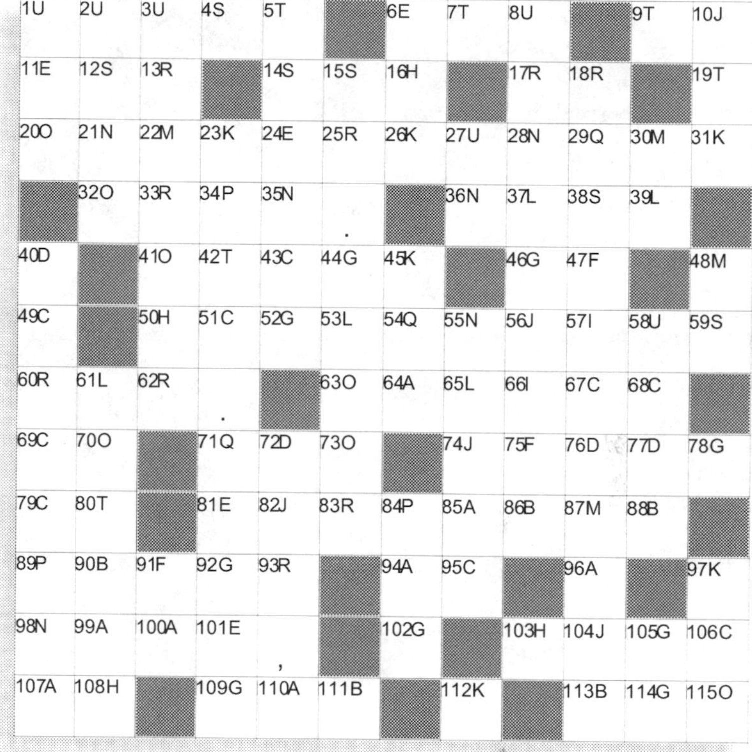

1U	2U	3U	4S	5T		6E	7T	8U		9T	10J
11E	12S	13R		14S	15S	16H		17R	18R		19T
20O	21N	22M	23K	24E	25R	26K	27U	28N	29Q	30M	31K
	32O	33R	34P	35N	.		36N	37L	38S	39L	
40D		41O	42T	43C	44G	45K		46G	47F		48M
49C		50H	51C	52G	53L	54Q	55N	56J	57I	58U	59S
60R	61L	62R	.		63O	64A	65L	66I	67C	68C	
69C	70O		71Q	72D	73O		74J	75F	76D	77D	78G
79C	80T		81E	82J	83R	84P	85A	86B	87M	88B	
89P	90B	91F	92G	93R		94A	95C		96A		97K
98N	99A	100A	101E	,		102G		103H	104J	105G	106C
107A	108H		109G	110A	111B		112K		113B	114G	115O

P. They hit the ground running

___ ___ ___ ___
34 84 117 89

Q. "___ the season . . ."

___ ___ ___
71 29 54

R. Traveler's outline

___ ___ ___ ___ ___ ___ ___ ___ ___
33 83 60 18 93 13 17 25 62

S. Bloody Mary stalk

___ ___ ___ ___ ___ ___
38 15 59 12 4 14

T. Inhabited by a ghost

___ ___ ___ ___ ___ ___ ___
42 7 19 9 80 5 118

U. Grad student's dissertation

___ ___ ___ ___ ___ ___
1 2 3 27 58 8

Solution on page 228

Amy Bloom

1O	2O	3N	4L		5J	6C		7R	8R	9L	10Q
11P		12O	13O	14D	15H	16L		17N	18L		19G
20P	21J	22J		23A	24A		25B	26P	27C	28J	29L
30H	31I	32P	33P	34K	;		35M	36M	'	37F	
38Q	39C	40N	41P		42O	43F	44E		45O	46P	47E
48A	49B	50R		51O	52B	53I	54Q		55F	56Q	57M
58M		59I	60F	61C	62G	63A	64D	65B		66D	67G
	68C	69D	70L	71R		72I	73L	74E	75I	76A	
77A	78N	79F		80I		81G	82K	83H	84I	85M	86G
87C	88F		89K	90B	91G	92Q		93K	94R		95G
96L	97G	98K	99M	100H	101E		102L		103N	104D	105I
106O	107E	108H	109E	.							

A. Business person's motive

48 76 24 77 63 23

B. Joke reaction

49 52 25 65 90

C. Acting technique

87 68 6 39 61 27

D. Once more

66 14 69 104 64

E. Pick

107 74 44 47 101 109

F. Look without purchasing

55 79 60 43 37 88

G. Semiformal evening wear

95 81 91 97 62 67 86 19

H. Place for books

30 15 100 108 83

I. Lift between floors

75 59 84 53 80 31 72 105

J. Simple

28 5 21 22

K. Fool

82 34 93 98 89

L. San Francisco transport

18 73 29 4 96 16 70 102 9

M. Hand warmer

99 35 85 36 57 58

N. Flick

103 78 3 17 40

O. Medical site

51 2 12 45 13 42 106 1

P. Reception aid

32 26 11 46 41 33 20

Q. Sugary

10 38 56 54 92

R. Pickpocket

94 71 8 50 7

Solution on page 228

Carl Jung

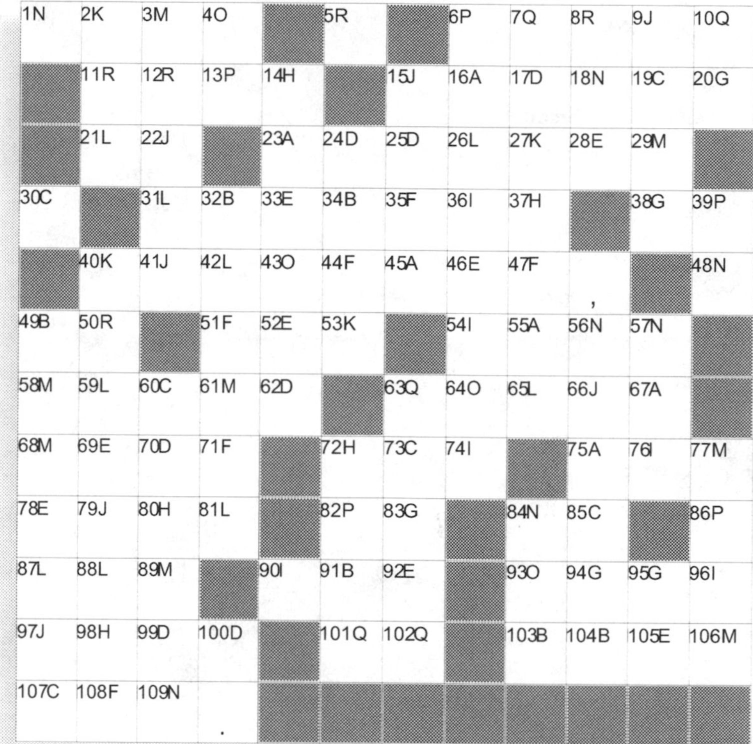

1N	2K	3M	4O	■	5R	■	6P	7Q	8R	9J	10Q
■	11R	12R	13P	14H	■	15J	16A	17D	18N	19C	20G
■	21L	22J	■	23A	24D	25D	26L	27K	28E	29M	■
30C	■	31L	32B	33E	34B	35F	36I	37H	■	38G	39P
■	40K	41J	42L	43O	44F	45A	46E	47F	,	■	48N
49B	50R	■	51F	52E	53K	■	54I	55A	56N	57N	■
58M	59L	60C	61M	62D	■	63Q	64O	65L	66J	67A	■
68M	69E	70D	71F	■	72H	73C	74I	■	75A	76I	77M
78E	79J	80H	81L	■	82P	83G	■	84N	85C	■	86P
87L	88L	89M	■	90I	91B	92E	■	93O	94G	95G	96I
97J	98H	99D	100D	■	101Q	102Q	■	103B	104B	105E	106M
107C	108F	109N	.	■	■	■	■	■	■	■	■

A. Field

75 45 16 67 55 23

B. Spring or summer

34 32 104 103 91 49

C. Brewing whistler

73 107 30 60 19 85

D. Manifest ___

100 99 70 25 24 17 62

E. Ten to the third

92 52 69 28 46 33 78 105

F. Evening disappearing act

108 35 44 47 71 51

G. Parade component

83 95 38 94 20

H. Nephew's sister

80 72 14 98 37

I. Response

96 90 74 54 76 36

J. Louisiana's state bird

9 22 66 79 15 41 97

K. Hawk's opposite

40 27 2 53

L. Cookout staple

26 59 31 21 65 88 81 87 42

M. Dumbo or Babar

89 68 3 61 58 77 106 29

N. Fish in a tin

109 48 56 57 84 18 1

O. Door opener

43 4 64 93

P. Slight odor

86 6 82 39 13

Q. Side road

101 102 63 7 10

R. Tartan pattern

8 11 5 12 50

Solution on page 228

Buddha

1Q	2R	3Q	4G		5L	6P		7M	8Q	9L	
10N	11N	12O	13K	14K		15H	16A	17R	18P	19B	
20J	21Q	22O	23P		24O	25A	26M		27D	28A	29O
30R	31D	32O	33I	34A		35P	36H		37I	38H	39Q
40K	41L	42A	43A	44F	45C		46F	47L	48G		49Q
50N	51O		52Q	53P	54E	55L	56B	57H	58E		59J
60M	61B	62E	63A	64C	65P	66K		67O	68K	69F	70E
71P		72C	73D	74D		75C	76G	77J	78K		79R
80D	81L	82I	83E	84I	85P	86B			87J	88H	89B
	90C	91H	92F	93D		94J	95I		96M	97B	98J
	99F	100F	101G	102E	103M	104L	105M	106E		107R	108I
	109A	110A	111J		112D	113O	114O	115K			

A. San Francisco bread

___ ___ ___ ___ ___ ___ ___ ___ ___
34 16 110 42 43 109 25 63 28

B. Baby party

___ ___ ___ ___ ___ ___
19 97 61 86 56 89

C. Green Christmas decoration

___ ___ ___ ___ ___
64 72 90 75 45

D. Connoisseur of fine food

___ ___ ___ ___ ___ ___ ___
31 80 73 74 112 93 27

E. Car's idling position

___ ___ ___ ___ ___ ___ ___
106 54 62 58 83 102 70

F. King Kong's continent

___ ___ ___ ___ ___ ___
46 92 100 69 99 44

G. Revise

___ ___ ___ ___
101 48 76 4

H. Intl. Kid-helping org.

___ ___ ___ ___ ___ ___
88 57 91 15 38 36

I. Snowman of song

___ ___ ___ ___ ___ ___
108 84 82 95 33 37

J. Surrender

___ ___ ___ ___ ___ ___ ___
77 87 111 20 98 94 59

K. Shrove ___ (Lent preceder)

___ ___ ___ ___ ___ ___ ___
40 68 78 66 115 13 14

L. Nativity visitors

___ ___ ___ ___ ___ ___ ___
5 104 55 9 81 41 47

M. There may be a frog in it

___ ___ ___ ___ ___ ___
96 60 26 105 7 103

N. Ump's call

___ ___ ___
11 50 10

O. Legendary outlaw and benefactor

___ ___ ___ ___ ___ ___ ___ ___ ___
51 22 67 113 114 32 29 24 12

P. Dashboard counter

___ ___ ___ ___ ___ ___ ___ ___
85 71 35 23 18 65 6 53

Q. Songbird

___ ___ ___ ___ ___ ___ ___
39 52 3 21 8 49 1

R. Speech source

___ ___ ___ ___ ___
17 107 30 79 2

Solution on pages 228–229

Erich Fromm

A. November choice

___ ___ ___ ___ ___ ___ ___ ___
108 109 80 14 93 74 105 42

B. Caesar salad topper

___ ___ ___ ___ ___ ___ ___
54 47 28 32 46 94 9

C. T-shirt material

___ ___ ___ ___ ___ ___
40 82 22 77 78 61

D. Country bordered by the English Channel

___ ___ ___ ___ ___ ___
62 83 48 68 59 104

E. Stumbling block

___ ___ ___ ___ ___ ___ ___ ___
75 79 73 58 91 65 35 56

F. Statue of ___

___ ___ ___ ___ ___ ___ ___
63 64 81 85 88 70 92

G. Unsettled land

___ ___ ___ ___ ___ ___ ___ ___
106 25 39 102 66 21 96 15

H. Bakery quantity

___ ___ ___ ___ ___
90 60 34 87 45

I. Fundraiser

___ ___ ___ ___ ___ ___ ___
29 101 72 44 95 19 51

J. Silver medalist's place

___ ___ ___ ___ ___ ___
100 71 43 52 84 69

K. Public square

___ ___ ___ ___ ___
31 98 67 33 17

L. Hare's opponent

___ ___ ___ ___ ___ ___ ___ ___
49 41 13 38 12 7 103 97

M. A deadly sin

___ ___ ___ ___
50 76 20 89

N. Stand up to

___ ___ ___ ___
110 99 55 16

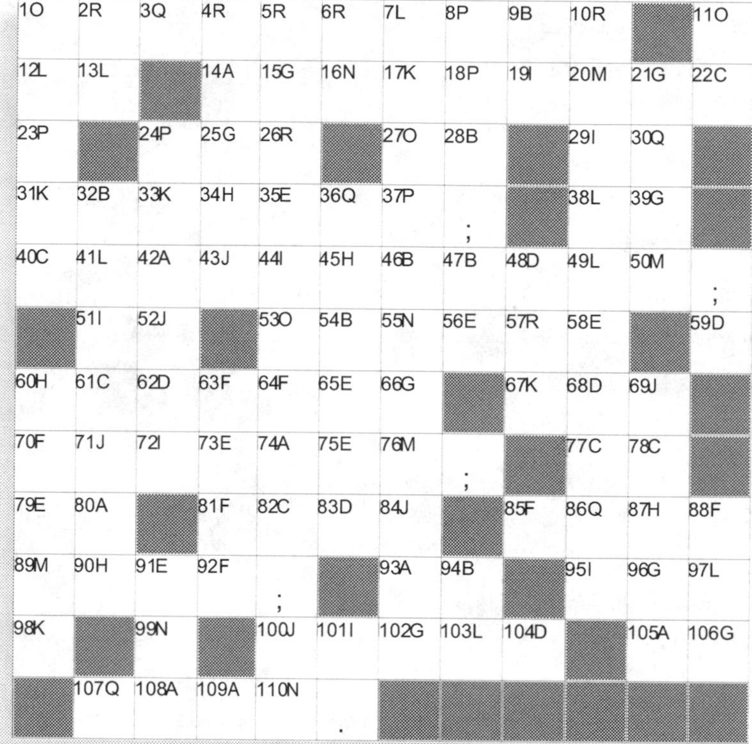

1O	2R	3Q	4R	5R	6R	7L	8P	9B	10R		11O
12L	13L		14A	15G	16N	17K	18P	19I	20M	21G	22C
23P		24P	25G	26R		27O	28B		29I	30Q	
31K	32B	33K	34H	35E	36Q	37P	;		38L	39G	
40C	41L	42A	43J	44I	45H	46B	47B	48D	49L	50M	;
	51I	52J		53O	54B	55N	56E	57R	58E		59D
60H	61C	62D	63F	64F	65E	66G		67K	68D	69J	
70F	71J	72I	73E	74A	75E	76M	;		77C	78C	
79E	80A		81F	82C	83D	84J		85F	86Q	87H	88F
89M	90H	91E	92F	;		93A	94B		95I	96G	97L
98K		99N		100J	101I	102G	103L	104D		105A	106G
	107Q	108A	109A	110N	.						

O. Fiction's opposite

___ ___ ___ ___
11 53 1 27

P. Morning television show

___ ___ ___ ___ ___
18 8 37 24 23

Q. Deadly sins number

___ ___ ___ ___ ___
107 36 86 30 3

R. Bank statement item

___ ___ ___ ___ ___ ___ ___
4 26 57 2 10 5 6

Solution on page 229

Henry Wadsworth Longfellow

1N	2Q	3O	4H	5O	6Q	7Q	8M	9G	10P	11E	12O
	13P	14L		15Q		16P	17K	18M	19O	20L	
21N	22O	23N	24L	25L	26M	27P		28F	29R		30P
31B	32D	33K	34E	35H	36F	.		37A	38J		39J
40G	41F		42L	43D	44J	45I		46A	47K	48J	49K
50C		51L	52M	53O	54H		55B	56A	57N	58H	59M
60A		61L	62D	63I		64J	65R	66L	67I		68C
69B	70O	71R	72H	73G		74D	75F		76K	77F	78H
	79B	80J	81N	82K	,		83D	84G	85N		86M
87A	88K		89A	90J	91F	92F		93H	94K		95Q
96E	97E	98F		99I	100J		101C	102C	103C	104F	105I
106D	107B	108G	.								

A. Psychiatrist, slangily

___ ___ ___ ___ ___ ___
89 60 87 37 56 46

B. Gentle push

___ ___ ___ ___ ___
69 31 107 79 55

C. Fire sign

___ ___ ___ ___ ___
101 103 102 50 68

D. Grand ___

___ ___ ___ ___ ___ ___
32 74 43 83 106 62

E. Wedding dessert

___ ___ ___ ___
11 96 97 34

F. Hideout on a limb

___ ___ ___ ___ ___ ___ ___ ___ ___
75 91 92 104 77 28 41 36 98

G. Google rival

___ ___ ___ ___ ___
108 9 73 40 84

H. Propose

___ ___ ___ ___ ___ ___ ___
4 58 72 54 78 35 93

I. Pal

___ ___ ___ ___ ___
105 99 67 63 45

J. Dirty dealing

___ ___ ___ ___ ___ ___ ___ ___
38 48 90 44 100 64 80 39

K. Tangible

___ ___ ___ ___ ___ ___ ___ ___
49 94 47 33 17 82 76 88

L. One and only person in life

___ ___ ___ ___ ___ ___ ___ ___
14 42 66 51 24 61 20 25

M. Halloween hue

___ ___ ___ ___ ___ ___
52 8 86 26 59 18

N. Hairpiece

___ ___ ___ ___ ___ ___
81 57 85 1 23 21

O. Rigby or Roosevelt

___ ___ ___ ___ ___ ___ ___
12 22 5 19 53 70 3

P. Bee's defense

___ ___ ___ ___ ___
30 27 13 10 16

Q. Use a loom

___ ___ ___ ___ ___
95 7 15 6 2

R. ET's craft

___ ___ ___
71 29 65

Solution on page 229

Chapter 2
Dropouts

Rearrange the letters in the vertical columns to fill the boxes directly below them. When you have filled in the grid correctly you will see a quote.

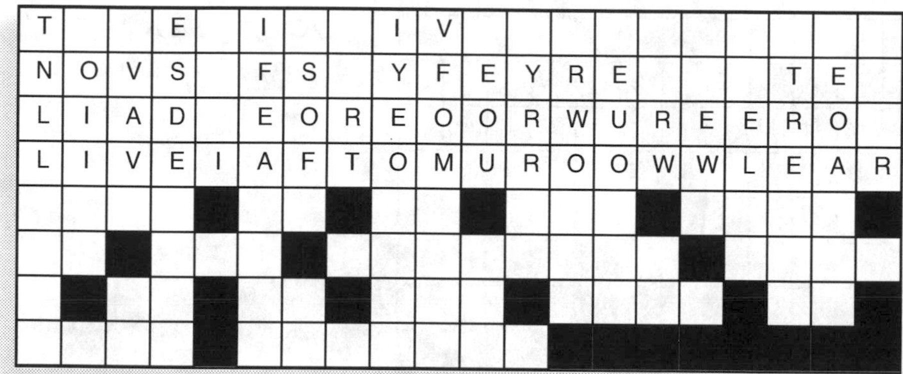

T E I I V
N O V S F S Y F E Y R E T E
L I A D E O R E O O R W U R E E R O
L I V E I A F T O M U R O O W W L E A R

Mahatma Gandhi

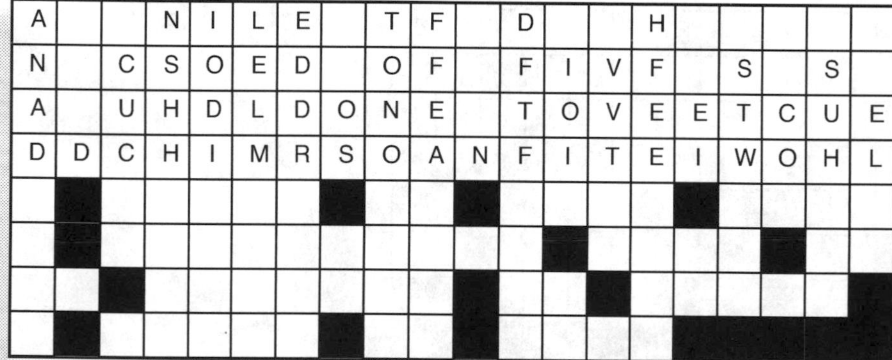

Groucho Marx

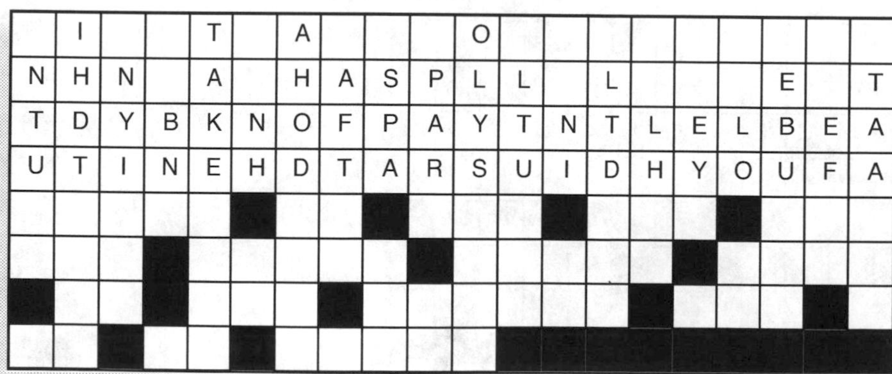

Anne Frank

Solution on page 229

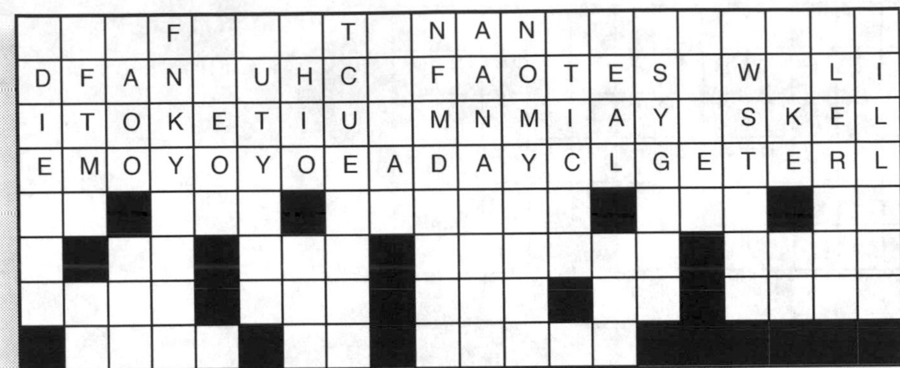

George Bernard Shaw

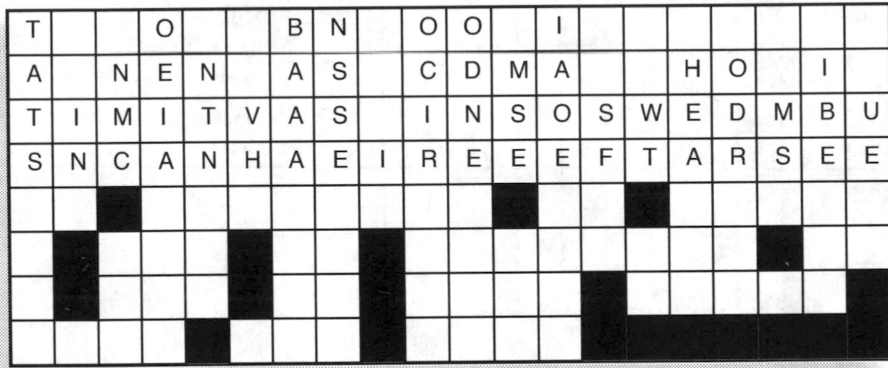

Victor Hugo

T E O
G U N P T T W I K E I V
O H I T S R A O T M C E O F O U R I N
I S L T G R O C M A A K E A Y L A R T S

Kurt Vonnegut

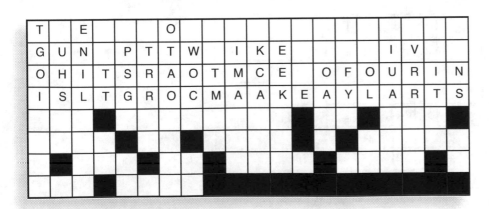

Solution on page 229

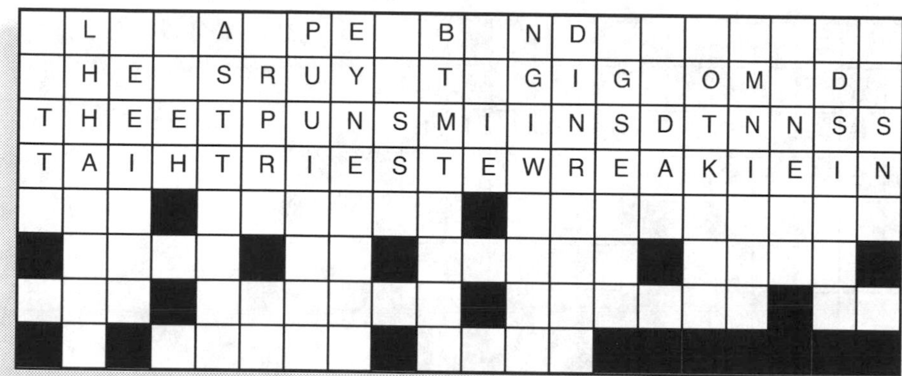

Ella Wheeler Wilcox

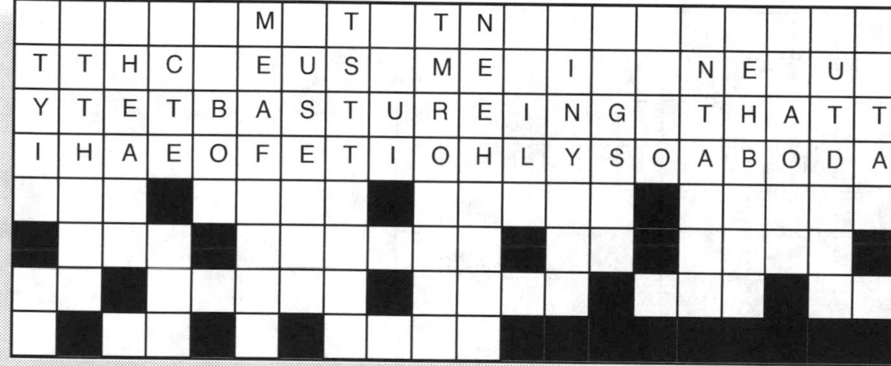

Abraham Lincoln

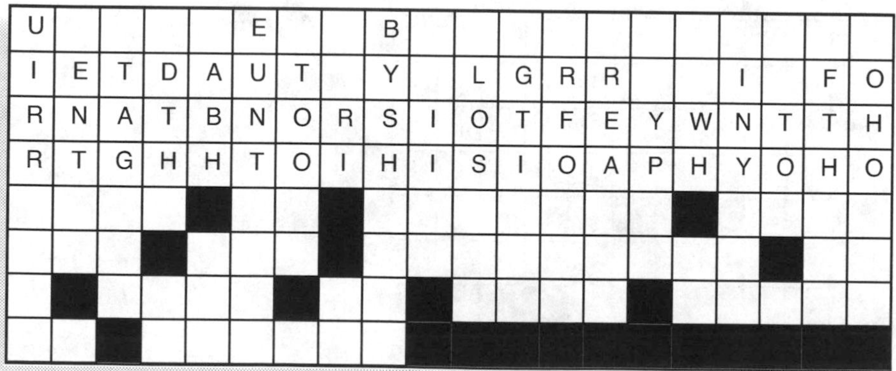

Benjamin Disraeli

Solution on pages 229–230

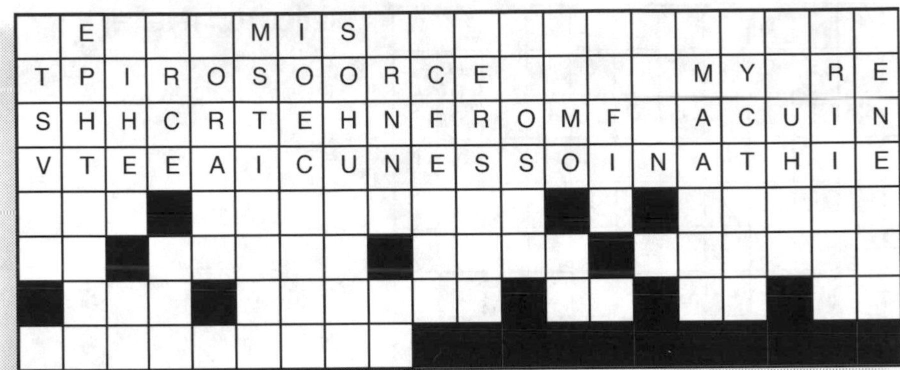

Claude Monet

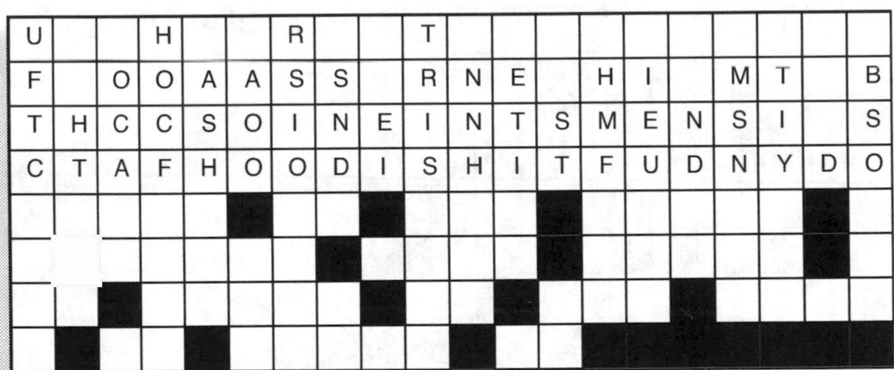

Steve Martin

S			S	F		P	I			I	C								
S	S		I	L	M	P	M	I	I	I	S		U	I	O	R	T	C	E
K	N	W	W	S	D	D	G	L	F	N	E	A	A	I	N	F	O	H	T
I	R	O	O	I	E	O	L	E	L	I	G	S	T	P	P	N	A	C	E
									■			■		■					
		■			■							■			■				
								■					■			■			
		■															■	■	■

Martin Fischer

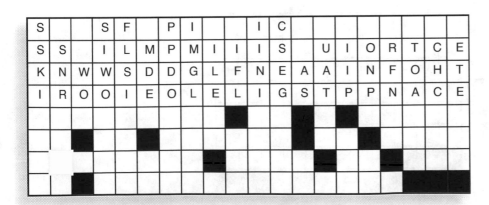

Solution on page 230

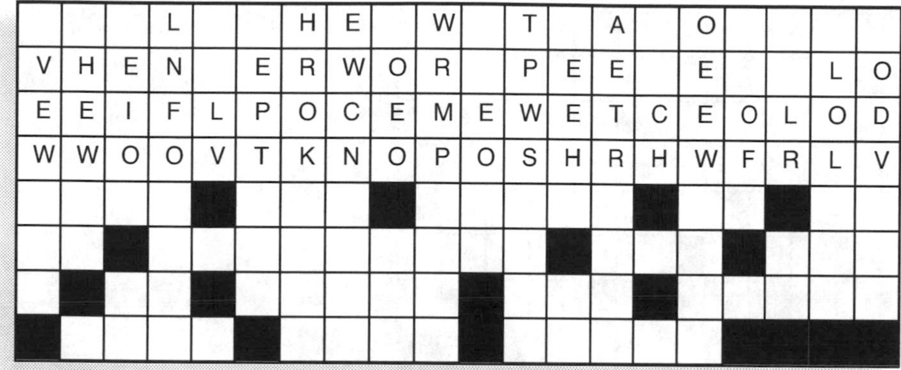

			L			H	E		W		T		A		O				
V	H	E	N		E	R	W	O	R		P	E	E		E			L	O
E	E	I	F	L	P	O	C	E	M	E	W	E	T	C	E	O	L	O	D
W	W	O	O	V	T	K	N	O	P	O	S	H	R	H	W	F	R	L	V
				■				■						■			■		
		■										■				■			
	■			■						■				■					
■					■					■						■	■	■	■

Jimi Hendrix

E	I	E							N		T	L	S		G				
H	V	E	S	A	T	O	F		F		E	H	M	E	B	I	H	G	
O	E	M	N	T	O	I	E	B	E	E	M	N	I	N	N	E	N	E	P
P	L	N	R	Y	T	N	T	H	E	O	A	O	N	O	Y	T	N	A	V
								■						■					
					■			■								■			
				■			■			■									■
			■			■				■							■	■	■

C.S. Lewis

	B	M	L		N				I	T									
	O	A	G		N	A	E		A	N			W	I	S	S		T	O
Y	I	N	O	A	T	O	S	L	E	R	Y		P	P	O	E		S	A
A	L	N	E	S	H	C	E	V	E	S	S	O	W	I	S	E	I	T	E
						■						■					■		
				■				■			■								
■				■			■					■					■		
■								■			■	■	■	■	■	■	■	■	■

George Santayana

Solution on page 230

William James

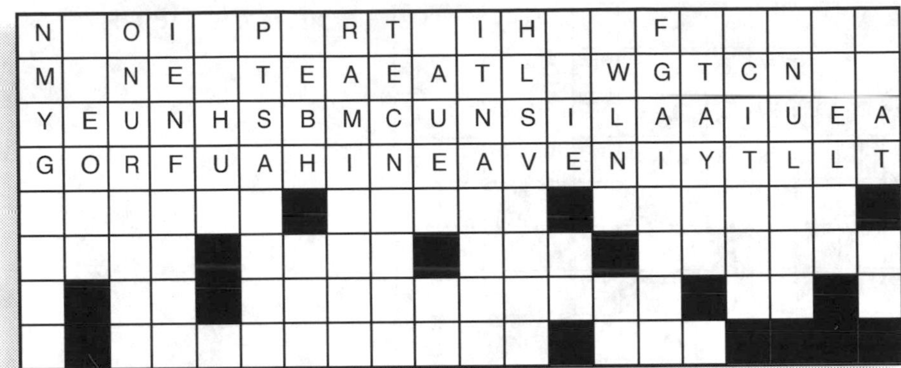

N		O	I		P		R	T		I	H			F					
M		N	E		T	E	A	E	A	T	L		W	G	T	C	N		
Y	E	U	N	H	S	B	M	C	U	N	S	I	L	A	A	I	U	E	A
G	O	R	F	U	A	H	I	N	E	A	V	E	N	I	Y	T	L	L	T

Harry Truman

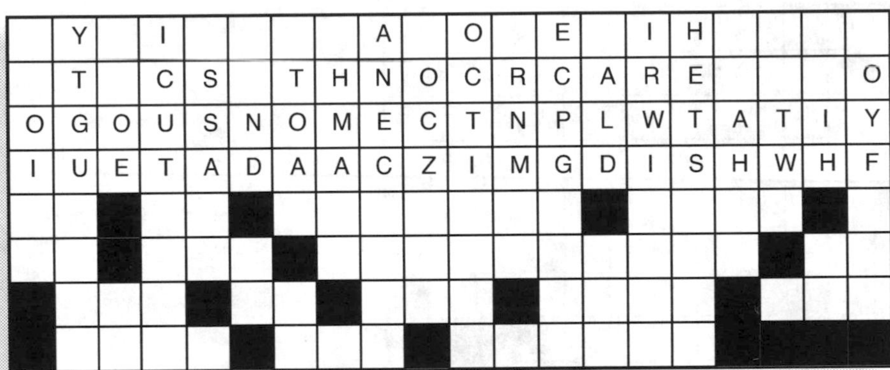

	Y		I					A		O		E		I	H				
	T		C	S		T	H	N	O	C	R	C	A	R	E				O
O	G	O	U	S	N	O	M	E	C	T	N	P	L	W	T	A	T	I	Y
I	U	E	T	A	D	A	A	C	Z	I	M	G	D	I	S	H	W	H	F

Anaïs Nin

E	P	N				R	S	O	L										
Y	O	L	D		I	T	S	T	D		T		L	A	F	S		D	E
P	A	N	Y	P	E	I	V	E	O	A	A	R	U	T	Y	S		B	X
T	H	E	D	S	L	I	N	E	N	F	L	L	W	I	H	E		E	E

Solution on page 230

Robert Frost

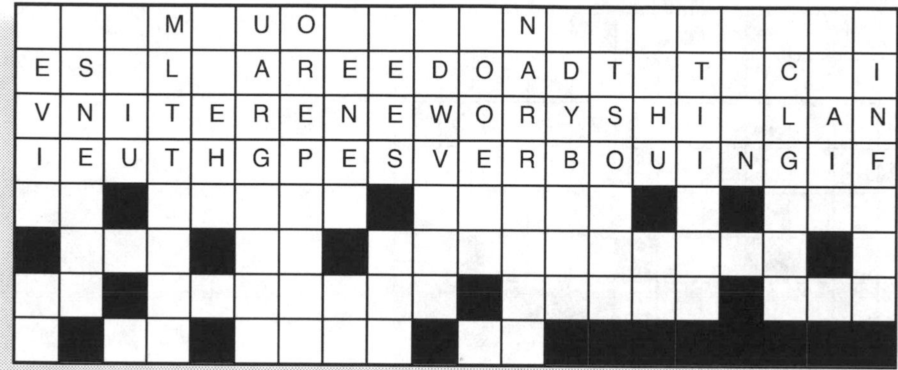

			M		U	O					N								
E	S		L		A	R	E	E	D	O	A	D	T		T		C		I
V	N	I	T	E	R	E	N	E	W	O	R	Y	S	H	I		L	A	N
I	E	U	T	H	G	P	E	S	V	E	R	B	O	U	I	N	G	I	F

Buckminster Fuller

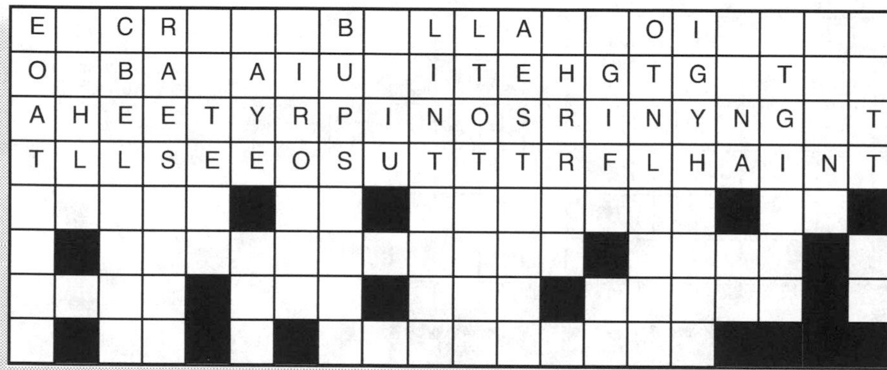

E		C	R				B		L	L	A			O	I				
O		B	A		A	I	U		I	T	E	H	G	T	G		T		
A	H	E	E	T	Y	R	P	I	N	O	S	R	I	N	Y	N	G		T
T	L	L	S	E	E	O	S	U	T	T	T	R	F	L	H	A	I	N	T

Ring Lardner

R	R					T	G						I		Y				
N	E		M	O	I	S	N	T		O	Y	O	A	L	C		M	O	
F	T	E	A	S	A	M	I	L	Y	F	S	M	I	M	E	O	R	E	A
T	H	O	G	F	I	N	H	E	T	A	A	H	U	V	P	O	Y	T	U

Solution on page 230

Andy Warhol

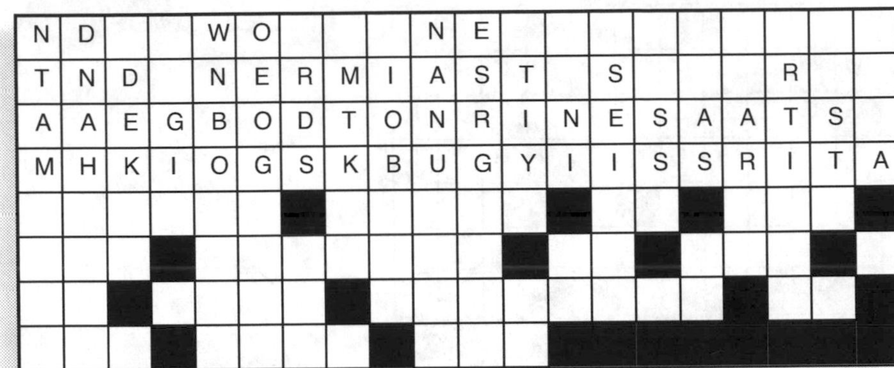

Mark Twain

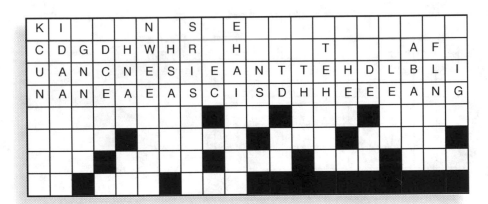

K	I				N		S		E										
C	D	G	D	H	W	H	R		H				T				A	F	
U	A	N	C	N	E	S	I	E	A	N	T	T	E	H	D	L	B	L	I
N	A	N	E	A	E	A	S	C	I	S	D	H	H	E	E	E	A	N	G
								■			■				■				
				■						■				■					■
			■					■				■				■			
		■				■				■	■	■	■	■	■	■	■	■	■

Elbert Hubbard

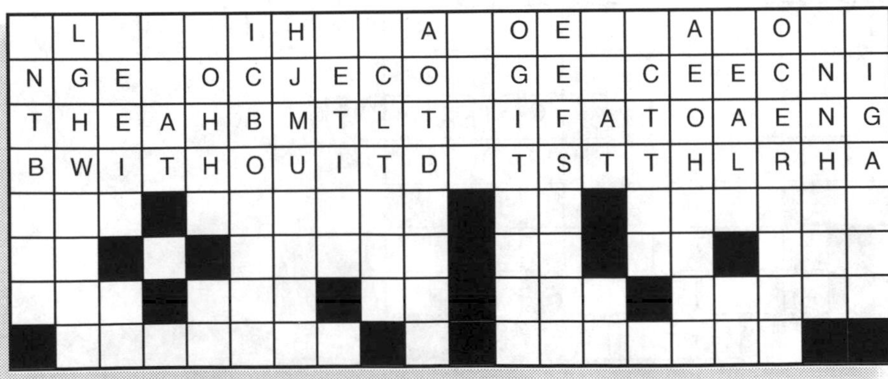

Solution on page 230

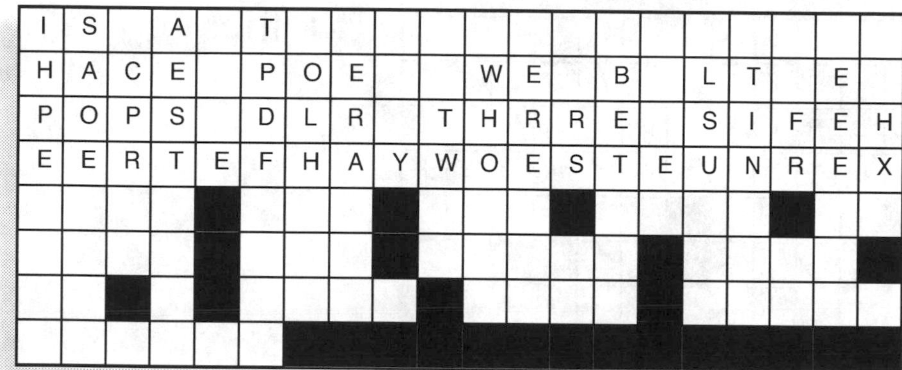

Mel Brooks

			H		E		N												
A		S	I	S	I		O	D	F		O	S		S		E	M		E
I	S	T	F	R	F	R	A	A	S	O	G	E		F	R	O	M	I	E
S	U	W	E	A	N	E	M	M	N	H	I	L	T	E	N	M	O	R	H

Baltasar Gracian

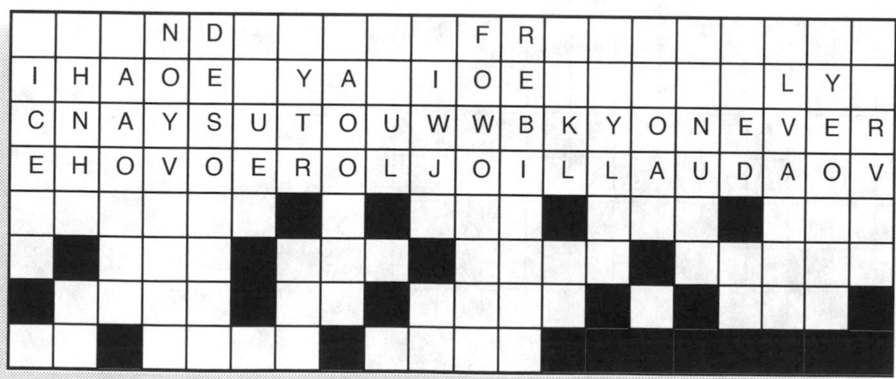

Confucius

Solution on page 230

Mother Teresa

	H								M	R	E	A							
T	I	N	A	E	D	E	S		P	R	E	C		A	U	N		N	
T	E	A	N	N	H	O	R	W	B	R	L	E	I	F	O	R	G	L	O
V	H	E	R	T	F	I	A	P	O	O	R	D	D	H	T	I	O	E	R
					■			■					■						
■			■				■						■				■		
		■				■													■
				■				■						■	■	■	■	■	■

Alan Bennett

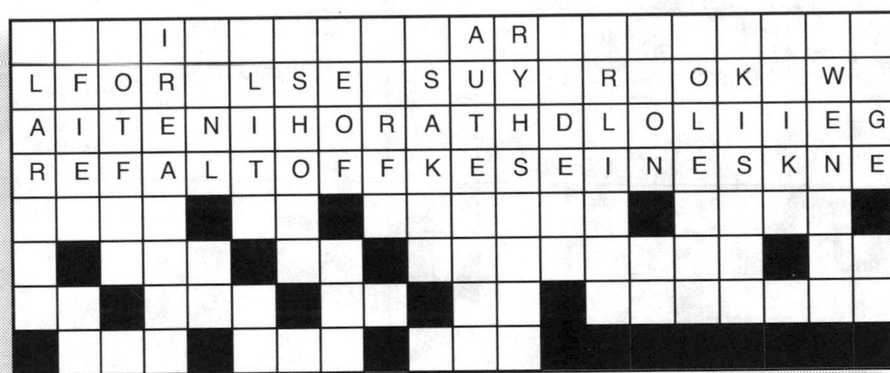

			I							A	R								
L	F	O	R		L	S	E		S	U	Y		R		O	K		W	
A	I	T	E	N	I	H	O	R	A	T	H	D	L	O	L	I	I	E	G
R	E	F	A	L	T	O	F	F	K	E	S	E	I	N	E	S	K	N	E
				■			■							■					■
	■				■			■									■		
		■				■			■			■							
■				■				■				■	■	■	■	■	■	■	■

Mary Oliver

C	I					E		T	O										
O	U	O	L	L	N	N		W	E		T			W			P		Y
O	E	R	P	S	A	L		F	I	L	D		A	N	I	I	T		Y
T	U	L	U	O	M	E	I	W	H	A	D	O	I	S	D	T	H	R	E
				■			■					■			■			■	
		■					■			■			■					■	
			■				■					■				■			
					■					■	■	■	■	■	■	■	■	■	■

Solution on pages 230–231

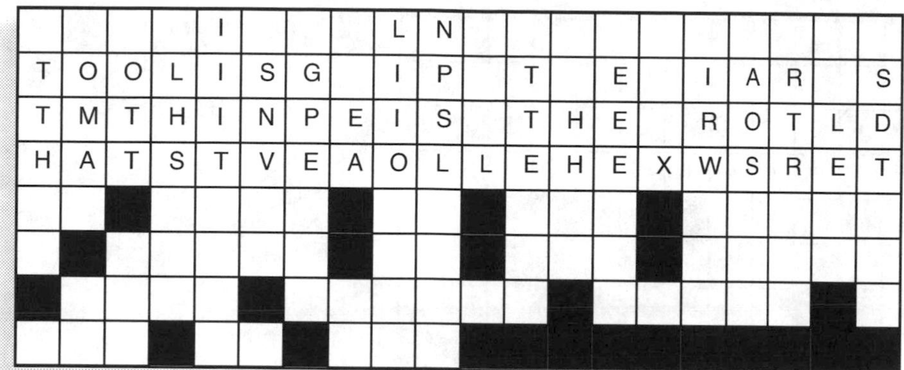

Oscar Wilde

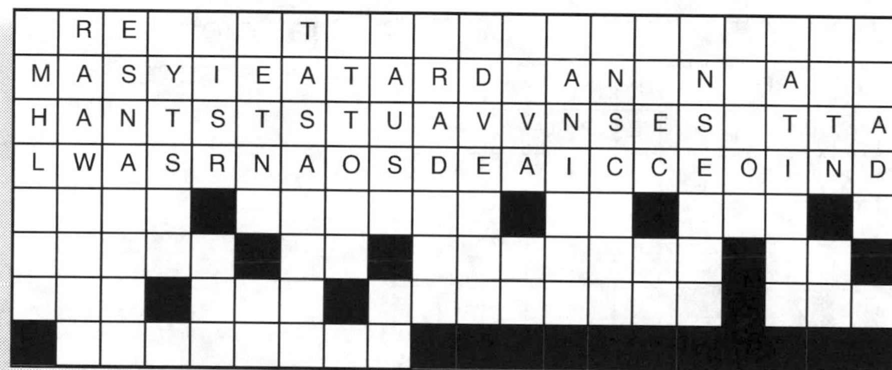

Blaise Pascal

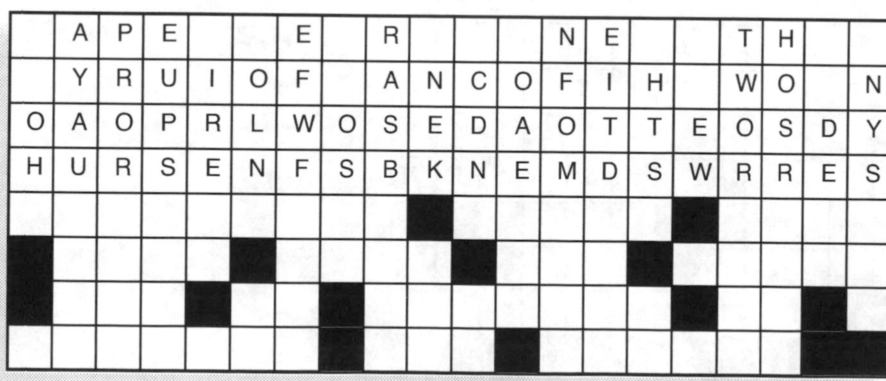

Buddha

Solution on page 231

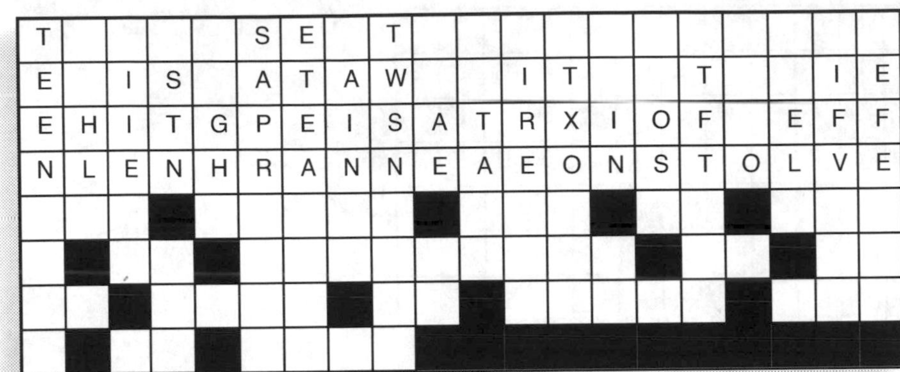

Lord Byron

T					S	E		T											
E		I	S		A	T	A	W			I	T			T			I	E
E	H	I	T	G	P	E	I	S	A	T	R	X	I	O	F		E	F	F
N	L	E	N	H	R	A	N	N	E	A	E	O	N	S	T	O	L	V	E
			■						■				■			■			
	■			■										■			■		
		■					■			■						■			
	■			■					■	■	■	■	■	■	■	■	■	■	■

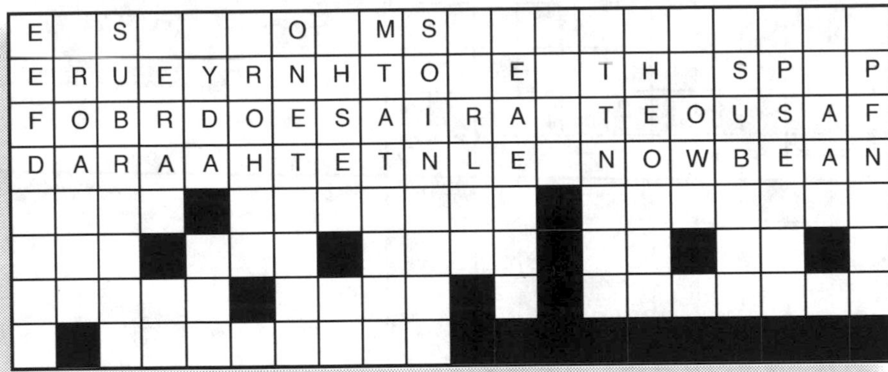

Napoleon Bonaparte

E		S				O		M	S										
E	R	U	E	Y	R	N	H	T	O		E		T	H		S	P		P
F	O	B	R	D	O	E	S	A	I	R	A		T	E	O	U	S	A	F
D	A	R	A	A	H	T	E	T	N	L	E		N	O	W	B	E	A	N
				■								■							
			■				■					■			■			■	
					■					■		■							
	■									■	■	■	■	■	■	■	■	■	■

Oscar Levant

	H	H	I	E			I		F										
S	A	N	E	E	N		G		N	I	V	E		E	N	A			D
T	T	E	I	S	S		A	N	E	A	N	S		L	R	D	E	I	B
E	T	W	R	T	Y	L	I	E	H	I	U	E		A	I	N	S	E	N
						■		■					■					■	
						■							■				■		
						■		■					■						
■					■					■	■	■	■	■	■	■	■	■	■

Solution on page 231

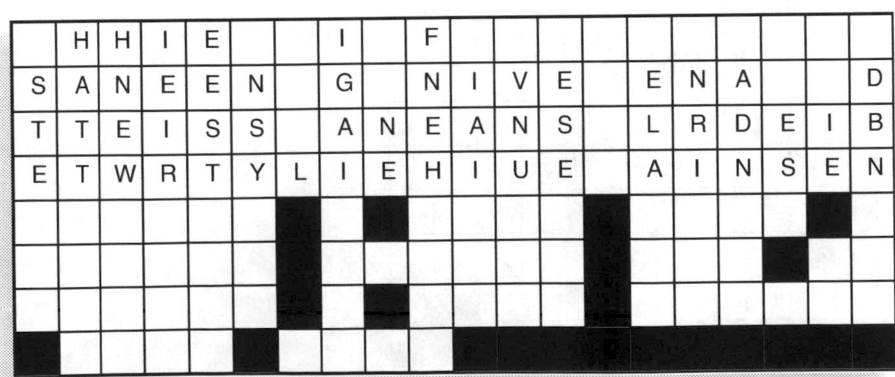

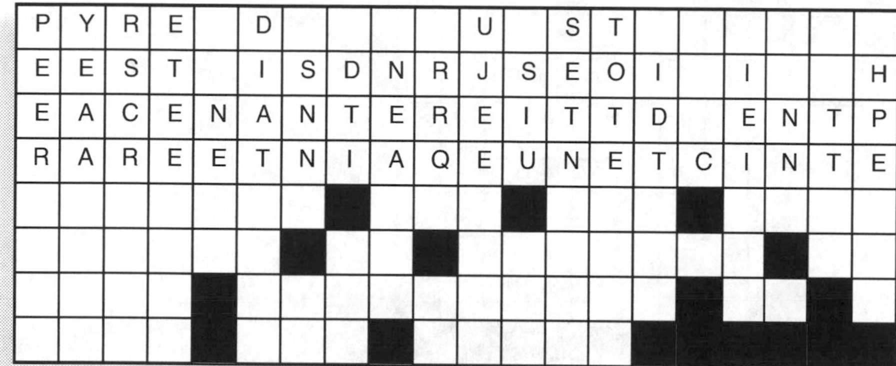

Bill Cosby

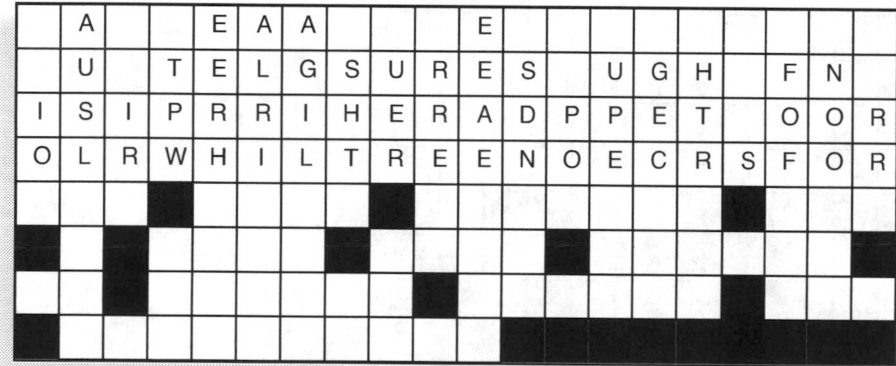

T.S. Eliot

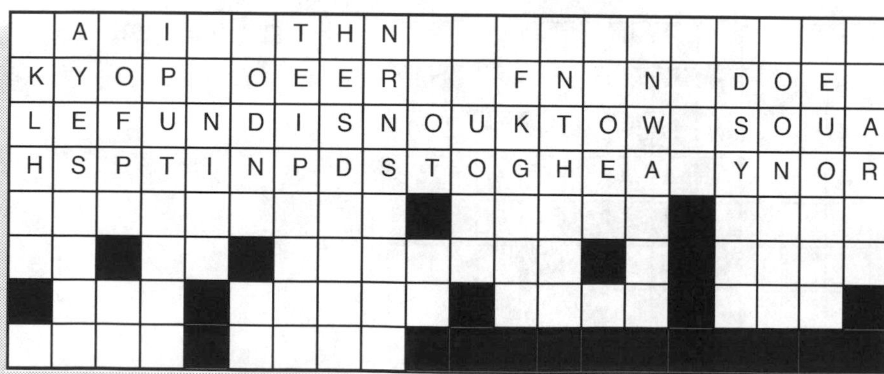

John Barrymore

Solution on page 231

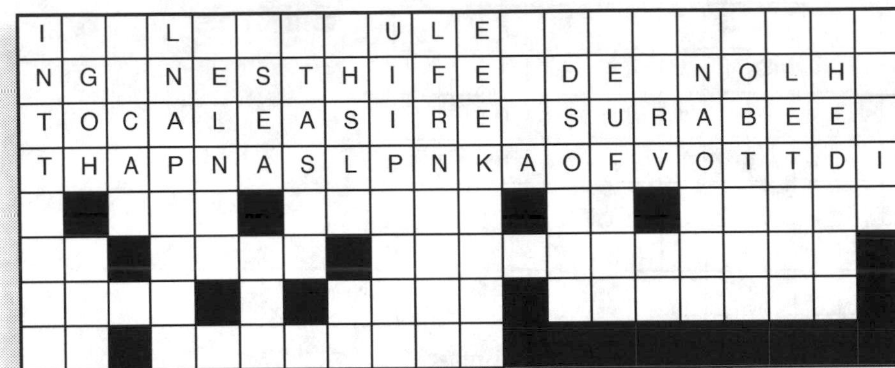

John D. Rockefeller

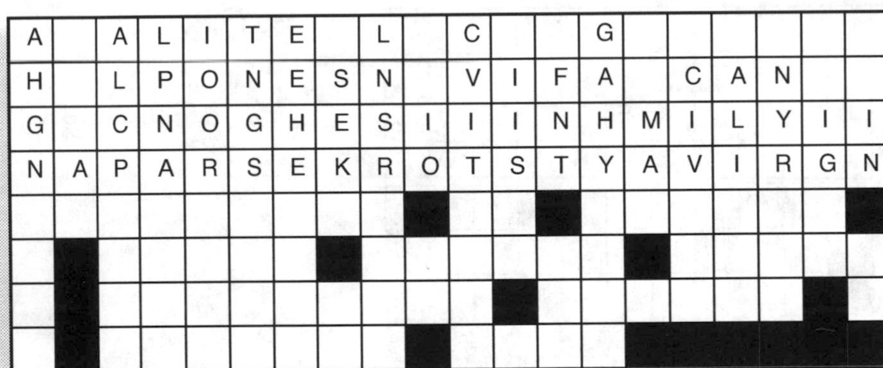

I			L					U	L	E									
N	G		N	E	S	T	H	I	F	E		D	E		N	O	L	H	
T	O	C	A	L	E	A	S	I	R	E		S	U	R	A	B	E	E	
T	H	A	P	N	A	S	L	P	N	K	A	O	F	V	O	T	T	D	I
	■				■						■			■					
		■					■												■
				■		■					■								■
		■									■	■	■	■	■	■	■	■	■

George Burns

A		A	L	I	T	E		L		C			G						
H		L	P	O	N	E	S	N		V	I	F	A		C	A	N		
G		C	N	O	G	H	E	S	I	I	I	N	H	M	I	L	Y	I	I
N	A	P	A	R	S	E	K	R	O	T	S	T	Y	A	V	I	R	G	N
									■			■							■
	■						■							■					
	■										■							■	
	■								■					■	■	■	■	■	■

Rita Rudner

H	A				C	A	R		E	T				E					
Y	L	V	Y		P	R	G		O	N	S	U	H	R	M		S		
L	K	E	E	O	U	H	I	L	N	F	O	N	G	H	H	I	L	E	I
A	O	U	R	C	A	N	E	E	D	R	E	T	A	W	E	T	O	T	T
				■									■						■
				■								■				■			
		■						■							■			■	
			■					■			■					■	■	■	■

Solution on page 231

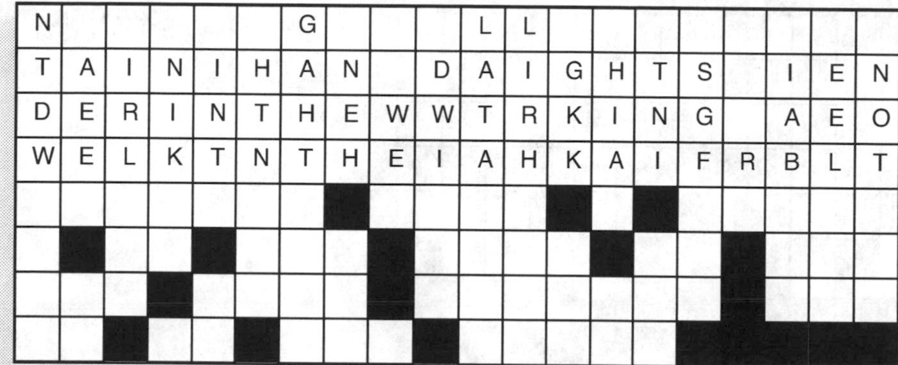

Helen Keller

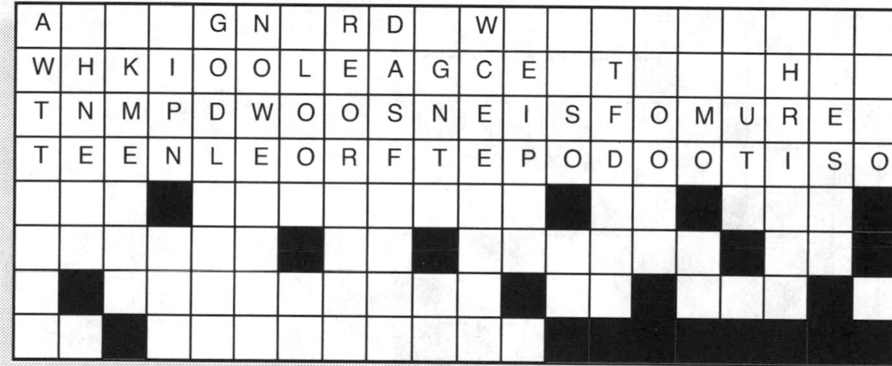

Benjamin Franklin

Albert Schweitzer

Solution on page 231

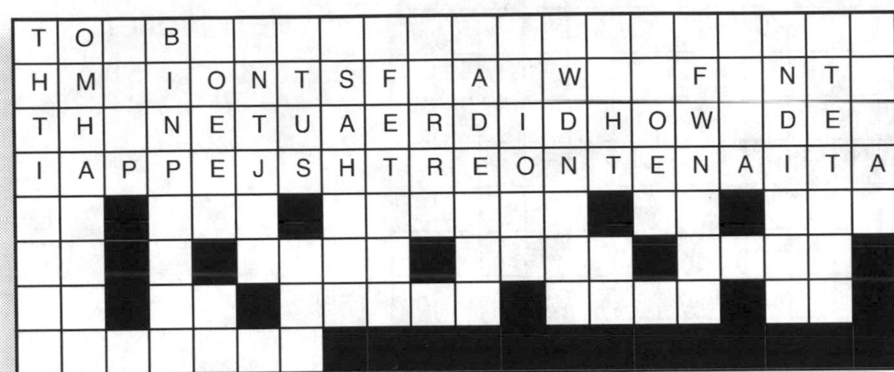

T	O		B																
H	M		I	O	N	T	S	F		A		W			F		N	T	
T	H		N	E	T	U	A	E	R	D	I	D	H	O	W		D	E	
I	A	P	P	E	J	S	H	T	R	E	O	N	T	E	N	A	I	T	A
		■				■							■			■			
		■		■					■					■					■
		■			■						■					■			■
							■	■	■	■	■	■	■	■	■	■	■	■	■

Woody Allen

L	O	T			R		L	U	N										
R	E	N		R	E	R	A	W	Y		L	Y	B	T		S		S	
Y	O	L	G	Y	O	U	P	L	E	L	B	O	V	E	H	H	A	L	E
N	T	U	Y	E	D	A	R	S	L	L	F	O	F	E	W	E	I	T	T
			■									■			■				
				■						■			■				■		
						■					■			■					■
			■							■					■	■	■	■	■

Rumi

	F		T			L					D		V	O					
	F	A	F			A	S	W	S		T	I	E	R		F	O	L	
W	L	O	I	T	D	O	C	H	E	O	L	I	T	E		M	A	R	E
I	H	I	R	E	E	I	E	S	N	O	T	H	F	F	I	C	U	K	T
				■			■			■					■				■
		■			■			■				■			■				
■					■					■									
■				■					■						■	■	■	■	■

George Eliot

Solution on page 231

Chapter 3
Fill-ins

Each letter in the grid is the first or last letter in a five- or six-letter word. All of the middle letters are missing. Select the three- and four-letter pieces from the list and complete the words in the grid. There is a place for every set of letters. Words read both across and down.

Fill-in 1

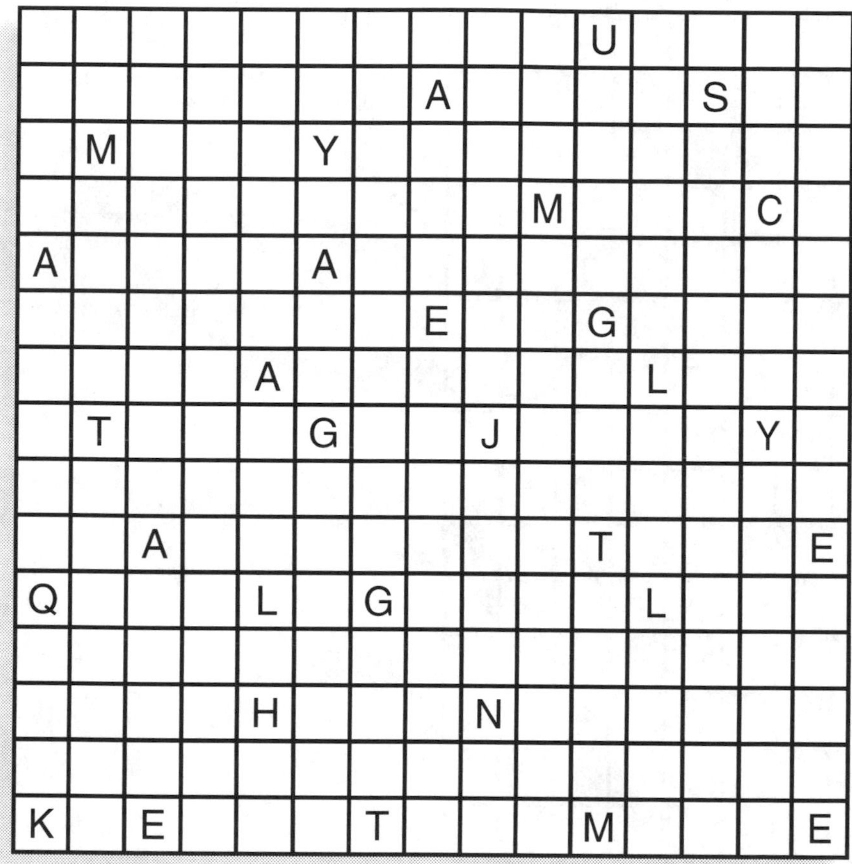

Clues

ABL
RON
BOD
NNU
OCA
HIN

UMA
UEL
AMU
IGH
ONT
UMM

USI
UAC
ERAT
MOEB
ALOP
OMEN

ARGO
MEND
UROP
NSUN

Solution on page 232

Fill-in 2

				F								B		
	A				E				A				L	
		G					S							
												T		Q
	R			Y		B					M			
									L					
			S					D						
							D							
T					T				R					T
	Y										E			
			D											
							S					E		
	A				E									
									E					

Clues

TAN
MBL
RIT
CUT
VAI
IGO

EEME
OSAR
EFUS
RUAN
EDDL
UAIN

QUAR
PPAL
ELEN
LOOZ
ROUP
HOWE

EDLA

Solution on page 232

Fill-in 3

F				S				F						W
							M					N		
	A					E								
			R					E		S				W
				S										
							N					Y		
	L				H									
						B				H				S
	D											P		
			A		O					D				
							D							
	A					N			D					T
			A		A					T		D		

Clues

ORC
ERT
OUT
OGM
YNC
PER

IGI
ORT
ORM
IDO
HRE
STER

EARL
LACE
IGES
NNEA
PIRI
PENE

ODER
ECED
EEDE
ERIE
VERS

Solution on page 232

Fill-in 4

		S									B		R	
	S					P				R				H
U				A				S						
		H				S					R		D	
												A		
G		M				A								
				T				R		T				C
									F					
T				D								N		
					R					O				
		E				N								
									L					Y
L					R									

Clues

LTR
OPI
SIN
SPE
OTA
RES

OCH
AJA
INA
RIA
ARGE
AZAA

OMAN
OUNT
UMME
OBIL
ANCI
CTIO

BDUC
OMBE
CRIM
IKEL
COTC

Solution on page 232

Fill-in 5

G					R				A					E
						T					E			
			T											
S				D					E					
								S		A				A
											Y			
	A					Y				S				
			Y				A					S		
				C										
			B					T				B		D
	O				E					L				R
T				T				R				Y		

Clues

GAT
IRL
PIN
AWD
LPH
ARL

EAD
ENE
OWE
TOO
RTER
RIAG

CHOO
AINE
WENT
RABL
LLIE
ORBE

OAST
ASAL
DAGI
ANNO
BACU

Solution on page 233

Fill-in 6

									A					
	B				G					E			B	
			B											
							I				E			
R					T									
	T								A				E	
					C									
			C					H				B		
							T							
	G					L			D					T
					A					E				
M				E								Y		
	L													
				R					E					

Clues

EGE
ELE
MAG
AVE
ELL
PAC

RMAD
ETIR
OOGO
HURC
ILAT
MPAC

IONI
IVES
LEAR
ALOR
EPOR
RGYL

UPOL

Solution on page 233

Fill-in 7

		A		S					D					
												P		
	R					E								
								W					W	
				S										
		A			C				E			Y		
A														
			H				T					D		
									C				N	
														W
					A					T				
M				L										
			S					S				P		
										E				H

Clues

CRA
OGU
ERS
ART
ABI
EEM

ROX
ANO
AUS
UMMU
ABAN
RETC

NEMI
INDO
ENEG
ECON
SYLU
OLLO

OCIL
SSEN

Solution on page 233

Fill-in 8

			W					N		S				
						R		C					D	
C				D										
			E		E					S				
		A					D			M				D
						D							R	
S				L				B				A		
													P	
		N					L			S				N
										T				T
			C					R						
							R		B				Y	

Clues

DOR
ILE
ATE
OVE
HOL
ALE

ALM
RYS
HIL
COR
HOA
ALS

ENTE
CCOR
ORMA
GRES
ALLE
AUCU

ITHI
RISS
EGAR
ICKE

Solution on page 233

Fill-in 9

	A						S					S		
				D										
			B					R						
										C				S
												E		
	M					F								
				R										
					F					S				
	H											M		Y
				P					S					
						D								
								I					D	
P					E									
	T			E								R		
					A				M					

Clues

XIO
OST
ENS
EAC
RAS
LORI

TRIU
OINT
ANNE
YSEL
AMPE
YSTE

TATE
ARLO
CANT
ARKE
ORCE
OLIC

SLAN

Solution on page 234

Fill-in 10

B														
		S					G		S				S	
				R						C				T
N					N									
							P			A				N
		E						G					D	
	Q					M					E			
B				T										
													A	
				A				O		S				Y
	R					E			T					Y
I				S				B					T	

Clues

DEA
TEP
GAI
REA
MIG
ROU

OUR
TUD
ROW
UIL
UMB
EVER

DROI
EREF
OTGU
ATIO
OOTH
OMBO

OUSS
UAVE
ORDI
SSES
PRIN

Solution on page 234

Fill-in 11

				P						F				A
		T					O							
									T					G
						L				T		H		
		S		E			R							
										C				E
	B				S									
							D					Y		
			A											
F					R				A					P
						A				E				
	D													
			L				R							
									Y					R

Clues

LOR
EAS
USS
THE
GIL
YPE

APE
TOL
LIS
ABO
AST
IRS

LLA
AUG
OLED
RYIN
ARKL
AMME

EYON
AGGE
OSTE
LAGU

Solution on page 234

Fill-in 12

C				R										B
							T					A		
			Z					R		C				
				O					S					D
E												R		
		R					E							
								C						
					C					E				M
W				E										
					B		I					F		
		L				L								
								N		F				E
D					W					D		E		

Clues

ROT
ADI
AYB
LUK
ELO
ASE

MOU
LUM
EVE
OLO
ECOI
EFUG

REBL
AJOL
INGE
RAUM
HOUL
HARG

ANTE
RETI
TSEL
HOIC
ORKE

Solution on page 234

Fill-in 13

						R					E			
		S												
A					T									
							S					G		
P				E							Y			
					A					S				
		T												
							K							
			A									C		
C					G			T						
										M				M
	A				R		B					Y		
			O					C						
									S					Y

Clues

IEC
TOC
URK
BON
ONI
MON

ADD
ODE
LDE
OMIN
TREE
TRON

TTES
IGAM
HANT
UBLI
IKID
EBUK

HALO
DONI

Solution on page 235

Fill-in 14

												R		
G					R			M					D	
		B												
	B					M			B				G	
							B					D		D
					F					E				
M														
		N									T			
									E					H
			A				D							
S				E				S					F	
											E			
			R					T						

Clues

TAT
LTA
EAT
EIN
CRI
ECAM

ARNE
ONTH
OTUN
ANYA
CRUF
ARIU

EBUF
NOUG
LEEC
ETHO
EJEC
ONGU

EHIN

Solution on page 235

Fill-in 15

			F				Y			A				L
	A													
S					Y		T					Y		
			M					R		E				
											S			G
	T				E		E					T		
			L					Y						
									C				L	
	R							A			E			
R					E									
						C				N				
B					E									
	P							F					H	

Clues

HES
ECA
HOS
ORK
ROO
NVI

LOO
TON
ORU
ABA
NTIR
CQUI

HEOR
ENTO
XPEC
ENGT
ANGL
CURV

CRIB
IVIN
RENC
ITAN
EPOS

Solution on page 235

Fill-in 16

			R					P						
						C				D				
S				E									D	
			E					E						
				M										
		T					S							
						N				R				M
E		E						S					E	
														S
B				N		P				P		T		
								L						
		R					N		U					D
						N				E		H		

Clues

RUN
RUD
RIM
TAG
ANG
RAW

HAR
OUL
OOT
TIL
ATO
EAL

EDIA
APPL
HERE
ITHE
NITE
IMPL

ENOW
AREE
EVAM
APPE

Solution on page 235

Chapter 4

Groupies

Groupies have lots of blanks and no clues. Actually, there is one clue, the one word supplied for you in each puzzle. This word is a member of the category from which all of the other words belong. For example, if the word is POKER, then the other words to be fit in the blanks could be card games.

Groupie 1

Groupie 2

Solution on page 236

Groupie 3

Groupie 4

Solution on page 236

Groupie 5

Groupie 6

Solution on page 237

Groupie 7

Groupie 8

Solution on page 237

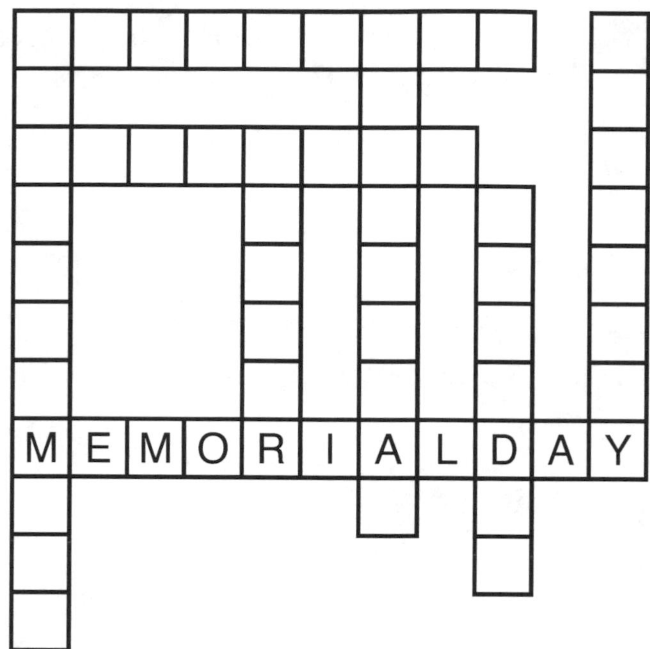

Groupie 9

Groupie 10

Solution on page 238

Groupie 11

Groupie 12

Solution on page 238

Groupie 13

Groupie 14

Solution on page 239

Groupie 15

Groupie 16

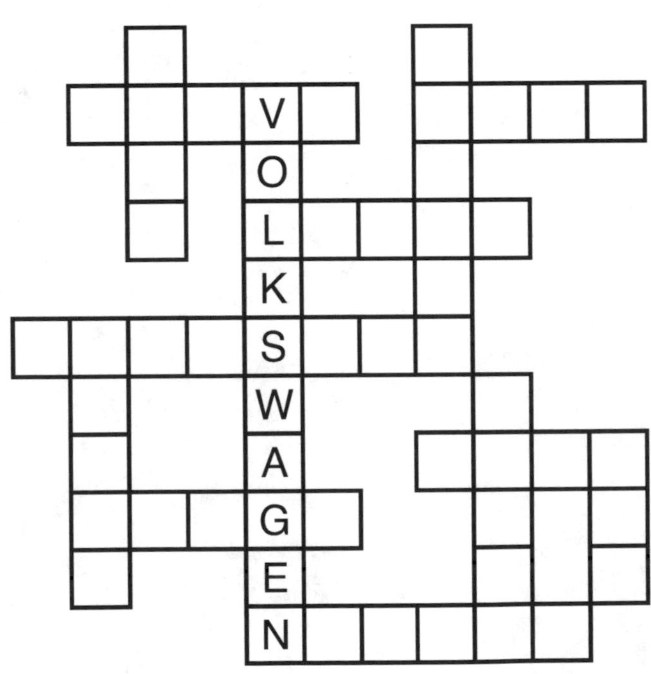

Solution on page 239

Groupie 17

Groupie 18

Solution on page 240

Groupie 19

Groupie 20

Solution on page 240

Groupie 21

Groupie 22

Solution on page 241

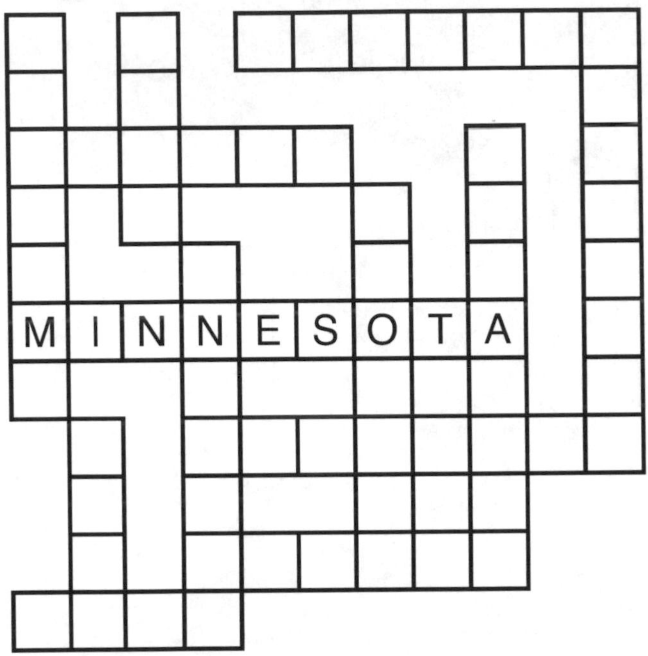

Groupie 23

Groupie 24

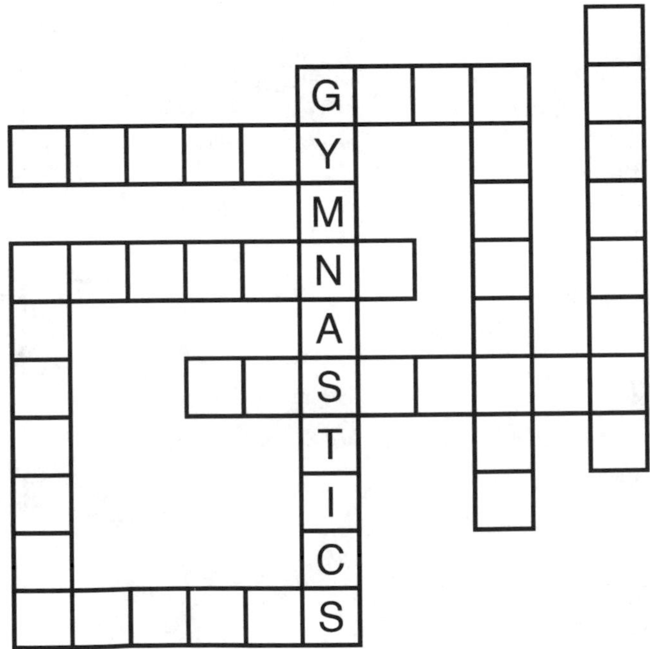

Solution on page 241

Groupie 25

Groupie 26

Solution on page 242

Groupie 27

Groupie 28

Solution on page 242

Groupie 29

Groupie 30

Solution on page 243

Groupie 31

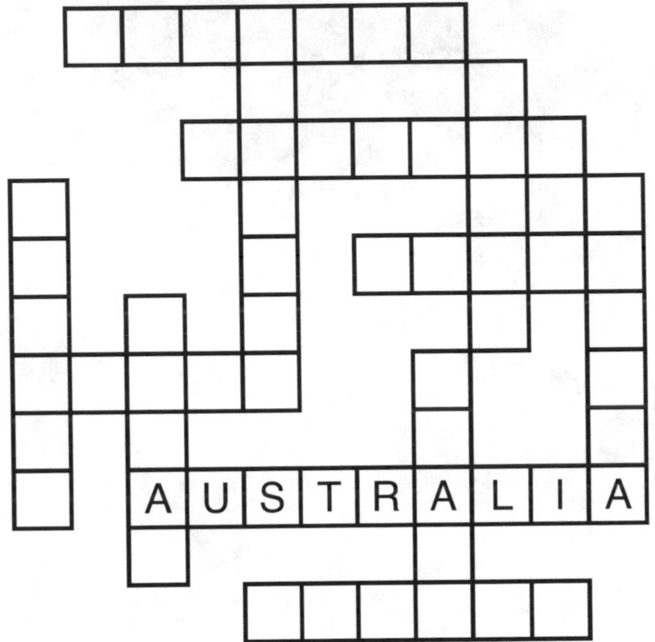

Groupie 32

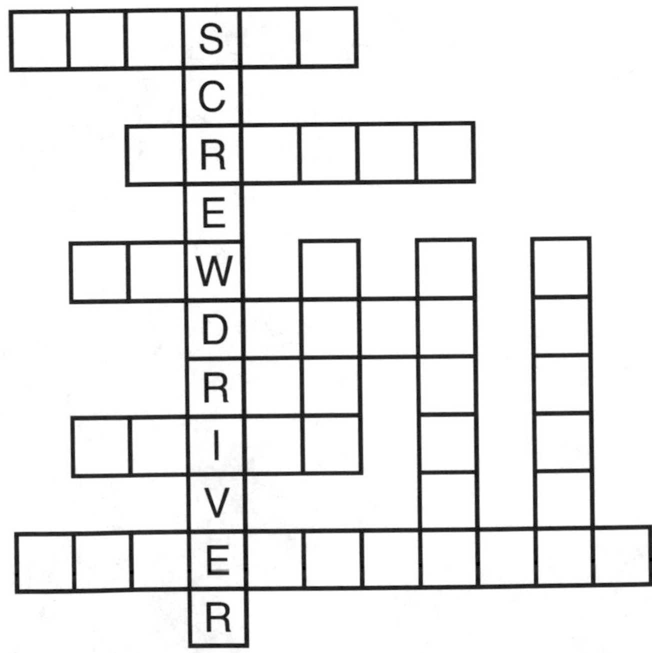

Solution on page 243

Chapter 5

Word Search

The puzzles in this chapter are in the traditional word search format. Words are hidden in a grid in any direction: up, down, forward, backward, or diagonally. The words are always found in a straight line and letters are never skipped. Words can overlap. For example, the letters at the end of the word "MAST" could be used as the start of the word "STERN." Only the letters A to Z are used, and any spaces in an entry are removed. For example, "TROPICAL FISH" would be found in the grid as "TROPICALFISH."

Tree Forest

P Q Y L L I W P V H Z T J T Q O R R R D
E F G Y A S L L Q J M B L B W Q W G I E
B E H O M U Y G E R O M A C Y S S D L F
S G L C M Z R O I T C C O L L E K P G L
O V G H E O R E O J I C R S S V P Z X R
P V K Z O E E C L A O U C E D A R R K T
A E Y T L Z B C P N V A Q I D E Z H T J
G J S O H K L A U R P O K S S L R P G T
C Q Y R H S U T P Y L A C U E M A T I N
K M K A G G M A W R T U O A E M L U O C
K B A N A N A L S K A R M D D W P N C Z
R T R G E I P P U P E B A M B O O L K T
S Z V E S R R A O F E H M E N M P A A J
C U L U P H I U I U S N U A M F E W D Y
R P Z J X V C N A M V S Q I D T G A T Y
I P K L Z W O L L A T E S E N I H C H T
P F R T C C T E M L Y R R E H C U L C Z
Q V L U E E M B O S E E D S P V X Q R N
B K I M G O Y H N P U U M K O G K N I G
B W I O N F P P D B E K I N X K R A B L

ALDER
ALMOND
APPLE
APRICOT
ASPEN
AVOCADO
BALSA
BAMBOO
BANANA
BARK
BEECH
BIRCH
CATALPA
CEDAR
CHERRY
CHINESE TALLOW
COCONUT
CONIFEROUS
EUCALYPTUS
GINKGO
LAUREL
LEAVES
LEMON
LIQUIDAMBAR
MESQUITE
MULBERRY
OAK
ORANGE
PERSIMMON
PLUM
POPLAR
RINGS
ROOTS
SEEDS
SHADE
SYCAMORE
TEAK
WALNUT

Solution on page 244

Let's Go Shopping

```
K Q C S E L A S N O P U O C L O T H E S
Q E S A H C R U P G B I R D R V Y S O R
V F T L Y G O N G Y N E P E T S T O R E
A P P A R E L E W L S I F P S X S S E P
W O D N I W L M G T D U K A E A S H A P
C K G O K T W E A I N F W R M T Y O R O
Q W R S V W O U V D F U U T A Q M E C H
B O O A Z O R G V A E T S M G P R S A S
Q I C E D A D V E R T I S E M E N T S N
K R E S N F K J O N R O S N E T O O H R
R F R T R V A T X H G E R T R W I R R U
B U Y O X E S S C R C L T S C N H E E T
V S T C D C M V T N K Y Y T H P S S G E
E Y I A I U L O A F S E G O A L A W I R
Q O R S N S L R T O O N Z R N A F O S I
T T U L K B A B Y S T O R E D S V R T O
J M C R E E M K B M U M D S I T S B E E
T Q E F L W E G N A H C X E S I N S R X
C L S C X M E S L A E D I R E C T O R Y
C B N V U G Y J L F G M L H N H U I E R
```

ADVERTISEMENTS
APPAREL
BABY STORE
BROWSE
BUY
CASH REGISTER
CHRISTMAS
CLEARANCES
CLERKS
CLOTHES
COUPONS
CUSTOMERS
DEALS
DEPARTMENT STORE
DIRECTORY
ELEVATOR
EXCHANGE
FASHION
FAST FOOD
GAMES
GIFTS
GROCERY
JEWELRY
KIOSK
MALL
MERCHANDISE
MONEY
MUSIC STORE
NEGOTIATE
PARKING
PET STORE
PLASTIC
PURCHASE
REFUND
RESTAURANT
RETURNS
SALES
SEASONAL
SECURITY
SHOE STORE
SHOPPERS
TOYS
WINDOW

Solution on page 244

Scientifically Speaking

```
T C X S M J C S W I T E S T T U B E O T
X B H O X Y G E N S U R O H P S O H P F
C O M P O U N D O A N J N E G O R D Y H
W N P P Z D U X I L H B E R Y L L I U M
T D P O Q C I N T P V K D M X P F Q C T
I I D S T D V O C H E Q S O D I U M S R
T N Q I A A A I A A L V N M T A S Z E E
K G O T R N L S R D T F I E N A I K T F
P N I I E O C I F E Y R O T A R O B A L
M O A V K T H L F C Q K U E A O N O N E
N N Y E A O E L I A U M F R D G S R O C
T K T H E R M O D Y N A M I C S E O B T
B Q I B B P Y C M U I L E H J C D N R I
E S V A W Y U C M A G N E S I U M F A O
R Z A L R J R B G V S L A C I M E H C N
A A R A C C E L E R A T I O N O I T O M
D Q G N D R I V I N G F O R C E B M L V
I N Z C R Y S T A L I Q U I D S S A L G
A M P E R E U Q R O T A E H E L X J S I
L A S E R W A S C G X G U W Q B D C M E
```

ACCELERATION
ALCHEMY
ALPHA DECAY
AMPERE
BALANCE
BASE
BEAKER
BERYLLIUM
BONDING
BORON
CARBONATE
CHEMICALS
COLLISION
COMPOUND
CRYSTAL
DIFFRACTION
DRIVING FORCE
FUSION
GLASS
GRAVITY
HEAT
HELIUM
HYDROGEN
INDUCTION
INVARIANT
IONS
LABORATORY
LASER
LIQUIDS
MAGNESIUM
MOTION
NEGATIVE
OXIDATION
OXYGEN
PHOSPHORUS
POSITIVE
PROTON
QUANTUM NUMBER
RADIAL
REFLECTION
SODIUM
TEST TUBE
THERMODYNAMICS
THERMOMETER
TORQUE

Solution on page 244

Have a Drink

R N P S H T M S K I E D L X B W V N P G
B E E C B T R G I B W A L D O R F N O F
S Z P F C C Y J N B I Y Q I M Z G W X X
E N S P C A R B O N A T E D A E M I L C
K S I Z E P E L U J T N I M Y T X C R K
L O I L H P B O U R B O N P X G K E T I
L W B R L Y R O O W T R X E U J I C A R
I H Q E N O V D E C I U J E G N A R O S
R L E E C U C Y J P T Z G O R G E L G C
I C B B W E S M D U A T S A H S M V H H
O M C T K G N A O U X L M D G D N C E P
E A H O L P I R L T G D M I R J T Y X S
E R E O L Q R Y G I N A N D T O N I C Q
T T S R U A A D X A U G P L C C R K B O
R I P I R T D K R U E Q U S A G Y E P E
W N R R A O N G N R H T E D A N O M E L
L I E C T A A T A M O U N T A I N D E W
G B S B C T M L H C O D T N E O W M B D
Z U S E E T E Z O O B P D T R T O V A Z
M B O K N E R N T C K R J B C H E L A Q

BLOODY MARY
BOOZE
BOURBON
CARBONATED
COCKTAIL
DAIQUIRI
DR PEPPER
ESPRESSO
GIN AND TONIC
GINGER ALE
GRAND MARNIER
GROG
KIRSCH
LEMONADE
LIMEADE
MANDARIN
MARTINI
MINT JULEP
MOUNTAIN DEW
MUSCAT
NECTAR
ORANGE JUICE
PEPSI
RC COLA
ROOT BEER
SCOTCH
SEVEN UP
SHASTA
TEQUILA SUNRISE
TOM COLLINS
WALDORF

Solution on page 244

Raining Cats and Dogs

```
N M S H N R E V E I R T E R N E D L O G
W W M C A U C Q R Y Y A B M O B Y C A E
C O R N I S H R E X L U A T R K E E B S
P H X S T S I K H E T P V N W S S R Y E
U C G R A I H S C I T O X E E E I L S N
R W R E M A U H S P M X K N G T X E S I
J O V S L N A E N L G E A N I Y T I I L
O H J E A B H E I E Y V I S A R U N N A
Z C L M D L U P P K A K H G N W R A I B
M N N R E U A D N J E S S R F H K P A L
A A A U V E I O A P H I Q E O I I S N O
I I I B O T J G M O A C H Y R P S R R O
N R N N N E G E R M A N S H E P H E R D
E E A A R S C T E O A S V O S E A K E H
C B R E E S H S B E C N P U T T N C X O
O I E P X A E F O L L H X N C F G O O U
O S M O I B T R D J C G S D A L O C B N
N W O R B A N A V A H H A L T A R A K D
G U P U A M N A I T P Y G E E J A N D H
O R I E N T A L W V I F N K B W Z M A Q
```

ABYSSINIAN
BALINESE
BASSET
BEAGLE
BLOODHOUND
BOMBAY
BOXER
BRITISH SHORTHAIR
CHIHUAHUA
CHOW CHOW
COCKER SPANIEL
CORNISH REX
DALMATIAN
DEVON REX
DOBERMAN PINSCHER
EGYPTIAN MAU
EUROPEAN BURMESE
EXOTIC
GERMAN SHEPHERD
GOLDEN RETRIEVER
GREYHOUND
HAVANA BROWN
JAVANESE
KELPIE
MAINE COON
MANX
NORWEGIAN FOREST CAT
ORIENTAL
PEKINGESE
POMERANIAN
PUG
RUSSIAN BLUE
SHEEPDOG
SIAMESE
SIBERIAN
TURKISH ANGORA
WELSH CORGI
WHIPPET

Solution on page 245

Making Music

```
N I O U F F A R P H M N X N U D S V W L
L P M U R D O G N O B B F C V E V O A K
G S T R A V I N S K Y Z T E M P O C G N
P A G A N I N I C C U P B I D V D A N O
Z S H O S T A K O V I C H P F N Z L E K
H A R M O N Y E N L K C E E O A T E R N
C X K J R T I L S K C O R S C N P S O S
S O Y N T R N O E P G M K C E O C T T D
C P E P O O I R R H A C O M I T P E C N
W H N G M M S A V T A R E L X M P R U I
T O T A M B S C A J D G L S A H I Y D W
G N R E Y O O U T I N A A H E E T O N D
A E A R D N R L O A C C L N A C E U O O
W F C O O E I N R I Z E F E U U K N C O
H I C C R M T R Y J N O O S S A B G L W
I D M K S K A Z O O S O A B U T O N E A
S D L C E S E P I T C E L E S T A H F O
T L U I Y Q B L E R J U L E S T Y N E A
L E A H C I M R A C Y G A O H M F Y S Z
E T P C R I L I J O H N C O L T R A N E
```

ACCORDION
ARRANGEMENT
BASSOON
BEAT
BONGO DRUM
CALLIOPE
CAROLE KING
CELESTA
CHICK COREA
CHIMES
CLEF
CONDUCTOR
CONSERVATORY
FERMATA
FIDDLE
HARMONY
HOAGY CARMICHAEL
JOHN COLTRANE
JULE STYNE
KAZOO
LESTER YOUNG
LIONEL HAMPTON
MILT JACKSON
NOTE
PAGANINI
PAUL MCCARTNEY
PUCCINI
ROCK
ROSSINI
SAXOPHONE
SHOSTAKOVICH
STEPHEN FOSTER
STRAVINSKY
TEMPO
THELONIOUS MONK
TOMMY DORSEY
TONE
TROMBONE
TUBA
VOCAL
WAGNER
WHISTLE
WOODWINDS

Solution on page 245

Animal Kingdom

D Z A R E H P O G U R E T S M A H R Y J
Q U D O G S Z U A O L L I D A M R A E T
F B C G I I I C T T H U X R B Y N C K Z
E N W K J L R A D P R E H T N A P C R F
R E A E B T G A T R K Q G D Z Y B O U V
R K S Z T I M L F S I R T D M K O O T X
E C C I L O L A F F U B A E E H G N O V
T I W L O I Y L E I E B S V F H N T R N
S H A R A P B O E S I R M B D G I N R J
B C H N L O R R C D O W A R N R M A A V
O U P K L Q O O E H P F N T E N A S P E
L B N E I R C K P G X L I H K A L A O K
E E H E H I P P O P O T A M U S F E U F
O A M P C E P C L R F Y N T O M F H W T
P V F M N C H E E T A H D O Y O A P L V
A E T G I E N I T N O R E H S P S N E F
R R U N H N T J N O N E V A R I U E S J
D I D U C U G O A R B C I T N I B S A K
N Y Y Z C W E K A N S E L T T A R I E V
Q Q Z R H B C X N D M S D F S H R E W D

AARDVARK
ALLIGATOR
ANTELOPE
ARMADILLO
BABOON
BEAVER
BIRD
BISON
BUFFALO
CHEETAH
CHICKEN
CHINCHILLA
COYOTE
DOGS
DUCK BILLED PLATYPUS
FERRET
FLAMINGO
FOX
GERBIL
GIRAFFE
GOPHER
HAMSTER
HEDGEHOG
HERON
HIPPOPOTAMUS
HORSE
HUMANS
KOALA
LEMMING
LEOPARD
LOBSTER
MOOSE
PANTHER
PARROT
PENGUIN
PHEASANT
PORPOISE
RACCOON
RATTLE SNAKE
RAVEN
SHREW
TASMANIAN DEVIL
TOAD
TURKEY
WEASEL

Solution on page 245

Bookish

```
W E S E R I E S X B A Q N T R A V E L Y
B R E F E R E N C E T R E V O C D R A H
M O L A I D E P O L C Y C N E L X C N T
A M F M S T E H S E G T C W N Z K A O D
H A H B J H B W S C G R E O T N Y E I E
S N E A N G E O E I H A I X O Y R O T S
F C L Q O I O L O Y L O P W T K B P C U
A E P N I R Y P F K D B L E E B I R I U
J U R R T Y O G O P S E U A L I O N F E
H S K E C P Q H M C D T C P S T V O G D
R S S V I O I B T G K E O I A T I E K B
E I L O F C V R E U I E T R M M I T R M
T P E C N O C M C G A E T X E A A C Y D
I B V T O J E Q N S K S I S B N L R Y O
R S O F N N O I T C U D O R T N I R D D
W T N O T X T I A L N N V S N Q A Q C O
T U E S E N B J L E P P A P E R B A C K
B I N D I N G I P F F N M M B G S X J U
Z P N R C H A P T E R S D I O E A Z T E
I I P H E C A F E R P Y L S O C X P L W
```

ACKNOWLEDGEMENTS
APPENDIX
AUTHOR
BINDING
BOOKSTORE
CASE
CHAPTERS
CONCEPT
COOKING
COPYRIGHT
DEWEY DECIMAL
DRAMA
ENCYCLOPEDIA
FICTIONAL
HARDCOVER
ILLUSTRATOR
INDEX
INTRODUCTION
ISBN
ISSUE
JACKET
LIBRARY
MANUSCRIPT
NONFICTION
NOVELS
PAGES
PAPERBACK
POCKET
PREFACE
PRINTING
PUBLISHER
REFERENCE
REVIEW
ROMANCE
SCHOLASTIC
SELF HELP
SERIES
SHELF
SOFTCOVER
STORY
TEXTBOOK
TITLE PAGE
TRAVEL
USED
WRITER

Solution on page 245

Play Sports

```
O B A S E B A L L M J J Y G N I C N E F
U I O U T E U Q O R C B G N I E O N A C
Q K L M A I N H E M A R T I A L A R T S
P I O N O U C S N C G N I D I R L L U B
M N P W P U S K K W N T W A C K F L V G
B G R L Q O N G B Y O R D E G B G A O N
N G E F R G A T Z A E G O L N L N B L I
T N T C K M N C A S L U W R I D I T L H
O I A D M S R I T I Y L N E L I T E E S
Y L W O N I W L D J N F H E D S F U Y I
E I N A C N I Y D D O C I H R C I Q B F
K A H K T N R A N O E F L C U U L C A G
C S E I G E R C T O D L L I H S T A L N
O T O L H T R B Y N T S S O M G H R L I
H E J C S E A S A C G N K B O B G B Y F
E J R W U L Y K K F L N I E O P I X R R
C A V B L B C D U I G I I M E B E N U U
I C E S K A T I N G I U N V D T W O G S
Y J I N R T C U R L I N G G I A U F B K
G N I T A K S D E E P S G B K D B T Y A
```

ARCHERY
BACKGAMMON
BADMINTON
BASEBALL
BIKING
BOB SLEDDING
BULL RIDING
CANOEING
CHEERLEADING
CRICKET
CROQUET
CURLING
CYCLING
DARTS
DISCUS
DIVING
DOWNHILL SKIING
FENCING
FISHING
FOOTBALL
HURDLING
ICE HOCKEY
ICE SKATING
LACROSSE
MARTIAL ARTS
MOUNTAIN CLIMBING
POOL
RACQUETBALL
RUGBY
SAILING
SKEET
SPEED SKATING
STICKBALL
SURFING
TABLE TENNIS
TRACK AND FIELD
VOLLEYBALL
WATER POLO
WATER SKIING
WEIGHTLIFTING
WRESTLING

Solution on page 246

Back to Business

R R R D Z D H W J B N J N I H Y D U O X
A E E L B A V I E C E R F C I G U Q H G
L M O T E S O S G J M G R E K O R B D N
L U Y N I G R A M A V E R A G E S D O I
Y L R E T R A U Q L I Q U I D I T Y W K
R O D F N S E T A R E L B A I R A V J N
C V Y R N O Y M E X P O R T Y P S A O A
A X T U A A M L E B E T S N P D X Y N B
S H I L C O M P A N Y R E P O R T S E U
H E L I D T B R K A T N A O L R D A S L
F X I A V N T G D V E F G C E V R V O L
L C T B O E U G I T T F U P Y M E I D M
O H A I R M E F H B O Q O N A X L N R A
W A L L S T R E E T E R A R D O U G E R
U N O I D S A Q S R P H K Y F O F S V K
M G V T E E S O H K H E T T P H N B E E
A E C Y M V C M D S T I R M L Z Y O N T
X F I N A N C I A L U O O A C I S N U P
E V L W N I B R Z Q P C H L A R E D E F
H U D G D H C V E R E S O U R C E S V G

AVERAGES
BANKING
BARTER
BEAR MARKET
BROKER
BULL MARKET
CASH FLOW
COMPANY REPORTS
COMPOUND
COST OF GOODS
CRASH
DAY TRADER
DEMAND
DOW JONES
EQUITY
EXCHANGE
EXPORT
FEDERAL
FINANCIAL
INVESTMENT
LIABILITY
LIQUIDITY
LOAN
MARGIN
MONEY
NYSE
PORTFOLIO
PROPERTY
QUARTERLY
RALLY
RECEIVABLE
REFUND
RESOURCES
RETIREMENT FUND
REVENUE
SAVINGS BONDS
THE BIG BOARD
VARIABLE RATES
VOLATILITY
VOLUME
WALL STREET

Solution on page 246

Turn on the TV

J J U D G E J U D Y N W O H S Y A D O T

K R O W T E N D O O F R U G R A T S S H

W D S E T H E W E S T W I N G Y G D T E

C O S U M H N U S A N E T W O R K X L J

A P T X N I G T E L E T U B B I E S E E

N T H S C D L I E N T O U R A G E L N T

L B E D E O A L L M Y C H I L D R E N S

S L S G A S M N I G V T T R U O C N A O

S O I E D Y A E C O N T R M T V S N H N

A O M H U A S M D E N I X G V A N A C S

K M P S E L G O E Y C A D A Y R O H R D

C B S S N E B R F S C H I I P B S C E I

A E O E A B R D O O T E A R U B W R H S

J R N Y B B C T P T U R N N E G A O T C

S G S E O R E H E Y C R E T N T D O A O

B S C I F I C H A N N E L E R E N D E V

U X G E N E R A L H O S P I T A L T W E

R P P T H E S O P R A N O S V B L U W R

C B I O G R A P H Y C H A N N E L O G Y

S S A W X Y G P V O Q U N I V I S I O N

ALL MY CHILDREN
BBC
BET
BIOGRAPHY CHANNEL
BLOOMBERG
BRAVO
COMEDY CENTRAL
COURT TV
DAWSONS CREEK
DAYS OF OUR LIVES
DISCOVERY
ENTOURAGE
ESPN
FOOD NETWORK
GENERAL HOSPITAL
GUIDING LIGHT
HEROES
INSPECTOR GADGET
JACKASS
JOE MILLIONAIRE
JUDGE JUDY
MSNBC
MTV
NYPD BLUE
ONE TREE HILL
OUTDOOR CHANNEL
PAX TV
PBS
RUGRATS
SCI FI CHANNEL
SCRUBS
SESAME STREET
SUNDANCE CHANNEL
TELETUBBIES
THE JETSONS
THE SIMPSONS
THE SOPRANOS
THE WEST WING
TNT
TODAY SHOW
UNIVISION
USA NETWORK
WEATHER CHANNEL

Solution on page 246

Treat Yourself

W Q L P N F E N C A R A M E L U V T U M

U V D I G E S L P G U M D R O P X O Z E

P A S Q C Q Z P P X E Q M R K V M R M Y

C T T Y F O E A I P K D P Y A I T T Z F

P P U P X T R U D H A S T U N T S E H C

E C N N I W I I Q R C D P C F F S S J X

P B D Z C D Z V C H D O E U B T W U E I

C H E E S E C A K E A M T I R A Y H C S

O R X L L A B E S E E H C A D Y C C O W

S X I M X E H C I A R N T O T N R T A E

E E M H I S O P T T B Y S E U O A O Q E

G A H B D O N P O P R T T P Y B P C E T

N D T X K I I F P R E R O D D U O S E S

I N K I K E F R E A G E R A N B P R W M

D U E P D E E B F L N S R P A B I E N F

D S M C E T N U Q I I S A G C L L T A L

U U N D Z A S P O N G E C A K E L T J G

P C H E R R Y P I E V D J S C G O U M G

K W L C O T T O N C A N D Y O U L B Y A

R S Q N O E H J D C M B T Z R M F B A Y

APPETIZERS
BUBBLE GUM
BUTTERSCOTCH
CANDIED APPLE
CARAMEL
CARROTS
CHEESE BALL
CHEESECAKE
CHERRY PIE
CHESTNUTS
CHEX MIX
COOKIES
COTTON CANDY
CRANBERRY TART
CUSTARD
DESSERT
GINGERBREAD CAKE
GUMDROP
KISSES
LICORICE
LOLLIPOP
MINCEMEAT PIE
MIXED NUTS
POTATO CHIPS
PRALINE
PRETZELS
PUDDING
PUMPKIN PIE
PUNCH
ROCK CANDY
SODA
SPONGE CAKE
SUNDAE
SWEETS
TOFFEE
TORTE

Solution on page 246

Dive In

P E K W N E E R C S N U S H A A X I A R
Y S L P A C O R E W O H S F L R W K A B
J Q Y D I T A O L F A F J N T A T L L V
T L L B D W E O O L O P O C R A M E L F
U O O C Q A K R L V S M U M C B L H E D
F O J O A N P O P W Y B P L D C M W R M
E P Z C P B W E K O R T S T S A E R B I
Q G O B O E A R I D L A J U M P Z E M F
S N A B N L I N A G E O M U J Y X M U R
V I P D A L D D A S G N I W R E T A W C
F D E N K Y R D D R A O B G N I V I D U
I A H E G F L N S I E U D R B I K I N I
N W T R X L U H P W K V A S Z W A V E H
S C A N N O N B A L L F A Z W H C H S L
U K B E O P E U L W T I U S M I W S I E
D L N B T I B T E W D C O Z E B E S C K
E Q U U U E T T D L A D D E R F T G R R
Q U S T R R P O I J E C H L O R I N E O
S B K F N T N H L E R E O F T F F L X N
C Q Q T Z R A D S H T N T G O G G L E S

BELLY FLOP
BIKINI
BREASTSTROKE
CABANA
CANNONBALL
CHLORINE
DIVING BOARD
DOGGIE PADDLE
EXERCISE
FINS
FLOAT
GOGGLES
HOT TUB
JACUZZI
JUMP
KIDDIE POOL
LADDER
LAPS
LIFESAVER
LOTION
MARCO POLO
MUSCLE
RAFT
SHALLOW END
SHOWER
SLIDE
SNORKEL
SUNBATHE
SUNSCREEN
SWIMSUIT
TREAD
TRUNKS
TUBE
UMBRELLA
WADING POOL
WATER POLO
WATER WINGS
WAVE
WET

Solution on page 247

Car Crazy

```
W E M I S S I O N S L O W R I D E R M R
X M E P R E R U O T D N A R G R Q D U M
N X T A E T A L P H C T U L C O D A F F
B O S I L O N T A I L L I G H T K S F R
X B Y N G R A C E L C S U M Y A G H L P
M O S T N I O J L A S R E V I N U B E N
W B G K A T R O A D S T E R I R V O R O
A W N R R N N R O H S H D N M E B A S I
C L I O W E L O T Y T G O Q D T R R N S
B A L T P M H F S R A I D D P L A D O N
B T O E E N D G A X T L G R E A K Y T E
F M O R E G N V B I I Y E I R R E R S P
E O C U J I E A D C O C D B F A S E I S
C T O B G L L N B A N N A R O C A T P U
I E Q R G A O E U M W E R E R I C S I S
N L A A N C X L M S A G T D M N K L C E
A H M C R U O T P H G R G N A G N O N S
C E I I R U S E E A O E T U N Q A H I U
S N A Y A W E E R F N M D H C Q R P C F
G N I T A E H B N T A E S T E K C U B L
```

AIR CONDITIONING
ALIGNMENT
ALTERNATOR
BALANCING
BEETLE
BRAKES
BUCKET SEAT
BUMPER
CAMSHAFT
CARBURETOR
CHARGING SYSTEM
CLUTCH PLATE
COOLING SYSTEM
CRANKCASE
DASHBOARD
DODGE DART GT
EMERGENCY LIGHT
EMISSIONS
FREEWAY
FUSES
GRAND TOURER
HEATING
HOOD
HORN
JEEP WRANGLER
LOWRIDER
MOTEL
MUFFLER
MUSCLE CAR
PAINT
PERFORMANCE
PICNIC
PISTONS
RACING
ROADSTER
STATION WAGON
SUNROOF
SUSPENSION
TAILLIGHT
THUNDERBIRD
TRAVEL GAMES
UNIVERSAL JOINTS
UPHOLSTERY

Solution on page 247

Wild Adventure

P D Z D O F I C X V S E K A L S P I C E

J H H E O N O Y N A C V T D K J R M W S

K N X A Y O I X T M K E S H C U C I B T

X J U B N L W L X I W R C H I S Y S F N

P S C Y A E I D P P S G E Y T H P T G E

L H C S O N L Z R R M R N V S A O L Z L

A R H U Y F A E A A Q E E R G L A E A L

N U I M K I T G V R H E R V N C Y T R E

T B P M I A U L K A B N Y T I U O O E P

S S M I E O L C A I T V J E K D G E G E

Y A U T C A S W E O Q I R E L N O E D R

C Y N S F E A N P S Z P O T A E L I A T

A A K N C T I O S F E G P N W W K I B C

M L I G S P G O E A Q E F S E G D O L E

O A K N E R M H K H B I N O C U L A R S

R M G T A D E C I D U O U S Q I G C I N

E I I P H Z Y W P Y U B Z B H N V B V I

L H H E F U R H O X Q F S T R E A M E P

W Y V J R E T A W H A D N O C A N A R X

Z O E J R U L B T C S E V L O W R L S W

ALPS
ANACONDA
ANTEATER
BADGER
BINOCULARS
BIODIVERSITY
BRAZIL
CANYON
CHIPMUNK
COUGARS
DECIDUOUS
ELEVATION
EVERGREEN
FIRS
GLACIER PEAK
HARDWOOD
HIMALAYAS
INSECT REPELLENT
LAKES
LODGE
MISTLETOE
MOSS
NEW GUINEA
PIKES PEAK
PLANTS
RAINFALL
RIVERS
SCENERY
SHOWERS
SHRUBS
STREAM
SUMMIT
SYCAMORE
TARZAN
TOPOGRAPHY
WALKING STICK
WATER
WHITE PINE
WOLVES

Solution on page 247

Home Construction

R X Y Q A C U P D F F R I W V B E Q S J
X E S Y S J A O T G N I B M U L P N S Q
E P J S H E O B R N U B I G H C G G Y H
V C B K R R H G I I A R Y R N O S A M W
P J V E S E Q C M N Z W O D N I W Y A B
S H O W E R I V T O E T R O W E L T E L
I C L M R T Y L F I P T A U V F E E L I
N E A I U I H U P T W P W I K R E A R T
K I D B T Q R M C I W S R R H R X R E O
S G D H C N P B P D T D L E U E E D P D
L M E U I B D E R N Z J A T W M C O A O
C D R T P N W R E O U T C L A M U W P S
F U U U B L S M L C E E H E L A C N D X
N R P F Y C E U E R T E A H L H O B N B
E S T B R C N X L I Y O L S P Y N E A G
P S G E O Y D R H A P P L I A N C E S G
Z M E A R A E C R E T U O R P L R B J B
H N W T R T R Y E N M I H C E S E A L R
S Z S L I A N D P S B R O I R E T X E D
R Z E M M R Y J H E A T I N G N E O B J

AIR CONDITIONING
APPLIANCES
ARCHITECTURE
BAY WINDOW
CABINET
CEMENT
CHIMNEY
CONCRETE
CUPBOARD
DOORS
DRIVEWAY
DUPLEX
EXTERIOR
FURNITURE
HALL
HAMMER
HEATING
INSULATION
LADDER
LUMBER
MASONRY
MIRROR
MITER
NAILS
PICTURES
PLIERS
PLUMBING
RAGS
ROUTER
SANDPAPER
SCREENS
SEAL
SHELTER
SHOWER
SINKS
SWITCHES
TEAR DOWN
TRIM
TROWEL
TUB
WALLPAPER
WATER HEATER

Solution on page 247

Chapter 6

Lost and Found

Fit all of the missing letters into the grids. If you put them in the right places, you'll find that every word crosses another, horizontally or vertically.

Lost and Found 1

Missing Letters

S	**I**	**A**	**A**
E	**E**	**R**	**A**
U	**P**	**R**	**Y**
L	**P**	**A**	**U**

I		C		O	F	F		O
N	Y		O	N				R
C		I		C		D		E
H				E	N		D	
	T		O					B
	T		S		G			
L		S	T	S		L		E
	C			E	W		N	
S	K			D		E	G	G

D	E	P				O	I	
I		O		A				
S				U	M	B		N
				L			P	T
	E	T				S		
T		H		S			C	E
E			S	T	I	C		N
R	E	T	A		N			V
	T		T	R	E	A		

Lost and Found 2

Missing Letters

E	**A**	**T**	**Y**
L	**S**	**T**	**A**
I	**L**	**H**	**H**
I	**T**	**L**	**A**

Solution on page 248

Lost and Found 3

Missing Letters

A	**R**	**G**	**E**
T	**I**	**S**	**D**
O	**D**	**T**	**F**
A	**O**	**L**	**P**

B	U	D		S		E	L	T
E		R		T			E	
A		E		A	C	I		
U						N		E
		S		T	R	I	E	
			F		E	T		I
	L	U	I	D		I		T
U			G			A		
L	A	W		C	O			R

Lost and Found 4

Missing Letters

A	**A**	**N**	**R**
T	**T**	**K**	**C**
N	**L**	**C**	**A**
C	**D**	**L**	**O**

A	L				P	R		Y
R		I	T	S			R	
	A		E		H		T	
H		E		T	E			
	E	L		E	S			
A		Y	E			I	L	
R			N			S		A
				E	P			V
			Y			S	E	A

Solution on page 248

Lost and Found 5

Missing Letters

N	D	E	F
D	E	A	I
E	R	N	N
A	A	M	K

E			A		F		I	R
X				O				A
	G	I		G		W		I
M		X			M	I	N	
I				C	A		E	
N		P		L			E	S
			N	E	D			
		E		A		P		G
A	N	Y	O				D	

	N	O	B			I	P	S
	O		I				I	
P				I	B		E	
	N		C		E	A		E
A			U	G		Y		
			I		S		W	S
L		F	T			R		
O		O		P	A	S	T	
W	A							R

Lost and Found 6

Missing Letters

X	S	L	O
S	S	L	I
I	E	L	A
A	E	L	K

Solution on page 249

Lost and Found 7

Missing Letters

T	R	E	B
I	I	R	A
C	S	B	A
A	N	S	Y

	I	N	C				S	E
B		U				R		
E	V		L		T	E		R
D				G	R	A		
	D		I	L			L	
P		N		A		W	E	
		C	A		C	E		A
S		E		E			I	G
	O		T					

Lost and Found 8

Missing Letters

D	T	E	P
R	C	E	S
B	S	I	O
R	E	D	L

M			C		T	U		
O		M	U	M			A	
	R					A		H
E		R		W	O		E	
R		A	P	A	R	T		
A	C	C				I	N	G
T	A		E			S		O
	L		M	E	N			
	L							

Solution on page 249

Lost and Found 9

Missing Letters

A	**E**	**O**	**U**
P	**W**	**O**	**A**
R	**P**	**A**	**Y**
W	**S**	**S**	**N**

O	W	L					L	
	H	O			L	E		F
N	O			D	A			
A			J			E	T	
T		B	A	N	G		E	
U			M			N	D	
		D	A	T				T
	Y	E			G			
		W		T	E	M		

Lost and Found 10

Missing Letters

E	**A**	**P**	**B**
C	**O**	**M**	**H**
E	**C**	**E**	**C**
N	**S**	**F**	**I**

	S			O	M	B		
S		Y						A
	E			R			A	P
A		H	I	E	V			
				A		F		S
E		F	E		T	I	V	E
	I	R			I	T		E
S	C		R	E	D			
Y		G		D		A	L	

Solution on page 250

Lost and Found 11

Missing Letters

B	**L**	**E**	**L**
A	**D**	**O**	**O**
R	**E**	**O**	**E**
L	**E**	**R**	**R**

B	U	I			S		E	
U			O			C		Y
	E	S	S		D			
	L		S	S	O	M	S	
	S	M	E		T		I	
G			S	E		T		Y
		D			A		N	
G			S	P		E		
		Y		Y	I		L	D

A	C	T		H			W	
	H			I		P	E	
P				S	U			
			A				D	D
			V	E	R			I
	T	O	E			A	G	
	I			O		B		S
F	A	R	E	W			L	
	N					E	L	

Lost and Found 12

Missing Letters

E	**O**	**E**	**B**
S	**L**	**I**	**F**
E	**N**	**N**	**S**
E	**U**	**R**	**R**

Solution on page 250

Lost and Found 13

Missing Letters

N	**R**	**N**	**A**
R	**E**	**I**	**E**
R	**S**	**Y**	**D**
G	**R**	**N**	**U**

	H	E	R	O				
	E					E		E
O			A	N		W	O	
	I		G		Y			
S	T	I			E	D		S
	A		E	S	S			
A	G	R		E		M	A	T
	E		D		Y		R	
				Y		E		D

Lost and Found 14

Missing Letters

U	**E**	**H**	**L**
L	**O**	**S**	**R**
P	**S**	**E**	**B**
S	**M**	**C**	**T**

	O	T	E			Z	I	
E				A	R	E		E
R		A		P				A
					S	O	N	
			I	T	E		A	
	E	E				I		S
	A	N	D		B		T	
A				A		L	Y	
	H		E		E			

Solution on page 251

Lost and Found 15

Missing Letters

L	S	O	O
R	T	N	F
G	I	Y	I
A	O	U	N

C	H	I				C		
A				N		I		O
R		B		A	N		R	Y
	H		W	L		A		S
G		D			A	R	D	
	R		B	S			R	
		E			G	I		N
	O		E	S			W	
	R		W			A	N	

M	A	R				S		
I				G	L		D	
D	I	G		R				
D				E		R		
			H	A	B	E	T	
		H				D		S
	J		B		A			I
		T		C	K			
		O	T		S	A		E

Lost and Found 16

Missing Letters

A	K	T	O
E	H	Z	S
I	A	Y	L
P	A	U	C

Solution on page 251

Lost and Found 17

Missing Letters

R	**S**	**A**	**S**
A	**H**	**E**	**Y**
T	**T**	**I**	**S**
E	**X**	**O**	**E**

		R	I	L	L		P	
				O			L	
	S		F			J		W
	T		E		P	E		
	O	P				T		D
	R		L	A	Y		A	
D		E		I	S		U	E
		L		L		I		
F	I		H		O		E	N

Lost and Found 18

Missing Letters

D	**A**	**E**	**R**
S	**S**	**L**	**I**
T	**O**	**O**	**A**
M	**R**	**E**	**E**

	D		E	F	F			
D	I	D		O			I	
R				R	O	A	D	
	L		O					C
G		T	O	R	C	H		R
	G	A			L	I	N	
R		N	E	W				W
I		C			R	E		S
		E	T		K			

Solution on page 252

Lost and Found 19

Missing Letters

D	A	E	V
Y	M	A	R
I	E	G	A
T	E	O	E

	G		P				R	
R	A			M	A	K		S
	S	O	L					
					O	I		
	H	I	K			V		T
R	E	M	E		B	E	R	
E		A		E				
L	E	G		N				
					H	E	R	

Lost and Found 20

Missing Letters

R	O	Y	E
N	L	M	Y
D	L	N	D
H	E	D	S

	A	D		U		A	D	
E			U		E			
L				U		O		E
P			B	A	B	L		
	A			L	E			
	F		F		Y		S	
A	T			Y	O		K	
N		A					I	
	E	T				U		P

Solution on page 252

Lost and Found 21

Missing Letters

S	K	P	I
M	E	E	R
I	R	M	P
R	D	L	U

H							O	
I		A			E	A	R	S
	O	M			L	I	D	
		E		A	I			
	W		O	N	G		R	
				K		T		A
O		C			O	A	D	S
A	M	A	T					
K		N			S			S

		B		D		P		H
T				E	F	O	R	
E		L			A	P	O	R
		O	M		T		B	
	O	W		L	A			R
			T		L	A	T	
O	A	S		S		I		D
O			L	I	S		S	
K	N	E						

Lost and Found 22

Missing Letters

E	T	L	H
I	E	E	R
T	B	B	O
T	V	X	I

Solution on page 253

Lost and Found 23

Missing Letters

D	**N**	**D**	**U**
T	**U**	**L**	**L**
T	**P**	**E**	**E**
C	**U**	**C**	**U**

O	U	T					G	
U					H	A		
	I	B			R		U	
		E	X			S	E	
		G		A	S	K		E
	F		N	C	T	I	O	N
		N	U	T				
					R	T	L	
	B	O	S	S				

Lost and Found 24

Missing Letters

L	**I**	**E**	**T**
A	**O**	**I**	**S**
I	**O**	**C**	**A**
R	**A**	**E**	**M**

			L		B		D	
	I	S				T		D
M			V	E	R			
I			E			B		T
S	H			S			S	
T		T			A	X		S
			L	O			O	
		M			M	O	N	G
	L	E	A	K				

Solution on page 253

Lost and Found 25

Missing Letters

S	**E**	**C**	**E**
O	**N**	**E**	**R**
O	**B**	**H**	**P**
O	**V**	**A**	**T**

A	S			C	U			
	E		U			O	U	
E		E	N			R		A
		X		E	R	N	A	L
I	N		O	M			P	
C						I	R	S
E			E	T	S			
		S		Y		U		G
					N		S	

	R			C	R	E		
H		M					L	
						O	U	R
S		N	S		U		M	
	L		E	U	R			E
O	T	H			S			A
U		I	N	G		D		G
				E	Q			
S		S				G		E

Lost and Found 26

Missing Letters

P	**T**	**O**	**R**
R	**E**	**A**	**U**
L	**P**	**S**	**E**
S	**F**	**U**	**P**

Solution on page 254

Lost and Found 27

Missing Letters

C	**U**	**E**	**D**
G	**R**	**N**	**N**
A	**R**	**S**	**E**
D	**O**	**O**	**A**

C				E	P	T	S	
	A		O		R		C	
	T		P	O				R
	H	A	Y			O	N	E
C		C				A	T	S
R		C		B		D		P
I	D				M			O
E		S			S	O	O	
			T	Y				

Lost and Found 28

Missing Letters

T	**T**	**E**	**T**
H	**C**	**L**	**U**
A	**L**	**R**	**G**
P	**C**	**S**	**R**

					P	L	O	
	U	B	I	C		I		O
H		A		O			A	W
O	C				S			E
	H	O	S	P	I			
H	O	N	E	S			W	
	I		F			E	A	S
		O	U	P			R	
						I	D	

Solution on page 254

Lost and Found 29

Missing Letters

O	**E**	**T**	**C**
E	**D**	**H**	**S**
I	**T**	**C**	**N**
A	**Y**	**G**	**O**

				C				
A		N				L	E	S
U		E		R				O
	U	I	D	E				
U		T			T	O	M	S
S				L	A	R		
	I	E	D			K	I	P
	T	R		U	T			A
			R		E	X		

Lost and Found 30

Missing Letters

H	**T**	**T**	**E**
L	**D**	**F**	**O**
B	**I**	**S**	**E**
N	**O**	**C**	**E**

S				U	P			
		I	L			T		U
A		N		S	A		L	S
R		T	O					K
		E			O	C	U	S
			E	A	T	H		
A		D				E	A	D
L		E	D	G		S		A
	A	D			R			

Solution on page 255

Lost and Found 31

H	A					R	A	
		E		W		U		O
C	E		T					W
				S	T		E	
		I	N		S	O		
H		C			E			
		E	S		L	A		K
M	Y			L	F		T	
	M		X					

Missing Letters

I	N	A	S
S	E	G	G
C	V	R	N
A	X	A	A

Lost and Found 32

J	A				K	I		
			I	N	N		A	
	I	G	N		E		W	
		E	C	R			S	E
B		T				I		
			A		E	D	G	
B	L	O			A			N
	S	W				E	S	T
		E			S			

Missing Letters

T	Z	A	D
E	Z	V	L
E	W	E	E
A	E	L	S

Solution on page 255

Chapter 7
Providers

Fit all of the words into the grids. To get you started, one of the words is already entered.

Provider 1

A L T S

3 Letters

ALE
ARB
ARE
ARK
ART
CON
DES
EAT
IRE
KAY
KIT
LEE
LOO
ORA
PAD
PEA
PIE
RET
RIA
SEA
SER
STY
TAR
TOT

4 Letters

ACME
ALAE
ALOE
ALPS
ALTS
APSE
ARCS
ARIA
ARTS
BANS
CASE
COAT
COKE
FLAT
HELP
LOAN
MANY
MATT
MOTH
OLEO
PANS
RATS
RIOT
ROOT
SEES
SELL
SERA
SOUP
STYE
TETS
TOLU
TOTE

5 Letters

AFORE
ARRAS
CAMEL
COOLS
MASSE
MASTS
PLOTS
SALSA
STELE
TENSE

6 Letters

ELAPSE
SESAME

Solution on page 256

Provider 2

P S S T

3 Letters

ALA
ANT
ARS
AVE
AYE
BOY
DAD
ERA
ERN
GAT
GEN
MAY
MOA
NAE
ORT
PAP
PUT
RAP
SAT
SET
TEN
TOM
TSK

4 Letters

AGEE
ALEE
AMPS
APED
APES
ASPS
BARE
BRAD
EYES
LAVA
NENE
ONES
PATS
PELE
PLEA
POLL
PSST
RARE
ROUT
SALE
SASS
SATE
SCAT
SEAS
SERE
SLOE
SLOG
SOLO
SPAT
STAB
TEED
TENS
TOIL
TORE

5 Letters

ALTAR
BLAST
ESSES
KAPPA
MINCE
ROAST
SEEDS
STABS
STEED

6 Letters

ARMADA
ASTERS

Solution on page 256

Provider 3

3 Letters

AGA
ANA
BRA
DOS
GAS
HES
MAD
MOB
MOP
NOR
OAT
ODS
ORE
PAS
POI
RIG
SAG
TAT
TOE
YEA

4 Letters

AEON
AERO
AGIO
AMAH
ARID
CARD
DEAL
DRAT
ELSE
EPEE
ERGS
EVES
HERO
HITS
MAGS
OARS
OSES
OTTO
OWED
SEGO
SETA
SNAG
SODS
TARS
TEEN
THAT
TOMS
TOPE
TRIM
TSAR
TYNE
WOES

5 Letters

DENSE
RAGES
RAVEN
STATS
STOAT
TRESS

6 Letters

ARENAS
ARREST
PESETA
ROASTS
STREET
THRONE

7 Letters

CAMERAS
NEATENS

Solution on page 256

Provider 4

L A B

3 Letters

ACT
AGE
AGO
AHA
ALS
ASP
ATE
BAM
COO
EON
HOP
LAB
LAS
LAT
LIE
MAT
MIL
NUN
OBI
RAS
RES
ROD
SEN
SHY
SPY
TAS

4 Letters

ABLE
ACHE
AGAR
AGUE
ALBS
ANTE
APER
ARBS
BRAE
BRAG
BRAS
BROS
CORE
GLEE
KEEL
LEER
LOCI
LOOT
MANE
METE
MOPE
OAST
ODES
RACE
RATE
ROTE
SANS
SASH
SEAL
SEMI
SOAK
SOMA
SOTS
TEND
THEE
VISE

5 Letters

GATOR
GESTE
MATES
PSALM
SATES
SAVER
SLATS
TREED

Solution on page 256

Provider 5

T	A	E	■				■			

3 Letters

ALL
ANE
BAY
BOO
ELD
ERS
HAY
HON
HUH
ICE
LAG
LET
MED
MEN
OCA
OHO
OLE
PAL
SON
SPA
TAE
TAN
WIN

4 Letters

ABET
AGED
ALAS
ALIT
ANSA
AURA
BOWS
CORN
DICE
ELLS
EPOS
ERAS
GOBS
LAIN
LANE
MADE
OLDS
PREP
ROAN
ROSE
SAIL
SCAD
SEAT
SHAD
SHES
SHMO
SHOO
SLAM
SLED
SONS
SYNE
TAEL
TAPA
THEM
TOLE
TOON
TRIO
YENS

5 Letters

ANGST
ASSES
BESTS
PANED
PICOT
RESTS
SLATE
SNARE
TASSE

Solution on page 257

Provider 6

3 Letters

AAH
AMP
ARM
ASS
BEE
BOA
EEL
ELS
EMS
ERE
HAE
ION
LEA
OPS
OPT
PAR
PEE
ROB
ROT
SEE
TAO
TEE
THE
TIS
WET

4 Letters

ABRI
ALMA
ANTS
AREA
ASEA
BARN
CELL
ETHS
HEAT
IOTA
LAMP
LAPS
LASE
LASS
LOAM
OATS
OLES
OPES
OPTS
PEEP
PHAT
PROA
PSIS
RENT
SABE
SARI
SEAM
SEAR
SEER
SEPT
SETS
SIRE
SOON
TENT
TONE
TOOL
TORA
TWAS

5 Letters

ALINE
CASAS
MATTE
SPARS
STARS
START
TESTS

Solution on page 257

Provider 7

D A B

3 Letters

AMA
AMI
AWE
BEG
DAB
DOR
MAN
OWE
RED
REF
SIT
TAM
TED
TIN

4 Letters

AGER
AKIN
ALAN
ALAR
AMID
CAKE
CLAY
CREW
EARN
ELAN
FLEE
GAME
HERE
IDES
LOOS
LOPE
LUNA
MANO
NAVE
ORES
ORLE
PANE
PENS
SAVE
SCUP
SLOT
SONE
SURE
TAPS
TERN
THRU
TOWS
TROP
TUBE
UNIT
WANE

5 Letters

ACRES
AWARE
CRESS
CRONE
ECRUS
MASON
SPATS
STETS
STILE
TONES

6 Letters

ENISLE
LETHAL
OBEYER
PSEUDO

8 Letters

REGAINED
RHEOSTAT

Solution on page 257

Provider 8

3 Letters

APE
ARC
BEN
BUY
COS
DOM
EYE
FIB
FLU
FRO
LAW
LUV
OOH
RAH
SAW
SRI
THO
TOY
WAD
WAG
WEB
WOO
YES

4 Letters

ACES
AMIE
ARES
ARFS
AWED
AWLS
AYES
COVE
GENE
HOES
HOOT
LACE
MILS
MORT
OHMS
OMIT
OOPS
PAPA
PARA
PFFT
REST
RILE
ROUE
SETT
SHOW
SILO
SLAT
SLAW
SORE
STAR
STET
TARE
TEST
TODS

5 Letters

BROOD
IMAMS
MOCHA
POSTS
REAPS
RESEE
SEEPY
SPATE
TESTY

6 Letters

EMBRYO
TRADER

Solution on page 257

Provider 9

3 Letters

AAS
ABA
ALP
AND
CAP
ELK
EWE
FOE
GOD
HAS
HIE
HOE
IDS
ILL
LAM
LEI
NOT
OAR
OVA
PSI
SHA
SHE
VIA

4 Letters

AFAR
AIDE
ALES
ALLS
ALSO
AVOW
BRIT
BYTE
CHIS
CONE
DIME
EAVE
GREW
HOBO
ILIA
IRES
LOSS
MALE
MITE
NEAT
PATE
PEPS
PEST
POLE
READ
RUES
SAKE
SEIS
SHAG
SKIP
SOPS
SPAS
STOA
SWAT
TEES
TELE
TOGS
YULE

5 Letters

ADAPT
AREAS
PASEO
RECAP
SETAE
SHRED
SOAKS
TASTE
TEETH

Solution on page 258

ASDFGHJKL

Provider 10

F	O	I	L

3 Letters

ACE
ANI
APT
AWL
BAA
CUM
DOE
FAS
GOT
INN
KOI
LOP
OHM
ONE
ORS
OSE
PAX
REP
RHO
RUN
SAE
SOS
TAP

4 Letters

ACRE
ADDS
AGON
ANEW
ANNA
APEX
ARCO
AWOL
BAKE
BANE
BORE
DADA
DEAN
ELMS
FOIL
FRAT
HARE
HAST
LOCA
LOUT
MASS
MORE
OBOE
OUTS
PASS
PLAT
PROS
RETE
ROPE
SALT
SENT
SHUN
SLAP
SLIM
SNIP
SOME
STEW
TUNA

5 Letters

ALONE
BASED
LATHE
LEFTS
SCOLD
SHAMS
SLASH
TESTA
TREES

Solution on page 258

Provider 11

F	A	R

3 Letters

ADO
AVA
BAD
BOS
DAP
EVE
FAR
FOB
HAH
HEP
NET
ODE
PIS
TAB

4 Letters

ALFA
ALMS
AMEN
ANTA
BEAR
CITE
CLAM
CLOD
DRAY
DROP
DRYS
ERRS
ERST
EYRE
FEAT
ISMS
LAMA
LAWS
LEAN
LEAS
LILT
LIMA
MARS
MELD
OMER
OYER
PEAL
PEAS
PERT
RIEL
ROTA
SCAB
SOLI
STAY
TATE
VANE

5 Letters

ARCED
AVERS
MODES
SASSY
SETTS
SLAMS
SLAPS
SOLAR
TEENS
TORSI

6 Letters

AMERCE
ENSILE
REDONE
WISEST

8 Letters

RESTATED
TOOLSHED

Solution on page 258

Provider 12

H M M

3 Letters

ALB
ALT
AXE
BID
BRR
CAD
EAU
EFT
EKE
EMU
HEH
HIT
HMM
HUE
LAC
LAD
MON
NAN
OKA
ROE
SAL
SOT
SOU
SOW
TEA
WIG

4 Letters

ABED
ALBA
ALEF
AMAS
ARMS
ASHY
AWES
AXON
BASE
BATE
BEST
BIKE
BLOB
BRAT
DELE
EGER
EWES
MAID
MAMA
MARE
MOUE
MUTE
NAME
ORAD
ORCA
PEND
PESO
REBS
REES
ROLE
SAKI
SAND
STAT
SULK
TSKS
TUBS

5 Letters

ANTES
BASER
BASTE
OREAD
REMAP
SERAC
SLEEP
STYES

Solution on page 258

Provider 13

3 Letters

ADD
ASK
DAY
ELM
ETA
ICH
LIN
ORC
OUR
OXO
OXY
PEN
PER
PHI
PIA
POP
POW
PRO
RID
RUE
RYE
TWO
URN
WOE

4 Letters

ACTA
ACTS
ALGA
ANAS
ANIL
ARIL
BEER
CARE
CODE
COPE
DEAR
HIRE
IDLE
INNS
LEST
NOES
ODDS
ORCS
PALE
PIED
PLUS
PORK
PORN
RIDS
SCAM
SHAY
SPUD
TELS
TOGA
TRAM
URGE
WIDE

5 Letters

ASSET
ATRIA
EGEST
LOSES
MESAS
MOLDS
ORCAS
ORLES
PASSE
SCABS

6 Letters

CASTLE
SEAMEN

T	W	O										

Solution on page 259

Provider 14

RUSE

3 Letters

BRO
CHI
CUE
EAR
EGO
ELL
GHI
GNU
HEW
IVY
LED
MOM
NIP
RUT
SEX
SKI
SOL
TWA
USE
UTA
WRY
YAR
YOU

4 Letters

AGHA
ALEC
ALTO
AUTO
AVER
AWRY
BALL
BEAM
BEGS
BOIL
CYST
DOOR
DRUM
DYNE
HAKE
HEAR
IDOL
IRIS
LENT
LIMB
LOIN
MILT
MYNA
OGLE
ORAL
ORTS
PHEW
RUSE
SALS
SCUM
SLAY
SUPS
TEAR
TEXT
TOYS
TREE
USES
YAWP

5 Letters

ALPHA
ESTER
IONIC
LAMBS
MADRE
RASPY
SABRA
SANTO
TATES

Solution on page 259

Provider 15

O H S

3 Letters

ABS
ANY
BYE
CAN
DEE
DIP
DUG
DUI
DYE
ERG
GOA
HOW
LIB
NEE
NUB
OHS
OPE
PRY
REB
RUG
SUE
TUG
URB
YAY
ZOO

4 Letters

ABBE
ADOS
ADZE
ALLY
ASKS
BADE
BIOS
BOSS
DEED
EELS
EGGS
EGGY
EWER
GUNK
LEAP
LIDO
OGRE
OWES
PLAN
POPS
POUT
PURR
SAGS
SECS
SEED
SINE
SLUE
SOAR
SOUR
SPOT
STEP
SUNS
TARO
TONG
TROT
TRUE
ULNA
WEBS

5 Letters

ADAGE
APERS
CREST
SLUES
SPACE
SPEED
STATE

Solution on page 259

Provider 16

3 Letters

AIL
DEN
DEY
END
ERR
FEY
FIR
FLY
FRY
IMP
LYE
MAE
PAT
PIT
REC
SIP
TRY
WHA
YET
YON

4 Letters

ANDS
ANES
ANON
ANTI
ATOP
AVES
CRAW
DESK
EMIR
ENDS
EURO
GLAD
GRAD
HONE
LATE
LINT
LONE
OPED
RACY
ROVE
SAME
SCAN
SITS
SOLD
SPEC
SPRY
STUD
TIFF
TILE
TOUT
WYES
YETI

5 Letters

CLASS
CRATE
DESKS
EASTS
STOIC
YOWLS

6 Letters

APTEST
ASPIRE
AURATE
EYELET
NESTLE
STELLA

7 Letters

ATLASES
TESTATE

G R A D

Solution on page 259

Chapter 8

Words Within Words

Make words using only the letters in a given word. Each letter can be used only once per word. For example, if the word is HAPPINESS, then you could make the words *phase*, *snap*, *pipe*, and many others. Your words should have at least four letters. Words that are always capitalized or require a hyphen or an apostrophe are not included in the answer lists. For each puzzle, see if you can make ten (or more) words.

BARRISTER

British trial lawyer.

1. ________________
2. ________________
3. ________________
4. ________________
5. ________________
6. ________________
7. ________________
8. ________________
9. ________________
10. ________________

ABORIGINE

The first known inhabitant.

1. ________________
2. ________________
3. ________________
4. ________________
5. ________________
6. ________________
7. ________________
8. ________________
9. ________________
10. ________________

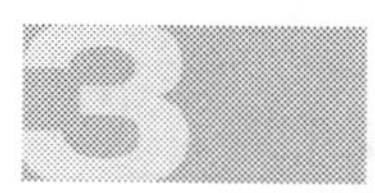

ACCRETION

Growth by a gradual buildup.

1. ________________
2. ________________
3. ________________
4. ________________
5. ________________
6. ________________
7. ________________
8. ________________
9. ________________
10. ________________

TOROIDAL

Doughnut-shaped.

1. ________________
2. ________________
3. ________________
4. ________________
5. ________________
6. ________________
7. ________________
8. ________________
9. ________________
10. ________________

Solution on page 260

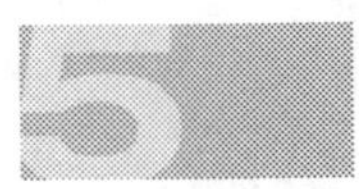

QUINQUAGENARIAN

A person between the ages of 50 and 60.

1. ____________
2. ____________
3. ____________
4. ____________
5. ____________
6. ____________
7. ____________
8. ____________
9. ____________
10. ____________

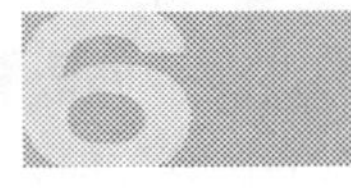

PLANGENT

Having a loud reverberating sound.

1. ____________
2. ____________
3. ____________
4. ____________
5. ____________
6. ____________
7. ____________
8. ____________
9. ____________
10. ____________

DIADROMOUS

Able to migrate between salt and fresh waters.

1. ____________
2. ____________
3. ____________
4. ____________
5. ____________
6. ____________
7. ____________
8. ____________
9. ____________
10. ____________

RECONDITE

Not easily understood by the average person.

1. ____________
2. ____________
3. ____________
4. ____________
5. ____________
6. ____________
7. ____________
8. ____________
9. ____________
10. ____________

Solution on page 260

ANACHRONISM

Thing that is chronologically out of place.

1. ____
2. ____
3. ____
4. ____
5. ____
6. ____
7. ____
8. ____
9. ____
10. ____

TRAVESTY

A ridiculous imitation of something.

1. ____
2. ____
3. ____
4. ____
5. ____
6. ____
7. ____
8. ____
9. ____
10. ____

PROSCRIBE

To condemn.

1. ____
2. ____
3. ____
4. ____
5. ____
6. ____
7. ____
8. ____
9. ____
10. ____

DACTYLOGRAM

A fingerprint.

1. ____
2. ____
3. ____
4. ____
5. ____
6. ____
7. ____
8. ____
9. ____
10. ____

Solution on page 260

CANTILLATE

To chant in a musical monotone.

1. ______________
2. ______________
3. ______________
4. ______________
5. ______________
6. ______________
7. ______________
8. ______________
9. ______________
10. ______________

SHEEPSHANK

A knot for shortening a line.

1. ______________
2. ______________
3. ______________
4. ______________
5. ______________
6. ______________
7. ______________
8. ______________
9. ______________
10. ______________

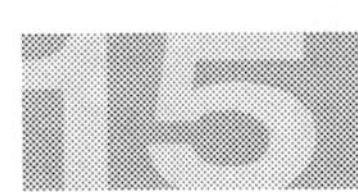

REFULGENT

Shining radiantly.

1. ______________
2. ______________
3. ______________
4. ______________
5. ______________
6. ______________
7. ______________
8. ______________
9. ______________
10. ______________

SORTILEGE

Divination by drawing of lots.

1. ______________
2. ______________
3. ______________
4. ______________
5. ______________
6. ______________
7. ______________
8. ______________
9. ______________
10. ______________

Solution on page 261

BLANCMANGE

A white sweet pudding made with milk and cornstarch.

1. ______
2. ______
3. ______
4. ______
5. ______
6. ______
7. ______
8. ______
9. ______
10. ______

ABSTRUSE

Hard to understand.

1. ______
2. ______
3. ______
4. ______
5. ______
6. ______
7. ______
8. ______
9. ______
10. ______

TELAMON

A supporting pillar in the form of a man.

1. ______
2. ______
3. ______
4. ______
5. ______
6. ______
7. ______
8. ______
9. ______
10. ______

ATOMIZER

Device for spraying liquid as a mist.

1. ______
2. ______
3. ______
4. ______
5. ______
6. ______
7. ______
8. ______
9. ______
10. ______

Solution on page 261

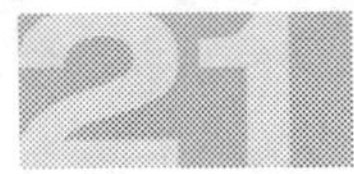

CALIGINOUS

Misty, dark, gloomy.

1. ______________
2. ______________
3. ______________
4. ______________
5. ______________
6. ______________
7. ______________
8. ______________
9. ______________
10. ______________

APIARIST

A beekeeper.

1. ______________
2. ______________
3. ______________
4. ______________
5. ______________
6. ______________
7. ______________
8. ______________
9. ______________
10. ______________

BANDORE

An ancient musical instrument resembling a guitar.

1. ______________
2. ______________
3. ______________
4. ______________
5. ______________
6. ______________
7. ______________
8. ______________
9. ______________
10. ______________

CASTIGATE

To criticize severely.

1. ______________
2. ______________
3. ______________
4. ______________
5. ______________
6. ______________
7. ______________
8. ______________
9. ______________
10. ______________

Solution on page 261

GOSSAMER

Something extremely light and delicate.

1. ______________
2. ______________
3. ______________
4. ______________
5. ______________
6. ______________
7. ______________
8. ______________
9. ______________
10. ______________

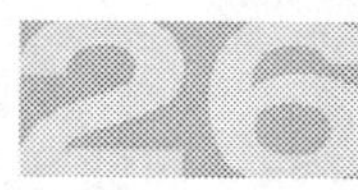

SCOTOPIA

The ability to see in dim light.

1. ______________
2. ______________
3. ______________
4. ______________
5. ______________
6. ______________
7. ______________
8. ______________
9. ______________
10. ______________

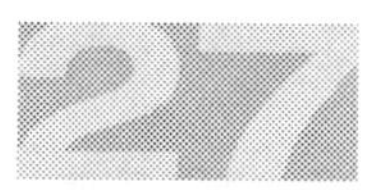

PLATITUDE

A trite remark.

1. ______________
2. ______________
3. ______________
4. ______________
5. ______________
6. ______________
7. ______________
8. ______________
9. ______________
10. ______________

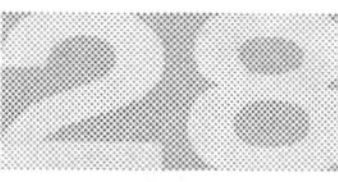

PRESCIENCE

Knowledge of things before they happen.

1. ______________
2. ______________
3. ______________
4. ______________
5. ______________
6. ______________
7. ______________
8. ______________
9. ______________
10. ______________

Solution on pages 261–262

SOLECISM

An ungrammatical usage of words.

1. ______________
2. ______________
3. ______________
4. ______________
5. ______________
6. ______________
7. ______________
8. ______________
9. ______________
10. ______________

SHIITAKE

An edible Japanese mushroom.

1. ______________
2. ______________
3. ______________
4. ______________
5. ______________
6. ______________
7. ______________
8. ______________
9. ______________
10. ______________

BLANDISH

To coax or influence by gentle flattery.

1. ______________
2. ______________
3. ______________
4. ______________
5. ______________
6. ______________
7. ______________
8. ______________
9. ______________
10. ______________

ADUMBRATE

To give a vague outline or representation.

1. ______________
2. ______________
3. ______________
4. ______________
5. ______________
6. ______________
7. ______________
8. ______________
9. ______________
10. ______________

Solution on page 262

ANGSTROM

A unit for measuring the length of light waves.

1. ______________
2. ______________
3. ______________
4. ______________
5. ______________
6. ______________
7. ______________
8. ______________
9. ______________
10. ______________

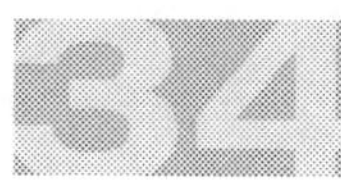

PRECOCIOUS

Unusually mature in mental development.

1. ______________
2. ______________
3. ______________
4. ______________
5. ______________
6. ______________
7. ______________
8. ______________
9. ______________
10. ______________

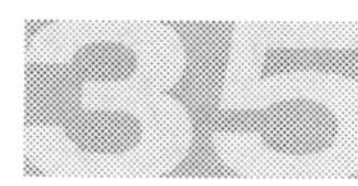

CAPRIOLE

A playful leap.

1. ______________
2. ______________
3. ______________
4. ______________
5. ______________
6. ______________
7. ______________
8. ______________
9. ______________
10. ______________

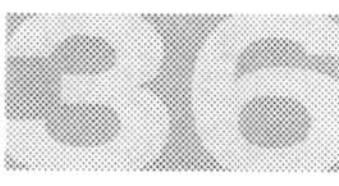

REPROBATE

A morally unprincipled person.

1. ______________
2. ______________
3. ______________
4. ______________
5. ______________
6. ______________
7. ______________
8. ______________
9. ______________
10. ______________

Solution on page 262

SOMMELIER

A wine steward.

1. ________________
2. ________________
3. ________________
4. ________________
5. ________________
6. ________________
7. ________________
8. ________________
9. ________________
10. ________________

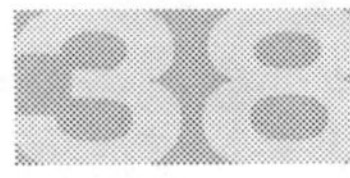

PRODIGAL

Wastefully extravagant.

1. ________________
2. ________________
3. ________________
4. ________________
5. ________________
6. ________________
7. ________________
8. ________________
9. ________________
10. ________________

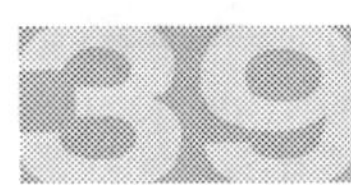

DILETTANTE

A dabbler in an art or field of knowledge.

1. ________________
2. ________________
3. ________________
4. ________________
5. ________________
6. ________________
7. ________________
8. ________________
9. ________________
10. ________________

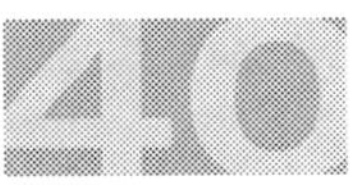

MOUNTEBANK

One who sells quack medicines.

1. ________________
2. ________________
3. ________________
4. ________________
5. ________________
6. ________________
7. ________________
8. ________________
9. ________________
10. ________________

Solution on pages 262–263

CARMINE

A vivid purplish red color.

1. ____________
2. ____________
3. ____________
4. ____________
5. ____________
6. ____________
7. ____________
8. ____________
9. ____________
10. ____________

APOSTASY

Abandonment of a former loyalty.

1. ____________
2. ____________
3. ____________
4. ____________
5. ____________
6. ____________
7. ____________
8. ____________
9. ____________
10. ____________

AD HOMINEM

Appealing to prejudices rather than intellect.

1. ____________
2. ____________
3. ____________
4. ____________
5. ____________
6. ____________
7. ____________
8. ____________
9. ____________
10. ____________

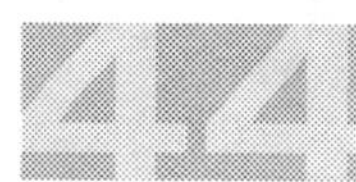

TELLURIAN

An inhabitant of earth.

1. ____________
2. ____________
3. ____________
4. ____________
5. ____________
6. ____________
7. ____________
8. ____________
9. ____________
10. ____________

Solution on page 263

PROPITIOUS

Presenting favorable conditions.

1. ______
2. ______
3. ______
4. ______
5. ______
6. ______
7. ______
8. ______
9. ______
10. ______

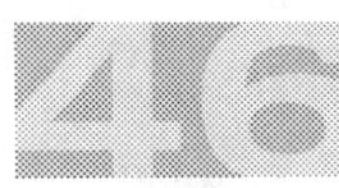

REMUNERATE

To pay or compensate.

1. ______
2. ______
3. ______
4. ______
5. ______
6. ______
7. ______
8. ______
9. ______
10. ______

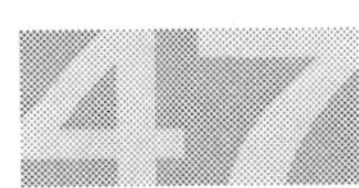

CARABINEER

A metal ring with a spring clip used in mountaineering.

1. ______
2. ______
3. ______
4. ______
5. ______
6. ______
7. ______
8. ______
9. ______
10. ______

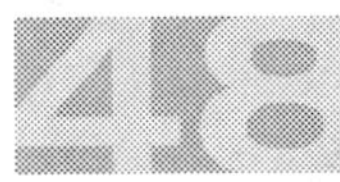

RECENSION

Revision of a text from various sources.

1. ______
2. ______
3. ______
4. ______
5. ______
6. ______
7. ______
8. ______
9. ______
10. ______

Solution on page 263

Chapter 9

Crosswords

Crosswords are probably the most common word puzzle in the world. Test your word power and trivia knowledge with these classic puzzles.

Crossword 1

Across

1. "Elephant Boy" actor
5. Lobster's feeler
9. Catches flies
14. Setting of "The Plague"
15. Director Petri
16. Matthew of "Friends"
17. "___ the east, and Juliet . . ."
18. ___ Piper
19. American Indians
20. Lets go
22. Least loco
23. Castor, to Pollux
24. Bombay dress
25. Has a bite of
28. Runner in the raw
32. Advanced degree tests
33. Conservative
34. It follows ka in the Spanish alphabet
35. Examine, with "over"
36. Climbs, as a pole
37. Bridegroom, for one
38. Guido's high note
39. British jackets
40. Flogged
41. Putting back on the payroll
43. Spuds
44. Yarborough, of NASCAR
45. Acoustic measure
46. Most ignoble
49. Grand Prix racer
53. Filibuster, in a way
54. Achings
55. "Pumping ___"
56. Marksman, e.g.
57. Being: Sp.
58. "Inter ___" (among other things)
59. Barcelona abodes
60. "Cheers" actor Roger
61. A whole bunch

Down

1. Evening, in Paris
2. "Laugh-In" comedian Johnson
3. Bondsman's concern
4. Agitate
5. Some sodas
6. "Star Trek" extra
7. "Sex, ___, and Videotape"
8. Bean holder
9. Grabbed with a toothpick
10. Cause of strain pain
11. Author Eliau
12. Some college tests, for short
13. Method: Abbr.
21. Amazes
22. Delhi dresses
24. Laurel and Musial
25. Drunkard
26. Play ___ in (be involved with)
27. Fergie, formally
28. "Every Breath You Take" singer
29. "The Family Circus" cartoonist Bil
30. "Oklahoma!" Aunt
31. Oboes, e.g.
33. Did superbly
36. Avocet's cousin
37. Dacron or denim
39. Pencil ends
40. Bat Masterson's weapon
42. Summer cooler
43. Coin flips
45. A votre ___!
46. Airline's former name
47. "Brava!" elicitor at La Scala
48. ___ Club (Costco competitor)
49. Word on a Biblical wall
50. "___ & Janis" (comic strip)
51. "There's nothing ___!"
52. "Much" preceder
54. "___ out!" (ump's call)

Solution on page 264

Crossword 2

Across

1. '50s toothpaste
6. Addition problems
10. Asian caregiver
14. Fabrics with metallic threads
15. Make a sweater, perhaps
16. Au naturel
17. Appropriate
18. Suffix meaning "collection"
19. "The Thin Man" canine
20. Mex. misses
22. Appetizer
24. "Aeneid," e.g.
26. Kenan's Nickelodeon pal
27. Agency of HHS
28. "Brian's Song" star
31. Clinch, with "up"
33. Beads on blades
35. Check fig.
36. Invitation to a hitchhiker
38. Closer to extinction
42. Steppe antelope
44. U.N. working-conditions agcy.
45. Banquo, e.g.
46. Leaves in, editorially
47. A chorus line?
49. Bach's "Toccata and Fugue ___ Minor"
50. Adage
52. His in Le Havre
53. Nabokov heroine and others
54. She-bear, in Seville
57. Anesthetize, in a way
59. ___ lily
61. Behave
63. Lee and Teasdale
66. ". . . ___ saw Elba"
67. Shakespeare, for one
70. Scarecrow's "guts"
72. ". . . ___ o'clock scholar"
73. In ___ of
74. Lustrous velvet
75. Ancient capital of Japan
76. "___ Brockovich"
77. Asks for, as advice

Down

1. They, in France
2. Frisks, with "down"
3. From the States: Abbr.
4. Spruce up
5. Get ___ on the wrist
6. Go downhill, maybe
7. A, in Acapulco
8. Belarus capital
9. Averred
10. "This guy walks into ___ . . ."
11. Mizzen and jigger, e.g.
12. Comic Johnson and others
13. "I ___ Rhapsody"
21. Worth a C, maybe
23. APBs, e.g.
25. Brown photo
28. "Mama" ___ Elliot
29. "Amo, amas, ___"
30. End in ___ (require overtime)
32. British prince, familiarly
34. Baby's bawl
36. Tries, with "at"
37. IOUs
39. Bookie's worry
40. City in central Sicily
41. Chiantis, e.g.
43. Fast sports cars
48. Simple sugars
51. Sing like a bird
53. Main arteries
54. Arctic, for one
55. In a way, slangily
56. Arab leader
58. A step up
60. Shocked reactions
62. ___ colada
64. "Comus" composer
65. Hit bottom
68. Old Portuguese coin
69. Demand payment
71. "Scream" director Craven

Solution on page 264

Crossword 3

Across

1. Carson's "Tonight Show" predecessor
5. Canadian pop singer Lavigne
10. "Buyer beware" warning
14. Earth, in Munich
15. Query before "Here goes!"
16. "___ Smile" (1976 Hall & Oates hit)
17. Hydrocarbon suffixes
18. Blood group known as the universal donor
19. "Avast!" responder
20. Be bested by
22. As a group
24. Boxing jab
27. "Star Wars" initials
28. Places for plaques
31. Ernie, of the PGA
33. Eastern Europeans
37. ". . . ___ penny earned"
38. British conservatives
41. "My ___, the doctor"
42. ___ and tuck
43. "Delicious!"
44. Word on either side of "-a-"
46. Sprechen ___ Deutsch?
47. Dutch commune
48. Back down
50. Word form for "height"
51. Blockheads
54. Historic women's gp.
55. On ___ (counting calories)
57. Some MIT degs.
59. "Lou Grant" actor
61. Newspaper accounts
65. Bolted together?
69. Hercules' captive
70. Barbie and Ken
73. Prefix meaning "wine"
74. "Animal House" association
75. "Adam Bede" author
76. Big dance
77. Shoe size
78. French cathedral city
79. Capital of ruins in Normandy

Down

1. Sound, as bells
2. "New Yorker" cartoonist Peter
3. Citrus coolers
4. Market again
5. Sun Tzu's "The ___ War"
6. "Oy ___!"
7. Blame, so to speak
8. "___ fixe"
9. Silk-producing city
10. Attack
11. Adages
12. Investment options, for short
13. Kemo ___ ("trusty scout")
21. Cantankerous
23. G.P.'s, e.g.
25. Designated
26. 151, in old Rome
28. ___ and dined
29. ". . . say, and not ___"
30. Blazer part
32. Breaks off
34. Very, in music
35. State, as an opinion
36. Hagar's dog
39. ". . . ___ daily bread"
40. Avarice, e.g.
45. Madame de ___
49. "___ note to follow sew . . ."
52. Cylindrical
53. Type of whale
56. Sags
58. Ceremonial dinner
60. Aeries
61. Separate, as flour
62. Razed, with "down"
63. "The Good Earth" character
64. ___ survivor
66. Feeling one's oats
67. An organic compound
68. Major ___
71. 52, in old Rome
72. Herbert of "The Return of the Pink Panther"

Solution on page 264

Crossword 4

Across

1. Cockpit guesses, for short
5. British philosopher
10. "Sabre Dance" composer Khachaturian
14. Actor Waggoner
15. Yoga posture
16. ___ di Como, Italia
17. Give it ___ (swing hard)
18. Accepted customs
19. Bart Simpson, e.g.
20. Annoy
22. Satisfies
24. Diving-bell inventor
26. The "bad" cholesterol
27. "American Graffiti" quaffs
30. Super ___: video game console
32. Barely gets, with "out"
36. Pasta terminator, often
37. Supermodel Banks
39. Greek markets
41. Airhead
43. ___ as a beet
45. B & B's
46. Christian of "Murder in the First"
48. "One ___ or two?"
50. "I Like ___"
51. Actor Morales of "NYPD Blue"
52. Country once part of the U.A.R.
53. Close, poetically
55. Kindergarten "time"
57. James ___ Carter, Jr.
59. New York Indians
63. "Look at Me, I'm Sandra Dee" musical
67. Peel, as an apple
68. "Over the Rainbow" composer Harold
70. "Liberal" studies
71. Anger, with "up"
72. Surveil, with "out"
73. "Keep it" notation
74. Reconditioned, e.g.
75. Presses the "Record" button
76. "Lights out" tune

Down

1. "Joie de vivre"
2. Ancient Phoenician seaport
3. Came down
4. Group of seven
5. 12th Hebrew letter
6. Bear, in Madrid
7. Be a nag
8. Doleful sounds
9. Reduced, as pain
10. Church robes
11. Like a day in June, to Lowell
12. Turkish bigwigs
13. Bon ___ (witticism)
21. After everyone else
23. Shake ___ (hurry)
25. Upperclassmen: Abbr.
27. Strindberg's "___ Julie"
28. Old womanish
29. Green beans
31. Like an eager guest, maybe
33. Japanese carp
34. "Sesame Street" character
35. Decaf brand
38. Shostakovich's "Babi ___" Symphony
39. Fleet commander: abbr.
40. Danish weight
42. "Harper Valley ___"
44. French department
47. "___ Kleine Nachtmusik"
49. Catherine ___, wife of Henry VIII
52. Ancient Athens rival
54. The Braves' div.
56. ". . . and ___ of thousands!"
58. Moorehead of "Bewitched"
59. "Je ne ___ quoi"
60. ___ Stanley Gardner
61. "___ I say more?"
62. Duel invitation, perhaps
64. Albanian river
65. "___ lively!"
66. Ballpark figs.
67. "Piece of the rock" company, informally
69. Barely earn, with "out"

Solution on page 264

Crossword 5

Across

1. Almost ready for the tooth fairy
6. Eschew food
10. Syrian city
14. Company whose reputation was "shredded"
15. "___ and the King of Siam"
16. Lupino, et al.
17. Common contraction
18. 100 dinars, in Iran
19. Big commotions
20. Salisbury Plain monument
22. "___ #1!"
23. Presidencies, to historians
24. "A ___ Born"
26. Click beetle
29. "Now you ___, now . . ."
31. Beaujolais, e.g.
32. Discourage
34. Action-film highlight
38. Prefix meaning "flower"
40. Medicinal plant
42. "This must weigh ___!"
43. Barely beat, with "out"
45. "There Is Nothing Like ___"
47. Chat room guffaw
48. ___ and raves
50. Disturbs
52. Barber pole feature
55. ". . . ___ is in heaven"
56. Donne, for one
57. New Mexico national monument
63. Florentine angel's instrument
64. Big top, e.g.
65. Blue eyes or baldness, e.g.
66. All-male
67. National anthem start
68. Bruce of comedy
69. Ancient Iranian
70. Ex-Washington baseballers, for short
71. Irregularly notched, as a leaf

Down

1. Watch readouts, briefly
2. "Don't bet ___!"
3. Catholic calendar
4. 14-line poem
5. Went in
6. Passengers
7. Has ___ (is connected)
8. Capture
9. "Honor Thy Father" author Gay
10. Longfellow subject
11. Pocket calculator, e.g.
12. Kiri Te Kanawa, for one
13. Ancestors of domestic donkeys
21. Brush critters
25. "___ Tac Dough"
26. "Blackboard Jungle" author Hunter
27. Floor covering, for short
28. Soldiers and carpenters, e.g.
29. Dispatches
30. Soprano Berger
33. Mammilla
35. Salt tree
36. Chimney accumulation
37. Photo processing choices (Abbr.)
39. Birthright
41. Entertain, in a way
44. One way to fish
46. Letter from Jude
49. Man of gravity
51. Gawking sort
52. Charley horse, e.g.
53. Nut cake
54. Add new cushioning to
55. ABA members
58. "___ real nowhere man . . ."
59. ___ the finish (competitive to the end)
60. "Billionth" word form
61. Big rackets
62. Eye affliction

Solution on page 265

Crossword 6

Across

1. CDX x V
4. Brauhaus brew
8. Summers, in France
12. Juillet follower
14. Antenna alternative
15. At the drop of ___
16. By ___ (from memory)
17. "Let's Make ___" (game-show oldie)
18. "Que" follower, in song
19. Spews out
21. Portable PCs
23. Carries
26. Hoo preceder
27. Hollered
30. Hebrew letter
32. Available for occupation
36. "Golden ___" (Drake's ship)
37. Pour into a carafe, say
39. Cameroon's cont.
40. Prefix for puncture
41. "A pox upon thee!"
42. "Now I ___ me down to sleep . . ."
43. Capote, briefly
44. Here, at Les Halles
45. Cleverly skillful
47. Canonized "femmes": Abbr.
48. Gunpowder ingredient
50. "___ 'em!"
51. Cut flowers
52. ___ Khan
54. "The Wreck of the Mary ___" (1959 film)
56. Completely consumed
60. Sporty Mazdas
64. "Private Lives" playwright Coward
65. 1966 Caine role
68. "Stormy Weather" Horne
69. Adolescent affliction
70. Brings up, as a child
71. Flying jib, e.g.
72. Reason for detention, maybe
73. Convenience store
74. Realtors' letters

Down

1. Colt's mother
2. ___ synthesizer
3. Cousin of a mandolin
4. Good, in the 'hood
5. "Can ___ dreaming?"
6. Airline that serves only kosher food
7. Baton-passing race
8. "For Your Eyes Only" singer Sheena
9. Kojak, to pals
10. Clanton gang foe
11. Depots: Abbr.
13. Did lab work
14. Throw, as dice
20. Director Browning
22. Sullen
24. Arab rulers
25. "Hold on a ___!"
27. Kind of letter
28. Theron's "Monster" co-star
29. Eskimo word for "Eskimo"
31. Evil intent
33. Coffee order
34. Zimbalist of "The F.B.I."
35. Supporting beam
37. Served, as time
38. "King" Cole
41. North Dakota city
46. Suffix meaning "sort of"
47. Great buys
49. Duffers' surprises
51. ___ Lanka
53. Cost ___ and a leg
55. "Aldrich ___: Traitor Within"
56. Anecdotal collections
57. "Livin' La Vida ___" (Ricky Martin hit)
58. Camera attachment
59. Ancient Greek City
61. "Go, ___!"
62. Blue dye
63. Actor Mineo et al.
66. "So ___, so good"
67. N.Y.C. line

Solution on page 265

Crossword 7

Across

1. Agenda
6. Daly of "Cagney & Lacey"
10. "Baby, it's cold outside!"
13. Highway markers
14. Trompe l'___ (visual deception)
15. Peau de ___
16. Breathing disorder
17. "Darn it all!"
18. "The Wizard of Oz" dog
19. Insect repellent ingredient
20. Sounds of hesitation
21. Cleans the slate
23. Marsh birds
26. Cockpit figs.
27. Actress Stone
30. Kind of shoppe
32. Medieval guild
33. Dugout
35. Drops bait
39. Suffix with expert
40. Jelly and jam
43. Norwegian rug
44. Condo units: Abbr.
46. People in Xings
47. "Love ___ you need" (Beatles lyric)
49. "Gorillas in the ___"
51. Sleeve band
52. In love
54. Macedonian city
57. Protect, as freshness
59. S.A.S.E., e.g.
60. Scissors beater, in a game
64. "___ a nice day!"
65. Point ___ return
67. 10th-cen. Holy Roman Emperor known as "the Great"
68. Angers
69. Au ___ (with milk)
70. "___ Entertain You"
71. AOL alternative
72. "Don't Tread ___"
73. Nature photographer Adams

Down

1. Carangid food fish
2. Long, easy stride
3. "___ of the Thousand Days" (1969 film)
4. Seesaws
5. Los Angeles Philharmonic director ___-Pekka Salonen
6. "The Velvet Fog" Mel
7. Baker's buy
8. Complaint that's "picked"
9. ". . . or ___!"
10. Climber's need, perhaps
11. ___ of passage
12. '20s autos
15. Went flat
20. "Ode on a Grecian ___"
22. "Cool!"
24. "Here ___ nothing!"
25. Carolina rails
27. Branch of Islam
28. Briefcase closer
29. Dill
31. "Put a ___ on it!"
33. Sharp, narrow ridge
34. Four-poster, e.g.
36. ___ Sea (Asian lake)
37. "Gomer ___, U.S.M.C."
38. Bagel topper
41. Afterthought afterthought (abbr.)
42. Bestowed titles
45. Says "Cheese"
48. Wise (up)
50. "Is ___, Lord?"
51. Cinematographers' org.
52. Blackens
53. Expert
55. Cutoffs fabric
56. F neighbor
57. Gap-filling wedge
58. Agnew's plea, briefly
61. Baseball's Mel and others
62. "Get over here, Fido!"
63. Canal to the Baltic
66. Aficionado
67. Suffix for "pay"

Solution on page 265

Crossword 8

Across

1. Filly's footfall
5. Arizona Indian
9. Droops
13. Ann and May
15. Fashion accessories on the Ginza
16. Cosmetics additive, often
17. Actress Gia
18. Spelling of "90210"
19. Arthurian days, e.g.
20. Chem. endings
22. "Lou Grant" star
24. NCOs two levels above cpl.
26. FDR or JFK
27. Merchandise: Abbr.
28. Bartender's "rocks"
29. Cash dispensers, for short
32. Smart, to sharp (abbr.)
34. Part of USNA
35. Holds, as a stadium
37. Data, for short
41. Egyptian queen, for short
43. Greek colonnades
45. Business letter encl.
46. Descartes and Magritte
48. "Annie Hall" director
50. Not wide: Abbr.
51. "Merry" month
53. Architect Saarinen
54. Doctor of rap
55. Proprietary symbols (abbr.)
58. Green parrot
60. Attempts
62. Short end of the stick
64. Dance site, perhaps
65. Pete Sampras, often
66. All atwitter
68. Out of favor, informally
72. Spiced tea
73. "Country" Slaughter
74. "If they could ___ now . . ."
75. Actor Rip
76. ___ and rave
77. Tie over, in music

Down

1. Dosage amts.
2. Fond du ___, WI
3. ___ Locka, FL
4. "Moby Dick" captain
5. Flower holders
6. Native Nigerian
7. Stuck, as in mud
8. Comments to the audience
9. "___ who?"
10. "___ came a spider . . ."
11. "It depends on whose ox is ___"
12. Crystal ball users, e.g.
14. December temps
21. ___ Park, CO
23. Irving and Tan
24. Actor's minimum wage
25. A natural, in craps
28. Price hike: Abbr.
30. ___ Hari
31. Lifted, so to speak
33. P.M. times
36. 12/26 event
38. "Biography" network
39. Russian rulers, once
40. Bone-dry
42. Computer reseller, for short
44. "We make the world's best mattress" sloganeer
47. "For goodness' ___!"
49. "McTeague" novelist Frank
52. Aviator Chuck
55. Area of land
56. "___ Man" (Village People hit)
57. Say "*&%@#!"
59. ___-Dale (Robin Hood friend)
61. "The Wreck of the Mary Deare" author Hammond
63. Albanian river
64. Woody fiber
67. Geometry suffix
69. ___ Air
70. ___ Darya (Aral Sea feeder)
71. "___ Bingle" (Crosby)

Solution on page 265

Crossword 9

Across

1. Manila hemp
6. ___-CIO
9. Destroy, as documents
14. "Smoking ___?"
15. "Mamma ___!"
16. Bay of Biscay feeder
17. Friend of Fran and Ollie
18. "Prince Valiant" character
19. Take ___ in the right direction
20. Barn attachment
21. Ko-Ko's dagger in "The Mikado"
22. Bake-sale sponsors
23. Lead/tin alloy
25. Bay area airport letters
27. Comic Soupy
30. Baker and Bryant
35. Twice, musically
38. Buffet patrons
40. Enameled metal
41. Berra and Bear
43. Pa. nuclear accident site, 1979
44. Fields, in "The Bank Dick"
45. "Inner" word form
46. Ribbed taffeta
48. "Maximum weight" unit
49. Gets cheeky with
51. Venetian blinds, essentially
53. Crux
55. A Beatle
58. "Meet Joe Black" star Brad
61. Physics units
64. Achilles' weak spot
66. Show again
67. Brazil-Paraguay border river
68. Greeting from Pooh
69. Edomite capital
70. Tomcat
71. Colonial announcer
72. Brew, as tea
73. Some TV sets
74. Abominated

Down

1. NASA affirmatives
2. Rumor
3. Bracelet site
4. Black and blue
5. "Falcon Crest" actress Alicia
6. "___ Called Horse"
7. Bad thing to be under
8. Bowling alley divisions
9. Quickly apply
10. Army
11. "Gilda" star Hayworth
12. "___ Tu" (1974 song)
13. Bank acct. entry
21. Ward of "House"
24. Scot's negatives
26. Mi followers
28. Kett, of the comics
29. 18-wheelers
31. "Am ___ believe . . . ?"
32. Ballyhoo
33. "And another thing . . ."
34. ". . . ___ and not heard"
35. Brief farewells
36. College in New Rochelle, N.Y.
37. Bilko and York: Abbr.
39. Brook
42. Hawaiian hawks
44. Paving stone
46. Home of the Seminoles
47. Aberdeen miss
50. Corner
52. African desert
54. Fort ___, NC
56. Began the fire anew
57. C.S.A. notable
58. Amanda of "The Whole Nine Yards"
59. ". . . can't believe ___ the whole thing"
60. Bias-ply, for one
62. Cap-___ (from head to foot)
63. Small amounts, as of cream
65. "___ of the Flies"
66. Rotation meas.
68. F.D.R.'s predecessor

Solution on page 266

Crossword 10

Across

1. Philippine island
6. Atlas contents
10. Chews the fat
14. "Drab" color
15. Done to ___
16. "Night" author Wiesel
17. Digs for ore
18. ___ majest
19. Cheese in a Greek salad
20. Land in the Thames
21. 90-degree shapes
23. Gas, in Greenwich
25. "___ for Alibi" (Grafton novel)
26. Assemble, with "up"
27. Carry-___ (small pieces of luggage)
28. Dismay
32. Hong Kong's Hang ___ Index
33. Bank offerings
34. USAF weapon
35. Did nothing
40. Bedevils
41. Marsh elder
42. Angle
43. Knocked for a loop
45. Investigator: Abbr.
46. Bel ___ (cheese)
47. Assayers' samples
49. Very funny joke
50. 1051, to Caesar
53. ___ deferens
54. "To ___ is human . . ."
55. Bridal paths
57. Indonesian islands
58. "Dear old ___"
61. "Red Balloon" painter Paul
62. Egyptian Christian
64. Condemned's neckwear?
66. Fat in a pat, maybe
67. ". . . sting like ___"
68. Comedian Fields
69. Bering and Baltic
70. "___ is more"
71. Clip, as sheep

Down

1. Body of an organism
2. "Et ___" (and others)
3. After-dinner candy
4. "___ Maria"
5. Closes again, as an envelope
6. Shopping centers
7. Old-time actor Roscoe
8. Footlike part
9. Enter slowly
10. Plundered, old-style
11. Certain Oldsmobile
12. Mountain climber's spike
13. Aquatic mammals
22. "___ Abner"
24. Caviar, essentially
26. Frame a photo again
28. "Betsy's Wedding" actor
29. Penniless
30. Book leaf
31. "As I Lay Dying" character
32. Goalie's stat
34. Adjuncts
36. "Down with," in Dijon
37. Secures, as a shoelace
38. First, second, or third
39. 1914 battle line
44. All you need, in a Beatles song
46. Mom and Dad
48. Imp
49. A doz. doz.
50. Powerful sharks
51. City in northern France
52. "___ bad moon rising . . ."
54. Art Deco pieces
56. Composer Janacek
57. "Planet of the ___"
58. Fuss over, with "on"
59. ___ Minor
60. Bambi, e.g.
63. Award bestowed by Queen Eliz.
65. "___ la la!"

Solution on page 266

Crossword 11

Across

1. Duke's conf.
4. Russian fighter jets
8. H.S. juniors' exams
13. Lindstrom and Zadora
15. Seat of Allen County, Kan.
16. Authorize
17. Dennis the Menace, to Mr. Wilson
18. Was inventive, and then some
19. ___ dish
20. Colorful ring
22. "Count me out"
24. Cir. bisector
25. Dish out gazpacho, e.g.
26. "Pippi Longstocking" novelist Lindgren
28. Bad-tempered goddess
30. Turned sharply
34. Mediterranean fruits
37. "___ on the Fourth of July"
40. Roman judge
41. Ball chaser?
42. Cowboys' gear
44. ___ Tin Tin
45. Growing out
47. Name in plus-size modeling
48. Bog fuel
49. Brownish horse
51. "Legally Blonde" character
53. Bakery assets
56. Biased writing?: Abbr.
60. ___ Spumante
63. "For Me and My ___"
64. Mini-simian
65. Sound of a spring
67. Mortgage, e.g.
69. Author Jaffe
70. French avenue
71. Blue-gray shark
72. "___ out?" (pet's choice)
73. "You've got mail" addressee
74. Assns.
75. "All My ___ Live in Texas" (1987 #1 country hit)

Down

1. Horrify
2. 1980s–'90s Olds
3. Checked out before the heist
4. "___ 18" (Leon Uris book)
5. "___ Dalmatians"
6. Hidden valleys
7. 1978 Nobel Peace Prize cowinner
8. Baby food
9. Traveled on snow
10. "Height" word form
11. When said three times, a W.W. II film
12. Do laps in the pool
14. Shoulder wraps
21. Celtic sea god
23. "48___" (Murphy movie)
26. Stick out like ___ thumb
27. France's ___ de Glenans
29. Hall-of-Fame basketball coach Hank
31. Karl Wallenda's "path"
32. "East of Eden" director Kazan
33. Minimal progress, so to speak
34. "Them"
35. Prefix with sphere
36. Cur "grr"
38. Backboard attachment
39. Appoints
42. Amorous gaze
43. ___ Aviv, Israel
46. Boot camp denizen
48. Russian czar known as 'the Great'
50. Cabin component
52. Back talk
54. Swedish port
55. "Are you calling me ___?"
57. "___ at last!"
58. Town near Tanglewood
59. Asterisks
60. Quatrain rhyme scheme, maybe
61. Aria, e.g.
62. Cash drawer
64. Years in Spain
66. Aus. neighbor
68. Heart chart, for short

Solution on page 266

Crossword 12

Across

1. Animal rights org.
5. Produce, as a play
10. "The King and I" country
14. Beach plaything
15. Flynn of "Captain Blood"
16. Former sneaker brand
17. High, in music
18. Blue ___ Mountains
19. "A ___ formality!"
20. Most acute
22. Hangmen's needs
24. Icelandic epics
25. Academy Awards
28. Crude shelter
30. Atkins diet no-nos
34. Cowboy's seat
37. Eyes, in poetry
39. Drill sergeant's syllable
40. Fertilizer chemical
41. Arles' river
43. Hire a decorator, e.g.
44. Diplomat's res.
45. Agronomy concern
46. N.Y. Yankees' division
48. Cannes cup
50. First-rate
52. Aswan Dam lake
54. Angle
58. "Chili today, hot ___"
61. '40s First Lady
63. Swan genus
64. Make ___ buck
67. Condition for some soap opera characters
68. ". . . in the pot, ___ days old"
69. Shaker's partner
70. Jack who played Jake in "Big Bad John"
71. Understands, as a joke
72. Barbecue rods
73. Animal lairs

Down

1. Said, old-style
2. ___ in comparison
3. Given a ticket
4. "M*A*S*H" star
5. Sun. messages
6. Son of Poseidon
7. Suffix for tank
8. Armageddon nation
9. "Marcus Wellby, M.D." actress Verdugo
10. Small stuffed triangular turnover
11. "As I was going to St. ___ . . ."
12. Billion follower
13. Actresses West and Murray
21. Donkey, in Dusseldorf
23. Imaginary monsters
26. Informer
27. "Hee Haw" humor
29. Aviation word starter
31. Actress Perlman of "Cheers"
32. Beginning blossoms
33. Ad
34. Bird feeder food
35. First word of "The Aeneid"
36. Ball belles
38. All in
42. Chart toppers
43. Put back
45. Close, as an envelope
47. "Heads I win, tails you ___"
49. Animal traps
51. Already ready
53. Baseball features
55. Chameleon
56. "___ is an island . . ."
57. Coal haulers
58. Grab, as ice cubes
59. "I cannot tell ___!"
60. ___ Blanc
62. Wd. parts
65. Beau Brummell
66. "Bird" word form

Solution on page 266

Crossword 13

1	2	3	4	■	5	6	7	8	■	9	10	11	12	13
14				■	15				■	16				
17				■	18				■	19				
■	20			21			■	22	23		■	24		
■	■	■	25				26	■	27		28	■	■	■
■	29	30				■	31	32		■	33	34	35	36
37			■	38		39			■	40				
41			42		■	43			■	44				
45					■	46			47		■	48		
49				■	50			■	51		52			■
■	■	■	53	54		■	55	56				■	■	■
57	58	59	■	60		61	■	62				63	64	■
65			66		■	67	68			■	69			70
71					■	72				■	73			
74					■	75				■	76			

Across

1. Four-posters
5. Riches preceder, sometimes
9. Campus buildings
14. "Able was ___ I saw . . ."
15. Celebes ox
16. ". . . had a farm, ___"
17. Ran, as colors
18. "___ pronounce you . . ."
19. Insipid
20. "Burnt" color
22. ". . . ___ thousand times . . ."
24. Acidity nos.
25. French queen
27. A couple of cups
29. Tabulae ___: clean slates
31. Chem., for one
33. City in Colombia
37. Confine, with "in"
38. Train stop: Abbr.
40. Leaves port
41. "___ Ben Jonson"
43. Chair part
44. Island off Scotland
45. "Peter, Peter, Pumpkin ___"
46. "Virginia" dances
48. Atl.-based cable network
49. Agitated condition
50. Any doctrine
51. "Life ___ short . . ."
53. Actress Taina
55. Blacksmith, at times
57. Army off.
60. Pah preceder
62. A Gandhi
65. "___ and the Night Visitors"
67. Author Sarah ___ Jewett
69. CBS eye, e.g.
71. Beat back
72. Laws, for short
73. Train line to N.Y.C.
74. Fussbudget
75. Arena shouts
76. Delight, as a comedy club crowd

Down

1. Baby's neckwear
2. Congers, e.g.
3. Eins, zwei, ___
4. Passover dinners
5. Cascades peak
6. Kofi of the U.N.
7. Baby syllable
8. Cut, as a log
9. Exclude
10. "Black gold"
11. Enjoy, as benefits
12. Ho Chi ___ City
13. Adds turf to
21. "___, My God, to Thee"
23. "Shogun" sash
26. Looks up to
28. "___ in every garage"
29. Aired over the summer, maybe
30. Violinist's heirloom, perhaps
32. Nicolas of "Con Air"
34. ___-ground missile
35. Gaucho's plain
36. "___ It a Pity?"
37. Farm implements
39. Some cameras, briefly
40. Answered impudently
42. Network of veins, e.g.
47. Elsa, for one
50. "___ to Extremes" (Billy Joel tune)
52. Warbles
54. Sucker, in Sussex
56. Door attachment
57. Dietary component, for short
58. Buddhist sacred mountain
59. "Dragnet" force: Abbr.
61. Italian statesman Aldo
63. Agitate
64. City near New Delhi
66. Pronominal contraction
68. Aunt or uncle: Abbr.
70. "Kid" of the jazz trombone

Solution on page 267

Crossword 14

Across

1. "Concentration" objective
6. Last NT book
10. Last year of the 14th century
13. Awesome hotel lobbies
14. Decrease
15. Arias, for example
16. Whisperer of sweet nothings
17. Dinner scraps
18. Bugs Bunny, e.g.
19. Aunts, cousins, etc.
20. ___ the good (beneficial)
22. Adhesive
23. Abbr. in many business names
24. Lady of rank
26. Belittles
29. Agent's 15%, e.g.
30. Pet store brand
31. Con games
35. Absorbs, with "up"
39. 1002
40. ___-night doubleheader
41. What an MC wears
42. "___ and Lovers" (D. H. Lawrence novel)
44. Columbus' port
46. Friend of Albert, Churchy, and Porkypine
47. Station closing?
49. Just about
51. Make rough
55. Writer LeShan et al.
56. "I'm ___ here!" (skedaddler's cry)
57. Alleviator
59. Bloom-to-be
62. ___-Tass (Moscow news agency)
63. Candied items
64. Early French coin
66. "Aida" backdrop
67. "Hard ___!" (helmsman's cry)
68. "The Crucible" locale
69. "Capeesh?"
70. ___ room
71. Adds to the pot

Down

1. "___ the Knife"
2. Yours, in Paris
3. 1982 Disney film starring Jeff Bridges
4. Co., in Caen
5. Capital of Zimbabwe
6. Mil. truants
7. Actor's need
8. "___ of Old Smoky"
9. Hwy. designers
10. ___ Jaw, Saskatchewan
11. Thickens, as cream
12. Attends a banquet
15. Fixed looks
21. At a ___ for words
22. ___ Wee Reese
23. Some four-year degs.
25. Flunking letters
26. Aspirations
27. "Charles in Charge" star
28. African dictator
32. Windy City train initials
33. Ice pick, for one
34. "O Sole ___"
36. 1847 Melville novel
37. "When ___ fly!" ("It'll never happen")
38. Robert Burns, e.g.
43. "Being and Nothingness" author
44. Joe-___ weed (perennial herb)
45. "Smooth Operator" chanteuse
46. Afts.
48. Cape Town's country: Abbr.
50. 50's singer Julius
51. Creates, in a way
52. Belly button type
53. "___ of Two Cities"
54. Aussie tennis star Fraser
55. Blissful couple?
58. "I'll drink to that!"
59. Cloth unit
60. "___'s Gold": Peter Fonda film
61. GOP rivals
63. Candied tuber
65. Disallow

Solution on page 267

Crossword 15

Across

1. Actress Charlotte and Explorer John
5. Baseball officials, for short
9. Dundee uncle
12. Bid one club, e.g.
13. Gondolier, e.g.
15. Dino's tail?
16. Army mascot
17. ". . . ___ bagatelle"
18. "___ calling"
19. Hitherto
21. 502, to Flavius
22. Speech sound
23. "___ a deal!"
26. Being, in Bordeaux
28. Police alert, for short
31. "Ew-w-w!"
33. Hanging tapestry
37. Not, for a Scot
38. Faxed, perhaps
39. Bucks
40. "You never had ___ good!"
42. Video game creator Sid
44. "To Autumn" and others
45. Conical dwelling
47. "All in the Family" creator
49. Edible tuber
50. "___ Is Born"
51. Camera technique, briefly
52. Bummed
53. Bird shelter
55. "Sheesh, ___ you read?"
57. Asian range
60. "Gimme ___!" (start of an Iowa State cheer)
62. Alternatives to Volvos
66. "___ we forget . . ."
67. Bird in "Peter and the Wolf"
70. Hillside, to Burns
71. Like Cheerios
72. Football coach Amos Alonzo ___
73. "___ Marlene"
74. RAM computer program
75. "Harper's Bazaar" artist
76. "___ for the poor"

Down

1. "Arrivederci ___"
2. Bird of Paradise constellation
3. Hard to grasp
4. Dirks
5. "___ Lazy River"
6. Addressee of many requests
7. Said "No contest," perhaps
8. Best of seven, e.g.
9. Attic window view
10. Atomic particle
11. Atlantic bird
14. Type of mutual fund: Abbr.
15. City near Naples
20. Harbor sights
24. ___ de menthe
25. Improve, as a skill
27. BBC's Italian counterpart
28. "Gentlemen Prefer Blondes" author Loos
29. Cracker spreads
30. Annoy
32. Backwoods booze maker
34. New stylings
35. Palm
36. "What a pity!"
39. "Law & Order," e.g.
41. Murkiness
43. Fed. job-discrimination watchdog
46. Leandro's love
48. Director Howard et al.
51. 100-member group
54. Former news org.
56. Indian drum
57. "Thanks ___!"
58. Grasslands
59. Copernicus' sci.
61. River to the Danube
63. Nutmeg cover
64. Aromatic ointment
65. Six, in Seville
68. Elev.
69. "___ before beauty"

Solution on page 267

Crossword 16

Across

1. Opera stars
6. Carrie and Louis
10. Ancestral stories and such
14. Give it ___!
15. Antidote
16. "Cry, the Beloved Country" author Paton
17. Hoarse
18. Irish exclamation
19. Prefix meaning "foreigner"
20. Keys in, as data
22. Vietnamese holidays
24. Adjective suffix
25. Aussie bounders
27. Discovers
29. White veggies
33. Banned bug killer
34. "An ill wind that nobody blows good"
35. Bruce and Spike
37. Sings like Torme
41. ___ TURN (road sign)
42. Casa rooms
44. Choreographer Lubovitch
45. "___ is human . . ."
48. Italian painter
49. "___ Enchanted" (2004 film)
50. N, E, W, or S
52. Lettering tools
54. Gives gratuitously
58. Lennon's in-laws
59. "Le Monde" article
60. "Bye!"
62. Chipped in
66. Breakfast, e.g.
68. Lomond, for one
70. Boatload
71. ___ de foie gras
72. Manny of the Dodgers
73. American dogwood
74. Not busy, at work
75. Loom part
76. Fort ___, Fla.

Down

1. "How ___ you!"
2. Dr. Seuss' "If ___ the Circus"
3. Buttoned item
4. Badmouth
5. "Sophie's Choice" author
6. M.Sgt., e.g.
7. Mongolian tent
8. Committed a faux pas
9. In a chair
10. Calif. airport
11. ___ acid
12. Attacked, in a way
13. Chemical compounds
21. Besmirches
23. Norms (abbr.)
26. Catch fish, in a primitive way
28. ". . . yadda, yadda, yadda"
29. Bridge, in Bretagne
30. "Peek" follower
31. Cad
32. Monica of tennis
36. ___ Domingo
38. "___ Ask of You" ("The Phantom of the Opera" song)
39. Seven-foot, e.g.
40. Ladies of Spain, briefly
43. City in Tuscany
46. Cereal box abbr.
47. "Norma Rae" director
49. Rapture
51. Domains
53. Sarge, e.g.
54. Gets rid of
55. "Paper Moon" actor or actress
56. "Awesome!"
57. "Cheers" chair
61. Entr'___ (theater break)
63. Canal of Sal, in song
64. The Ohre, to Germans
65. British bombshell Diana
67. "Ben Hur" novelist Wallace
69. Bale contents

Solution on page 267

Chapter 10
Diagramless

The diagramless crossword puzzle adds a bit of extra fun to your puzzling task. Not only do you have to know the answers to the clues, but you have to place them in the proper squares on the grid. Start with 1-across and work in pencil. These puzzles have regular crossword puzzle symmetry. You can learn the location of 1-across for each puzzle by turning the page upside down.

Diagramless 1

Across

1. The "L" of L.A.
4. UFO navigators
7. Relative of -arian
10. Birmingham's state: Abbr.
11. Wide shoe designation
12. Dentists' grp.
13. Highways: Abbr.
14. Compass pt. opposite SSW
15. Present and future
19. D.D.E. opponent
20. Open ___ of worms
22. Mauna ___ (Hawaiian volcano)
23. Bread with seeds
25. Some USN officers
26. Agent: Abbr.
27. Stallone title role
31. Uncovers
32. Certifies by oath
36. Layers of paint
38. "My Heart Skips ___"
39. Latin art
42. Mikhail of chess
44. Patriotic org.
47. Mothers
48. ". . . and to ___ good night!"
50. Furry foot
52. Avoid a trial
54. 1960s radical grp.
57. Money for old age: Abbr.
58. ___ Van Winkle
59. Vowel sequence
60. Sunday address: Abbr.
61. Ooh and ___
62. "___ port in a storm"
63. All ___ up (irate)

Down

1. ___ Flynn Boyle
2. ___ but wiser
3. Smart-mouthed
4. Nighttime, to a poet
5. Coffee-break time
6. "___ pin and pick it up . . ."
7. Bother continuously
8. Paradisiacal places
9. Competed in a marathon
16. Popular camera type, for short
17. Help-wanted abbr.
18. Syrup ingredient
21. Near miss
24. Tarzan creator's monogram
28. Motor-club letters
29. "The A-Team" muscleman
30. Place a wager
33. Cry audibly
34. Menlo Park inits.
35. Railroad stop: Abbr.
37. Avenue crossers: Abbr.
39. Mornings, briefly
40. Norma ___ (Sally Field role)
41. Concorde: Abbr.
42. Shire of "Rocky"
43. First Hebrew letter
45. Prone to imitation
46. Carnival show
49. Not on shore
51. Witch's blemish
53. La-la prelude
55. Lot of noise
56. Dim sum sauce

1-across starts in the 1st square from the left.

Solution on page 268

Diagramless 2

Across

1. Noah creation
4. "Otherwise . . ."
7. Lawyers' gp.
10. Property
11. Anchorman Rather
12. Leaky radiator sound
13. Georgia and Ukraine, once: Abbr.
14. Greek dawn goddess
17. Calendar abbreviation
19. Is the owner of
21. Helpers for profs
23. Was in possession of
24. "Are you a man ___ mouse?"
25. Loveseat
27. Kung ___ shrimp
28. ___ Lingus: Irish carrier
29. ACLU concerns: Abbr.
32. Knights' horses
35. Feedbag grain
36. "The best things in life ___ free"
37. Michigan's ___ Canals
38. Sugar: Suffix
39. Sure-footed work animal
40. Capone and Pacino
42. Catches sight of
44. Doctors' group: Abbr.
47. "Evil Woman" rock group
48. New York's ___ Island
51. Football great Dawson
52. Crude carriers
53. Dishonorable one

Down

1. One hundred percent
2. Alphabetic run
3. Lock opener
4. Hospital areas: Abbr.
5. Second notes of the scale
6. Lighten, as a burden
7. Commercials, e.g.
8. Go from pub to pub
9. Cochise portrayer Michael
13. But: Lat.
15. Extra play periods, for short
16. Ms. enclosure
17. "___ a Moon Out Tonight"
18. Mideast inits.
20. ___ Paulo, Brazil
22. Says
26. Golf ball support
29. Australian hopper, for short
30. Grad's cap attachment
31. "The Spectator" essayist
32. Former jrs.
33. 1950 Edmond O'Brien classic thriller
34. Note after fa
36. ___ in "Able"
41. Fully satisfy
43. Extremely long time
45. Sea: Fr.
46. Question's opposite: Abbr.
48. Assn.
49. Aunt in Madrid
50. City official: Abbr.

1-across starts in the 1st square from the left.

Solution on page 268

Diagramless 3

Across

1. CCL x X
4. Swiss river to the Rhine
7. German valley
8. Suffix with meth- or eth-
9. Rosary prayers
10. Putrefies
12. Bitter brews
15. Lousy grade
17. British brew
20. Mas' mates
21. Narrow waterway: Abbr.
22. Baltic or Bering
23. Airport screening org.
24. Light throw
25. Savannah summer hrs.
26. Moses' mountain
29. Letter addenda: Abbr.
31. Livy's lang.
32. Fri. follower
33. Wall St. trading group
34. First known asteroid
36. Calendar doz.
38. "Compos mentis"
40. Elbow's place
43. Sounds of doubt
44. "Boy, am ___ trouble!"
45. Narcs' agcy.
46. Opposite dir. from NNW
47. Basic version: Abbr.
48. Performed an aria
49. Spinning toys
52. Flimsy, as an excuse
55. Alliance since 1948: Abbr.
56. Smell ___ (be leery)
57. Cries of dismay
58. One of two hardy followers

Down

1. Dallas hoopster, briefly
2. Fannie ___ (federal mortgage agency)
3. Hosp. workers
4. Alpine river
5. Year in Yucatan
6. Not active: Abbr.
7. Carrier to Sweden
11. Ms. enclosures
12. Prone (to)
13. "Leaving ___ Vegas"
14. Those, in Toledo
15. Drunk's problem
16. Ambulance destinations, for short
18. Was in charge of
19. Have breakfast
21. ". . . or ___ thought"
24. "I tawt I taw a puddy ___!"
27. They, in Calais
28. Scottish negative
29. ___ for the course
30. French holy woman: Abbr.
32. Get a look at
33. Valuable possession
34. MSNBC alternative
35. Actress Thompson of "Family"
36. Month, in Madrid
37. Surprised exclamations
38. Command to a dog
39. Pitch in for
41. Stimpy's cartoon buddy
42. Periodical, for short
47. Radiator sound
48. Harden, as cement
50. Winning tic-tac-toe row
51. Foot the bill
52. "___-di-dah!"
53. Parseghian of football
54. Cause damage to

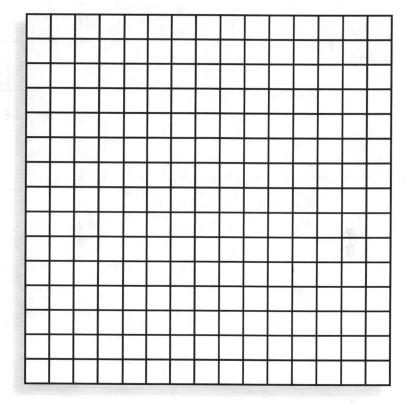

1-across starts in the 1st square from the left.

Solution on page 268

Diagramless 4

Across

1. Somalian fashion model
5. Library device
7. Corp. takeover
10. Dutch master Jan
11. EarthLink alternative
12. ___-mo (instant replay feature)
15. Gives a thumbs-up
16. Poisonous snake
19. Late columnist Landers
21. Brain-scan letters
24. Dove's sound
25. Stephen of "Michael Collins"
26. Navel type
28. Existence: Lat.
30. Krazy ___ of the comics
31. En ___: as a group
32. Fell behind slightly
36. Pro hoopster
39. Doo-wop syllable
40. Poker pair
44. Propelled a canoe
45. Lunch meat
46. 19th letter of the Greek alphabet
47. Pinup's leg
48. Hans of Dadaism
49. Cause friction
50. Find a sum
53. ___-Man (arcade game)
55. Scooby-___ (cartoon dog)
56. On ___ (winning)
61. G-man: Abbr.
62. "Gay" French city
63. Topers

Down

1. Driver's lic. and such
2. Small rug
3. Ended a fast
4. Jacqueline Kennedy ___ Bouvier
6. MD's helpers
7. ___ -Tzu: Taoist philosopher
8. ___ choy (Chinese green)
9. Mary-Kate and Ashley
13. Escapades
14. ___ a time (individually)
16. Highest card
17. Morse code message
18. Opposite of neg.
20. Boris' partner
22. "___ for Evidence" (Grafton novel)
23. "That's incredible!"
26. "___ Mine" (George Harrison book)
27. West Coast wine valley
29. Gen. Robert ___
33. Run-of-the-mill: Abbr.
34. Like some wits or cheeses
35. Florida port
36. Yuletide beverage
37. Lamb's cry
38. Naval fleet
41. Basketball position: Abbr.
42. Water: Fr.
43. Long sandwich
51. "Man's best friend"
52. Decimal point
54. Beanie
57. ___ Tafari (Haile Selassie)
58. Tijuana gold
59. Disappoint, with "down"
60. Brown with a Band of Renown

1-across starts in the 1st square from the left.

Solution on page 268

Diagramless 5

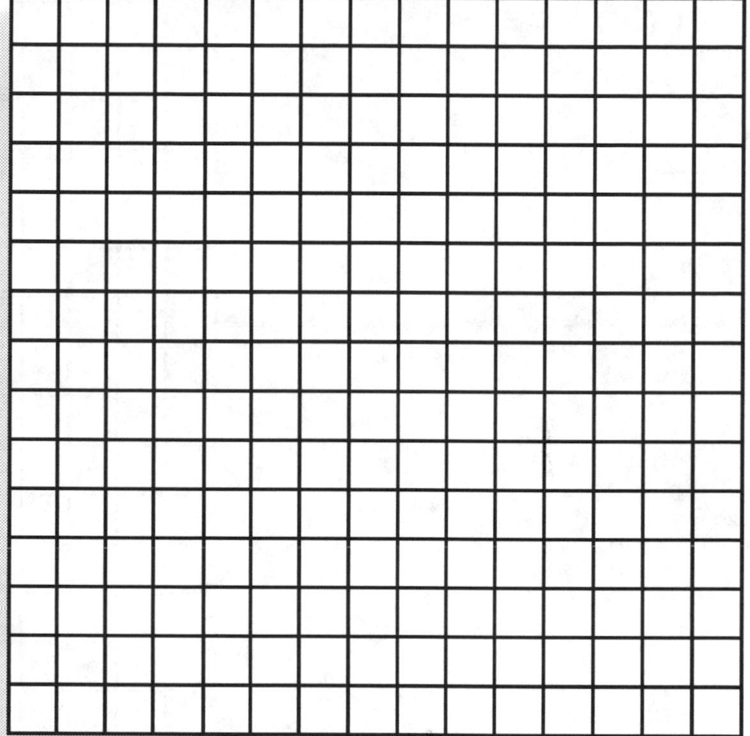

Across

1. "Yummy!"
4. Craft or skill
5. Nightclub routine
8. Caama
10. Extinct kiwi relative
11. The "I" of T.G.I.F.
14. Film director Lee
15. "It's ___ for Me to Say"
16. Thesaurus entries: Abbr.
19. Small bird
21. ___ tai (drink)
22. Typesetting mistakes
24. Feel regret over
25. Discontinues
28. Annapolis grad: Abbr.
29. TV reporter Donaldson
31. Silent film star Negri
32. ___ cit. (footnote abbr.)
34. Old what's-___-name
36. British rocker Brian
37. Three-strikes result
38. Prom-night safety gp.
42. Asner and Wynn
43. London lav
44. Japanese money

Down

1. Barnyard sound
2. "Is it Miss or ___?"
3. Rockies, e.g.
5. Amo, ___, amat
6. Not pro
7. Kids' running game
9. One, in Germany
12. Kiddie
13. Actor David Ogden ___
16. Tiny, in Troon
17. China's Sun ___-sen
18. Actress Long or Peeples
20. Makes level
23. Thrift-shop transaction
25. Corporate V.I.P.
26. Big picture?: Abbr.
27. Happy ___ lark
30. Tues. preceder
31. Attention-getters
33. Fortune 500 listings: Abbr.
34. Weed digger
35. Birth control option, briefly
39. Prince ___ Khan
40. Bambi's mother
41. Comic Rickles

1-across starts in the 1st square from the left.

Solution on page 269

Diagramless 6

Across

1. Downs' opposite
4. China's Mao ___-tung
7. Water cannon target
11. Elevations: Abbr.
12. Jefferson's Monticello, e.g.
13. Atlantic Coast states, with "the"
15. Bit of sunshine
16. WWII transport
17. Tooth pro's deg.
20. ___ Diego, CA
22. Three, on a sundial
23. Imbibe slowly
24. Sept. preceder
25. Emergency PC key
26. More statuesque
28. Slower, in mus.
29. Attached with glue
32. Wire diameter measure
35. Angry feeling
36. Sleep phenom.
38. "Put ___ Happy Face"
39. Pavement material
40. ___'wester
41. Highway: Abbr.
42. Prosecutors, for short
44. Captain Hook's assistant
46. Daylong marches
50. Coupe or convertible
51. Actress Lombard
52. Vienna is its cap.
53. Metal in pewter

Down

1. Ending for press
2. Detectives, for short
3. Drunkard
4. Dissertation
5. Radio interference
6. Double-curve letter
8. Small mountain lake
9. Airport posting: Abbr.
10. Spanish king
14. Football scores: Abbr.
16. Be deceitful
18. Dah's partner
19. Not dense
20. Seek damages from
21. Part of USDA: Abbr.
24. Changes
27. All fired up?
29. Actress Zadora
30. Departure's opposite: Abbr.
31. ___ gratias: Thanks to God
32. "The Island of Dr. ___"
33. Buries
34. New Guinea port
37. Juilliard subj.
39. Ivan, for one
42. Santa's mo.
43. One ___ time (individually)
45. Universal Studios' former parent co.
47. Stew vessel
48. ___ Lilly and Company
49. Japanese money

1-across starts in the 1st square from the left.

Solution on page 269

Diagramless 7

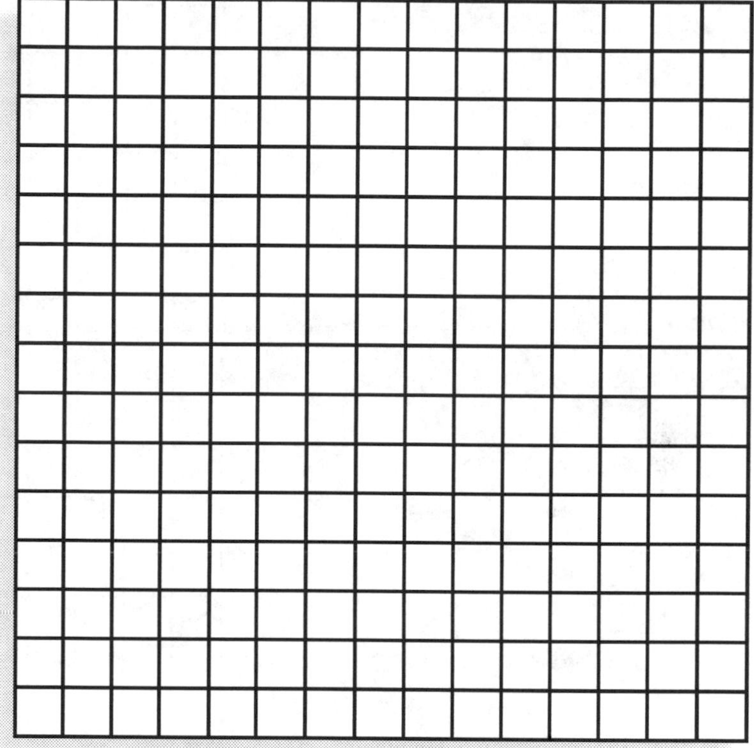

Across

1. Photo ___: publicity events
4. D.D.E.'s command in WWII
7. Cambridge sch.
10. Electrified fish
11. Beach composition
13. Polynesian tuber
14. Double-helix molecule
15. Correo ___ (Spanish airmail)
16. Eagerly expecting
17. French negative
19. Curved line
20. Covert WWII org.
21. Tiny bit
22. Stetson, e.g.
25. St. Louis clock setting
26. Cry to a calf
29. Plant pockets
31. Healthful retreat
34. Modifying word: Abbr.
35. Spring holy day
38. Throw again
40. Animal that beats its chest
41. Lille lily
43. Mrs. Dithers of the comics
44. Balloon-breaking sound
45. Letters on a cornerstone
47. ___ and outs
49. Derbies and berets
50. Comedian Bernie
53. Disencumber (of)
56. Big Band or Disco period
57. NFL team
58. Loud, as the surf
60. Some ALers
63. "Do I dare to ___ peach?": Eliot
64. Author ___ Christian Andersen
65. Debt acknowledgment
66. Lacking moisture
67. "___ Beso" (1962 song)
68. Bank device: Abbr.

Down

1. Multivolume ref.
2. Animal enclosure
3. Leans
4. Point opposite WNW
5. Scarlett's estate
6. Unique thing
7. "Welcome" sites
8. From Donegal
9. Blouse or shirt
12. One of the Seven Dwarfs
13. Lao-tzu principle
15. In addition
18. Feed bag contents
21. Summer coolers, for short
23. Nova Scotia clock setting: Abbr.
24. Asian weight
26. Big name in China
27. Pigs out (on), briefly
28. Breakfast quaffs, for short
30. Dernier ___ (the latest thing)
32. Tennis instructor
33. Ethereal: Prefix
35. "The Raven" monogram
36. Military mail drop: Abbr.
37. Aug. follower
39. Brownish
42. Mark with a branding iron
43. Dollar parts: Abbr.
46. Sports arenas
48. Do finger painting
49. Billy Joel's "Tell ___ About It"
51. Bar association member: Abbr.
52. R.E. Lee's org.
53. Pep-rally word
54. ""Dies ___""
55. Slips into
57. ___ Bartlet, president on "The West Wing"
59. Remark from Chan
61. Like stolen goods
62. Addition result

1-across starts in the 1st square from the left.

Solution on page 269

Diagramless 8

Across

1. Silent acknowledgment
4. "Either you do it, ___ will!"
5. Capital of Yemen
9. Elderly
12. Meeting: Abbr.
14. "The Giving Tree" author Silverstein
15. Actor ___ Ray
16. Hereditary
18. Miss Trueheart of "Dick Tracy"
19. Mlle.'s Spanish counterpart
21. Number-crunching pro
23. Kasparov's game
24. Mythical world lifter
28. Bear's abode
29. Highest-quality
32. Vietnamese festival
33. Long and slender
35. UK record label
36. Pharmacist's weight
38. Bygone car
39. She preceded Mamie
40. Swiss mountain
41. No longer fresh
43. "Soap" Family
45. Canoe paddle
47. Blue Jay or Oriole
48. Datebook entry: Abbr.
51. Noisy insect
55. Maximum
56. College grad
57. Pyramid scheme, for one
61. Uneaten morsel
62. Leak slowly
63. Hair coloring
64. ___ jiffy (quickly)

Down

1. Calculator figs.
2. It's north of Calif.
3. Malign, in slang
5. ID with two hyphens
6. "I have an idea!"
7. Amount after expenses
8. Oscar winner Guinness
9. Guadalajara "Rah!"
10. Mormon gp.
11. "Uno" + "uno"
13. Rests for a moment
15. Rat chaser?
17. "Illmatic" rapper
19. Clippers
20. Milk curdler
22. Game show host Sajak
23. 450, in old Rome
25. Inc., in Britain
26. Fill with fizz
27. Less up-to-date
29. Stinging insect
30. Letters after els
31. ___ boom bah
34. Campground letters
37. Army cops: Abbr.
39. Arthur who played Maude
42. Mississippi senator Trent
43. Slight amount
44. Sigher's word
46. Some DVD players
48. Start of a Latin 101 trio
49. ___ favor: please (Sp.)
50. Seattle clock setting: Abbr.
52. ___ de la Cit
53. Feed lines to
54. Unit of elec. current
58. 401, in old Rome
59. Author Rand
60. "Oh, give ___ home . . ."

1-across starts in the 1st square from the left.

Solution on page 269

Diagramless 9

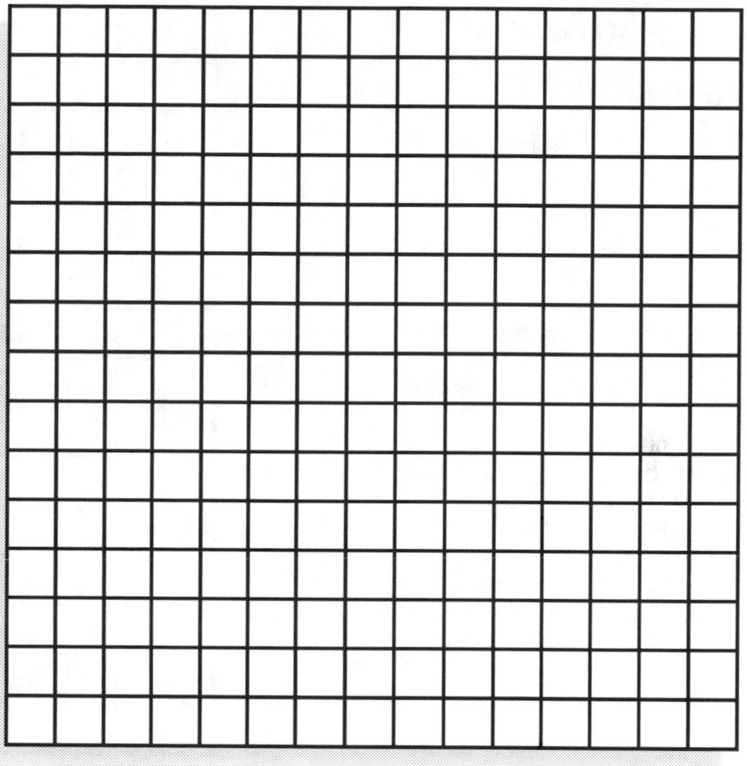

Across

1. Part of m.p.h.
4. Sibling, for short
5. High-school math course: Abbr.
8. Give ___ shot
11. Have the looks of
13. Crystal ball user
15. Maple fluids
17. Former San Francisco Mayor Joseph
19. Chick of jazz
20. ___- Magnon
21. CBS forensic drama
23. Schubert's "The ___ King"
24. Oft-swiveled joint
25. Keep an ___ to the ground
27. Tin ___ Alley
28. Whodunit's essence
31. Letter holder: Abbr.
34. Three, in Torino
35. Boyfriends
36. Capuchin monkey
37. Kazakhstan, once: Abbr.
38. USN bigwigs
39. Come out even
40. Patty Hearst's kidnap grp.
42. Jan. 1, e.g.
43. "The Lord of the Rings" monster
46. Tire pressure meas.
48. April 15 addressee
49. Freeways
51. Tampa neighbor, informally
55. Long-snouted fish
56. Tot's "little piggies"
57. Swedish car
61. NYPD figure
62. The "S" in R.S.V.P.
63. Gloomy ___
64. Son-gun filler

Down

1. Charlie Rose's network
2. Before, to a sonneteer
3. 1973 Supreme Court decision name
5. "Do ___ say, . . ."
6. Virgo's predecessor
7. Wreak vengeance on
8. "Equal" word form
9. Scale deduction
10. One who mimics
12. Sailors
14. Fabled bird
16. "My gal" of song
18. Cut off, as a branch
19. Spies' org.
20. Burns the surface of
22. Hardens, as cement
26. Puts back
27. Quart parts: Abbr.
28. ___ XING: crosswalk sign
29. On the ___ (fleeing)
30. Humor finale?
32. Symbols of hardness
33. Compete (for)
35. Sheep cries
41. '60s records
42. Great success
43. Part of NATO: Abbr.
44. Hope/Crosby title word
45. Guardianship
47. Art or novel add-on
50. "Spring ahead" letters
52. How-___ (instructional books)
53. Architect I.M. ___
54. Course for new immigrants: Abbr.
58. "Fourscore and seven years ___ . . ."
59. ___ Wiedersehen
60. Jamboree grp.

1-across starts in the 1st square from the left.

Solution on page 270

Diagramless 10

Across

1. Favorable vote
4. Soft shoe, for short
7. Tommy follower?
8. Hogs' home
9. Enzyme suffixes
11. '50s nuclear trial
13. PC linking acronym
15. Suffix with drunk or tank
17. Wagering place: Abbr.
20. Napoleonic general
21. Beauregard's boss
22. British big shot
23. Never, in Nuremberg
24. Outfield material
25. Collarless shirts
26. "___ it something I said?"
27. Electrically charged atom
28. Brother of Curly and Shemp
30. Gold measures: Abbr.
31. Anecdote collection
32. Boise is its cap.
33. L-P link
34. Lamb's dad
37. "At once!"
40. Average mark
41. Above, in poetry
42. Rocky outcropping
43. Snake that squeezes its prey
44. High, arcing shot
45. Collar, as a crook
46. Grain bristle
47. One hundred yrs.
48. A whole slew
52. Director Vittorio De ___
55. Lincoln or Vigoda
56. Took the bait
57. Try for apples
58. Wrong: Pref.

Down

1. Irish island
2. Interjections from Rocky
3. High season, on the Riviera
4. Wyo. clock setting
5. Taxonomic suffix
6. Songwriter Coleman et al.
10. Hair stylist's shop
11. Suffix with lemon or lime
12. Sound of music
13. Luke Skywalker's sister
14. Yeses at sea
16. One side in checkers
18. Sock front
19. Kids' ammo
20. Wind dir.
24. Cubs slugger Sammy
25. 4:00 social
27. "___ be my pleasure!"
28. Hair on a horse's neck
29. Yoko of music
30. Set of tools
33. Intends
34. Acting job
35. "___ Flux" (Charlize Theron movie)
36. Hazel's boss, to Hazel
37. Train stop: Abbr.
38. Ode title opening
39. Wall St. traders
40. Dairy animal
43. ___-relief
47. Lions and tigers
49. Auto for hire
50. Blood-type group
51. Cotillion girl
53. Apple competitor
54. LI doubled

1-across starts in the 1st square from the left.

Solution on page 270

Diagramless 11

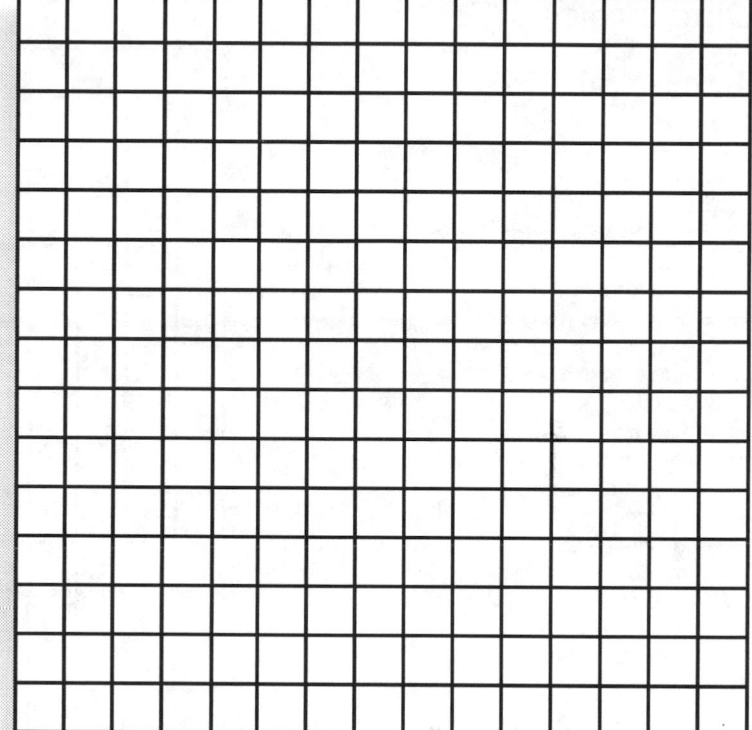

Across

1. Delivery room doctors, for short
4. U.S. soldiers
7. Coffee cup
8. Lab-maze runner
9. Hushed "Hey you!"
10. Genetic material: Abbr.
11. ___-Cat (off-road vehicle)
13. Many months: Abbr.
16. Bosom buddy
17. Floor-washing implement
19. One of Alcott's "Little Women"
20. Short race
23. Porcine pads
25. Having a handle
28. Part of A&P
30. Yang partner
31. Alleged spoon-bender Geller
32. Experimentation room
34. Coastal inlet
35. "___ seeing things?"
38. Bread with a pocket
41. Stag party attendees
42. Gas pump spec.
43. Height: Abbr.
44. Silkworm

Down

1. Mantra chants
2. Commuter vehicle
3. Lt.'s subordinate
4. Doberman's warning
5. Fleming who created 007
6. "Don't move, Fido!"
9. Roly-___
11. Outpourings
12. Asian arena, for short
14. Apt. ad abbr.
15. Bread, for stew
18. 7, on a phone
21. Firenze's land
22. Diarist Anaïs
24. Pronounce
26. "Open 9 ___ 6"
27. Doe in "Bambi"
28. Surrounding glow
29. The first "T" of TNT
33. Crimson Tide, briefly
36. Gibson of film
37. Savings acct. addition
38. Before: Prefix
39. Ending with cash or bombard
40. ___ Friday's: restaurant chain

1-across starts in the 1st square from the left.

Solution on page 270

Diagramless 12

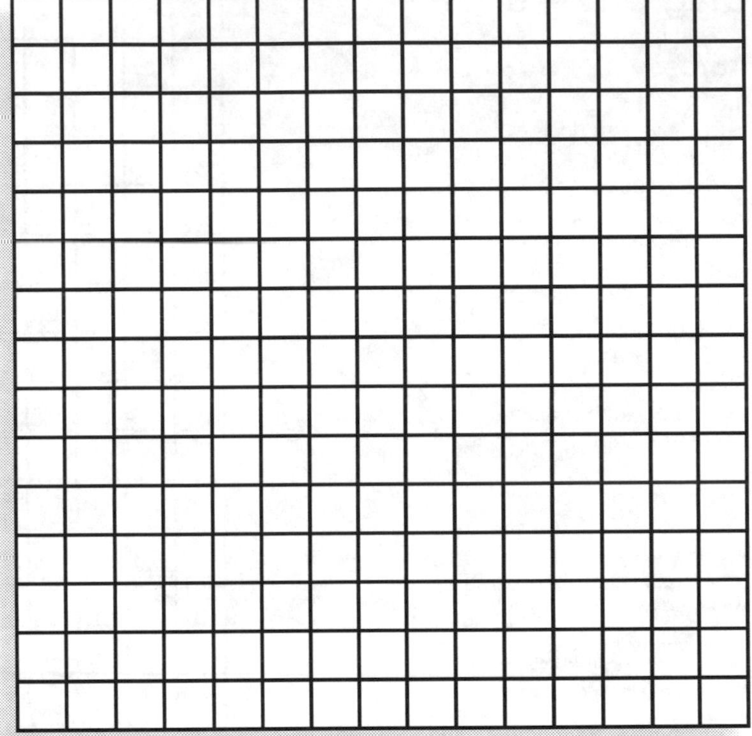

Across

1. Li'l Abner creator
5. Astronomical hunter
7. "Gunsmoke" network
10. The Titanic, e.g.
11. Yes, in Paris
12. Blaze remnant
15. Baseball VIPs
16. Naval noncom: Abbr.
19. Outdoor parking area
21. Kipling lad
24. French nobleman
25. Early afternoon hour
26. Kids with curfews
28. Massachusetts's motto start
30. Pod inhabitant
31. Van Gogh home
32. Comfy spot
36. Peer Gynt's creator
39. Computer in "2001"
40. Drove too fast
44. Bag carrier
45. Wind direction: Abbr.
46. Kwik-E-Mart owner on "The Simpsons"
47. Bygone airline
48. Chicago White ___
49. Morse code sound
50. Stanley Cup gp.
53. "___ a Rock": Simon and Garfunkel
55. Gaming cube
56. Strand
61. Topic for Dr. Ruth
62. "Tiny" Albee character
63. Every twelve mos.

Down

1. Rank above maj.
2. "Exodus" protagonist
3. Sewing-basket item
4. "The Murders in the Rue Morgue" writer
6. Org. for gun owners
7. Machine tooth
8. Bleacher creature?
9. Ebert's former partner
13. Feeds the pigs
14. Beehive product
16. B followers
17. Bit of wordplay
18. ROTC relative
20. Instructs
22. Suffix with Paul
23. Editorial submissions: Abbr.
26. Mai ___ (drink)
27. Makes a goof
29. Extreme shoe width
33. "Gimme ___!" (start of a Rutgers cheer)
34. Capital of Vietnam
35. "The Downeaster ___" (Billy Joel song)
36. Hairy TV cousin
37. Gift decoration
38. Bleachers
41. Paper holder
42. MPG raters
43. "That's obvious!" in teen talk
51. Hotfoot it, old-style
52. Superman foe ___ Luthor
54. CEO's degree, maybe
57. Ron of "Tarzan"
58. Atmosphere
59. A quarter of M
60. Attention-getting word

1-across starts in the 1st square from the left.

Solution on page 270

Diagramless 13

Across

1. Cyclops had one
4. Letter between pi and sigma
7. Actor Max ___ Sydow
8. Down for the count
9. Penny-___ poker
11. Doctor, at times
13. Cookbook abbreviation
15. Muscles to crunch
17. NHL legend Bobby
20. Friend's opposite
21. ___ de Janeiro
22. Where Switz. is
23. Bit of energy
24. "Nightline" host Koppel
25. WWII transports
26. Derek and Jackson
27. "The ___ Squad"
28. ___ Simbel
30. Word after jet or time
31. Omaha's state: Abbr.
32. Tape speed abbr.
33. Shipping unit: Abbr.
34. Kitten's sound
37. Breadth
40. Sp. woman
41. Like "to be": Abbr.
42. Op. ___ (footnote abbr.)
43. Bray starter
44. Mary ___ cosmetics
45. "Survivor" shelter
46. How to address a Fr. lady
47. Happened upon
48. Lots and lots
52. ___good example
55. "___ Yankee Doodle dandy"
56. "___ know you?"
57. Physique, briefly
58. 100 cts.

Down

1. Gabor and Peron
2. Hither and ___
3. Suffix for differ
4. "It's a Wonderful Life" studio
5. Santa's laughs
6. Pindar poem
10. Dog-___ (well-worn)
11. Mil. award
12. Caviars
13. Bullfight bull
14. Pleads
16. Auctioneer's quest
18. Boring routine
19. Train lines: Abbr.
20. Cupid's mo.
24. Clothes
25. Oil or grease: Abbr.
27. Atlas item
28. Pier
29. Actor Gazzara
30. ___ Yutang
33. Canadian Indians
34. Emcee's amplifier
35. The "E" in QED
36. Dryly humorous
37. Educ. institution
38. More, in music
39. ABA members
40. Theology sch.
43. ___ Pinafore
47. Letters and packages
49. Freedom, briefly
50. Comic Phillips
51. Money roll
53. Hall-of-Famer Roush
54. Furthermore

1-across starts in the 1st square from the left.

Solution on page 271

Diagramless 14

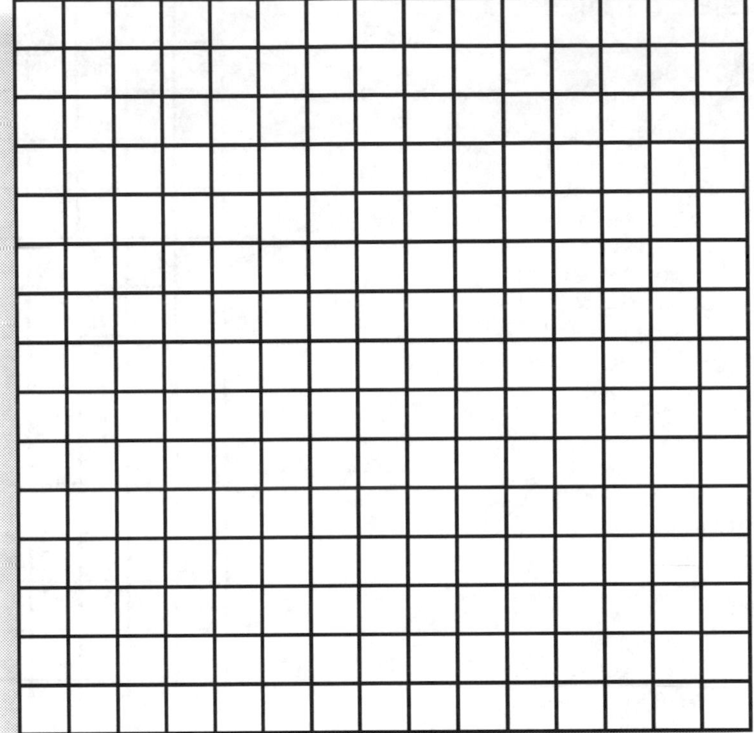

Across

1. Russian-built fighter
4. Apt. features
7. Unclose, poetically
8. Hiking paths
11. ___ Beta Kappa
14. Deep distress
15. Baby bird of prey
16. ___ Schwarz (toy store)
17. Fast fliers: Abbr.
19. Medieval poem
20. Anti-fraud agcy.
21. "___ a real nowhere man . . ."
22. Missing a deadline
24. Dockers' org.
26. President pro ___
27. Musical notes
28. Victrola company
30. Money
34. Hill-building insect
35. Chapel words
36. Floral welcome
37. Connery of film
39. Banquet hosts: Abbr.
40. Golfer Se Ri ___
41. Girl's pronoun
43. Believer
44. Movie-rating org.
46. Beatnik's exclamation
48. Airport overseer: Abbr.
49. Day: Sp.
52. General region
54. Harbor boat
55. Motor
57. New Orleans summer hrs.
60. God, in Roma
61. Parts of a play
62. Homer Simpson expletive
63. Boundary
64. "Eureka!" is one

Down

1. Cut the lawn
2. Nasdaq debut: Abbr.
3. Thousands, to a hood
4. Button material
5. Maid's cloth
6. Window ledge
8. Head, in France
9. Poetic meadow
10. Subway entrance device
11. Fizzling-out sound
12. Despise
13. Org. overseeing quadrennial games
18. California mount
23. HBO competitor
24. "Play ___ it lays"
25. Fishing cord
26. Southwest art center
28. Relative of hoarfrost
29. Atlanta-based public health agcy.
31. Type of skiing
32. Airplane assignment
33. Go on foot
38. Govt. code breakers
42. Pluto's realm
44. Hawaii's "Valley Isle"
45. When doubled, a Samoan port
46. Having hair like horses
47. Mars's Greek counterpart
48. 1-800-FLOWERS rival
50. Corporation abbr.
51. Onetime Time film critic James
53. Electrical letters
56. Place for the night
58. Beetle
59. Your, in the Bible

1-across starts in the 1st square from the left.

Solution on page 271

Diagramless 15

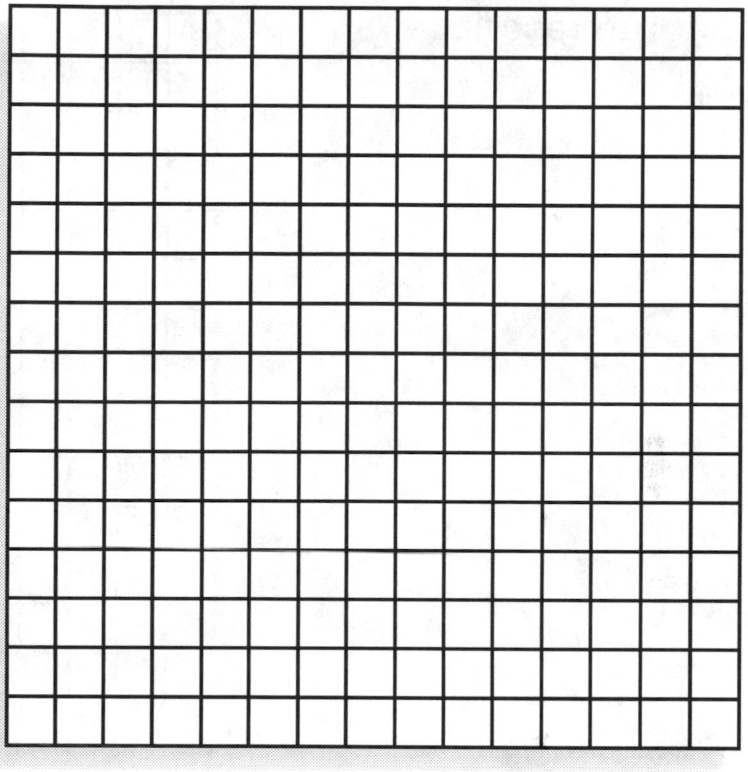

Across

1. Current rage
4. "Earth" word form
7. Deplete, with "up"
8. One-fifth of MMMV
11. Paper repairer
13. "Treasure Island" inits.
14. Turns on an axis
16. Not a duplicate: Abbr.
17. Haifa residents
20. Opposite of pos.
21. Auto Club offering
22. Workstation machines, for short
24. Gymnastics device
26. Trooper prefix
28. Thurman of "Kill Bill" films
29. Former Mideast alliance: Abbr.
30. Defense advisory org.
33. "I ___ You Babe"
34. Uncle: Sp.
35. Ad ___ committee
37. Bert Bobbsey's twin
39. Suffix with north
40. "Float like a butterfly, sting like a bee" boxer
41. Low voice range
43. Ryan of "When Harry Met Sally"
44. Not happy
45. Handheld computer, briefly
47. President after F.D.R.
49. Following orders
54. "The Virginian" author Wister
56. Fragrant East Indian wood
57. Network on the telly
60. Window glass
61. Lawyer's deg.
62. Polite word
63. Comic book punch sound
64. Chicken ___

Down

1. Mink or sable
2. Communication for the deaf: Abbr.
3. Arnaz of "I Love Lucy"
4. '60s muscle car
5. Brings home the bacon
6. Bee's nephew
8. Owed
9. Piece of animation
10. "It ___" ("Who's there?" reply)
12. Hard-boiled item
14. Broadway hit letters
15. Attorney's field
18. Layers of rock
19. It begins in Mar.
23. Campbell's container
24. Spying device
25. Egyptian deity
26. Couples
27. Elvis ___ Presley
29. Sport ___ (modern vehicles)
31. Tribal doctor
32. Merry old king
36. Smoke, informally
38. Hoopsters' org.
42. Noisy commotion
44. Dictation pro
45. Fruit-filled dessert
46. TV host O'Connor
47. Jump on one foot
48. Even trade
50. Dance, in France
51. House extension
52. Cabinet dept.
53. One of 16 in a cup: Abbr.
55. Freshly made
58. Life story, in brief
59. '80s–'90s Honda sports car

1-across starts in the 1st square from the left.

Solution on page 271

Diagramless 16

Across

1. "Boston Legal" fig.
4. Angry
7. Mardi___
8. Sounds of disappointment
9. Magazine magnate, familiarly
12. Burr or Copland
14. ___ room (den)
15. Author Peter
17. Family drs.
18. Dermal lead-in
20. Mixed-breed dog
21. High rating
23. Hi-speed connection
24. 1900
27. Actor Sparks
28. Abel's mom
30. Gangster's gun
31. Responses to a masseur
33. Wings: Lat.
35. Horse's home
37. Portable heat source
41. Good for what ___ you
43. Long-term S&L investments
44. Critic Reed
45. The "S" of CBS: Abbr.
46. TV sked abbr.
48. Actor Thinnes
49. Solo in "Star Wars"
51. Duffers' goals
53. "When I was ___"
55. Its cap. is Sydney
56. Folklore sprite
59. ___kiri
60. Hardly a beauty
62. Jazz singer Carmen
64. "Charlotte's ___"
65. Crazy eights spinoff
66. Calhoun of filmdom
67. ATM-making co.
68. Tongue-clucking sound

Down

1. Give ___ (care)
2. Old mariners
3. General on a Chinese menu
4. "Semper fi" guy
5. Knock the socks off of
6. U.S. Army medal
7. Comedian's bit
9. "Let me think . . ."
10. ___ Cologne
11. Domino or Waller
13. Educator's org.
16. City in Mo.
19. Operatic Lily
22. Author Le Shan
24. Brit. sports cars
25. Lion or leopard
26. NYC subway org.
28. Gobbles down
29. Flying geese formation
31. Actress MacGraw et al.
32. Loki's daughter
34. Psychedelic drug
36. San Francisco/Oakland separator
38. Grammar school basics, briefly
39. Prefix meaning "new"
40. Prefix with acetylene
42. Engine additive letters
43. Detroit products
45. Trapper's trap
47. Maine city
49. "That'll show 'em!"
50. "There oughta be ___!"
52. Personal ad abbr.
54. Perfume amount
56. Winged Greek god
57. Carefree episode
58. Hardly macho
60. Attila follower
61. Very old: Abbr.
63. Computer monitor: Abbr.

1-across starts in the 1st square from the left.

Solution on page 271

Chapter 11

Double Scrambles

Unscramble the letters to form words. Then, unscramble the first letters of the words you made to form a word related to the title. Some groups of letters can be unscrambled in more than one way. For example, the letters ASEHC can be rearranged to form CHASE. In these cases, part of the challenge is to determine the correct words so that the final answer can be formed using the first letters.

Example:

Breakfast Beverage

- NRABU
- EJWEL
- EXDIN
- HREAT
- AOCGR

The answer is:

- **U**RBAN
- **J**EWEL
- **I**NDEX
- **E**ARTH
- **C**ARGO

JUICE

Some Canines

- LHOET ______
- THIKN ______
- NEOYJ ______
- NKTAH ______
- EGAEL ______

______

Worthless Wheels

- CYERM ______
- AUHLG ______
- PEMYT ______
- NVEER ______
- OAISS ______

______

Rosetta Stone Language

- GERCA ______
- ATEEN ______
- NIKFE ______
- EHIGT ______
- NMAOR ______

______

Conversation Starter

- LTGIH ______
- DAYHN ______
- NARLE ______
- YMENE ______
- CAOEN ______

______

Solution on page 272

Diametrically Opposite

- IONNO ____________
- AVEIL ____________
- SLSAO ____________
- ALPNT ____________
- ANRCH ____________

____

Uncle Sam Feature

- ORPNA ____________
- EBYRR ____________
- TIDRY ____________
- RODAI ____________
- LUAEQ ____________

____

Dining Room Staple

- RCHTO ____________
- VELLE ____________
- ASESY ____________
- DBLEN ____________
- KENLA ____________

____

'70S Hot Spot

- SIAED ____________
- KLIYS ____________
- DLYLO ____________
- NAOGR ____________
- TARCF ____________

____

Solution on pages 272–273

One of the Deadly Sins

- IGRDI ____________
- EODNZ ____________
- TVENE ____________
- PLSEU ____________
- EILDA ____________

____

First Anniversary Gift

- PTIOL ____________
- AOUDL ____________
- RAYLO ____________
- ECAPE ____________
- EDRLE ____________

____

Cheese Choice

- FSTFA ____________
- SCEAR ____________
- EAGMI ____________
- WRROY ____________
- AKTSE ____________

____

Out of Practice

- ARDPI ____________
- ITHSG ____________
- TSATE ____________
- YHTAC ____________
- UIONN ____________

____

Solution on page 273

Syrup Source

- BOLRA ______________
- MAARL ______________
- XTEAC ______________
- PCINA ______________
- MIACG ______________

____

Tot Watcher

- DDADE ______________
- ENVLO ______________
- EIDYL ______________
- ONSEI ______________
- EVNER ______________

____

Up on a Map

- IGTHN ______________
- NOUCE ______________
- CEATH ______________
- PHAPY ______________
- XALRE ______________

____

Cold Covering

- SERUP ______________
- OTAIR ______________
- PTMOE ______________
- FOLOR ______________
- OIBRT ______________

____

Solution on page 274

Give a Hoot

- PHSAE ____________
- OVILE ____________
- IRTGE ____________
- ASUUL ____________
- ENHOY ____________

____

It's Stuck in the Corner

- NROIM ____________
- AYARR ____________
- ENLAP ____________
- STEAE ____________
- IPLLS ____________

____

Prepare for Surgery

- REMHY ____________
- ERUPP ____________
- OLROC ____________
- ABCON ____________
- EENVS ____________

____

Three, They Say

- AZORR ____________
- RMEAD ____________
- CEWRK ____________
- OCICM ____________
- NTFEO ____________

____

Solution on pages 274–275

Pasta Topper

- NTLUI ________________
- KEEHC ________________
- RESCO ________________
- TFEAR ________________
- TEREN ________________

____

Grown-Up Kids

- EGRAT ________________
- NILAE ________________
- ERTOH ________________
- FTHEI ________________
- TESPE ________________

____

Classroom or Poolroom Item

- LKNET ________________
- NATHU ________________
- EODGL ________________
- ARIES ________________
- ROCHI ________________

____

Fable Finale

- NTAGE ________________
- VRRIE ________________
- MIEVO ________________
- PRAEO ________________
- ALREG ________________

____

Solution on page 275

Charlie Chaplin Persona

- THCPI ______________
- GLANE ______________
- RMJOA ______________
- HERCA ______________
- DMITI ______________

____

Tie the Knot

- SAROT ______________
- MYAEB ______________
- THYUO ______________
- IAGAN ______________
- IONBR ______________

____

Rocker Site

- YAEDR ______________
- RCCUO ______________
- EOHUS ______________
- PIONT ______________
- RACHI ______________

____

Surgeon's Assistant

- RAYEL ______________
- NBLOE ______________
- LRRUA ______________
- UCELN ______________
- EPSLE ______________

____

Solution on page 276

Like Some Talk

- DLIES __________
- NLIEN __________
- LLAOC __________
- KAAEW __________
- MDALE __________

____

Weather Woe

- LSAIN __________
- MMYUM __________
- NTHET __________
- DLOEI __________
- TROEU __________

____

Sister's Attire

- VHYEA __________
- SISEU __________
- GEERA __________
- DBAER __________
- HEMTE __________

____

Field's Partner

- KEPSE __________
- ELAMC __________
- WETLO __________
- DAARR __________
- AEOLN __________

____

Solution on pages 276–277

Military Bigwigs

- RIEBF ________
- NYAON ________
- ESPDA ________
- OISLD ________
- ARGNE ________

____

Pleasing to the Palate

- UONGY ________
- BVEAO ________
- SEENT ________
- EPLLS ________
- KTHCI ________

____

One of the Senses

- HAMRC ________
- GREAE ________
- GAELL ________
- ITLMI ________
- KTSEA ________

____

Come Out of One's Shell

- TREHA ________
- RORWA ________
- MHUBT ________
- BHYOB ________
- CLOAR ________

____

Solution on page 277

Fuzzy Fruit

- ASELE ____________
- ITAPN ____________
- HEROS ____________
- ATSAL ____________
- CUGHO ____________

____

It's a Fact

- RATLI ____________
- PELYR ____________
- MNHAU ____________
- TIRLA ____________
- PUTSE ____________

____

Political Group

- TPCIO ____________
- ARISE ____________
- EAYRS ____________
- PEONH ____________
- TAITC ____________

____

Bouquet Tosser

- IRVLA ____________
- DEGES ____________
- RNENI ____________
- NKRDI ____________
- OABRD ____________

____

Solution on page 278

Funny Business

- OTRBO ________________
- ORFFE ________________
- UERTT ________________
- OYENM ________________
- DHARE ________________

____

Lighter Alternative

- LRETA ________________
- TIMRE ________________
- YOARM ________________
- ANOEC ________________
- HNORO ________________

____

Pulitzer Prize Category

- TBOUD ________________
- PAEPL ________________
- EADHA ________________
- CARTE ________________
- AELMT ________________

____

Rose Feature

- EBSRH ________________
- ERRDO ________________
- EYRAL ________________
- YOTDA ________________
- ONSUN ________________

____

Solution on pages 279–279

ASDFGHJKL

Kind of Blockade

- TLRIE ____________
- YEOSN ____________
- IVALT ____________
- BOATU ____________
- EAGNR ____________

____

Not on Deck

- HWLEA ____________
- SBANI ____________
- BOEWL ____________
- LAEBL ____________
- NEWRO ____________

____

Get Rid Of

- IHLLY ____________
- TIFRD ____________
- ESATX ____________
- ONRSI ____________
- NHACI ____________

____

Fire Starter

- PNSED ____________
- UDALT ____________
- OKNWN ____________
- YKCRO ____________
- ROEWP ____________

____

Solution on page 279

Chapter 12
Sudoku

Perhaps one of the secrets to sudoku's success is the puzzle's charming simplicity. Sudoku is played on a 9x9 grid. Heavier lines subdivide this grid into nine 3x3 boxes. The object is to fill in the grid so that every row, column, and 3x3 box contains the numbers one through nine with no repeats. The puzzle begins with some of the numbers already entered. There will always be just one solution for each puzzle.

Sudoku 1

		3	8				5	
1		2					8	7
			4		1			
7	6					3		
9				6				2
		1					7	8
			2		4			
2	4					7		9
	3				7	2		

Solution on page 280

Sudoku 2

8		4			1			
	1	5	4	8		3		
6		3						
	2			4			5	
			7	1	8			
	4			2			3	
						6		9
		7		9	5	2	4	
			2			8		5

Solution on page 280

Sudoku 3

		1			7			
3		8		4		2		
5				9	3			1
	6					1		
	1						7	
		5					9	
8			5	2				3
		4		1		7		2
			3			8		

Solution on page 280

Sudoku 4

7		4						2
						6		3
	6	8	1				7	
	4			3	6			
	9			4			1	
			2	1			4	
	3				5	7	9	
6		7						
5						4		8

Solution on page 280

Sudoku 5

		7	9	3				
		4					6	
2			1			9		4
5		3				2		7
	8						1	
1		2				6		8
8		6			7			2
	2					7		
				1	2	3		

Solution on page 281

Sudoku 6

			3	1			2	9
					5			3
				7	4	5		1
	8		6				1	
				2				
	5				1		4	
8		9	1	5				
6			8					
5	7			6	9			

Solution on page 281

Sudoku 7

			7	2		4		
4		6				1		
5					3		8	
6		8		9				7
		9				3		
7				4		8		1
	8		9					5
		7				9		4
		4		5	7			

Solution on page 281

Sudoku 8

5	6			3			7	
	8		1					9
4								1
6				9				4
			4	2	8			
7				6				8
1								6
3					4		1	
	9			1			2	5

Solution on page 281

Sudoku 9

1			9	8	4		7	
							1	
4	6				7			
7	2	3						
		9				8		
						9	3	7
			3				8	6
	1							
	3		8	4	5			1

Solution on page 282

Sudoku 10

1	7	6	5					
		4		1				
8		5	7			9		4
5	1	2						
4								6
						4	2	8
9		8			5	6		1
				6		2		
					2	5	7	9

Solution on page 282

Sudoku 11

	9	4		3	7		2	
				8				
1	8							4
4	3	8						
		2				9		
						8	1	5
9							8	7
				7				
	7		1	2		4	6	

Solution on page 282

Sudoku 12

	3	4	8	5		6		
	9				6			
6							5	1
4			7	1			2	8
				4				
2	7			9	8			3
7	4							9
			5				1	
		1		8	3	2	7	

Solution on page 282

Sudoku 13

4			1	9	2		6	
		9						3
					6		9	4
				5	1			
		1	9		8	6		
			3	2				
7	9		2					
3						1		
	1		7	4	5			2

Solution on page 283

Sudoku 14

	2		4	3		1		
4							9	
6	7			5			3	2
9	1	6						
	5						8	
						2	7	6
3	4			7			2	9
	9							4
		7		4	9		1	

Solution on page 283

Sudoku 15

4	9				6			
5			4	1			8	
3								
8	4	9					6	
	5			6			7	
	6					1	4	9
								5
	1			2	3			4
			8				2	1

Solution on page 283

Sudoku 16

3		4	1					
9								6
	1				5	7		
	2		9				1	
5			6		4			9
	8				2		6	
		8	4				7	
1								4
					1	9		3

Solution on page 283

Chapter 13

Cryptoquotes

In the following puzzles, each letter of the alphabet (A–Z) has been substituted with another letter. Your challenge is to break the code for each puzzle and decipher the quote and author. If you get stumped, there are hints for the puzzles at the end of this chapter.

Example:

U KLNV Q HLX. MV HLVA ZLCMUZX OLJ RLKUCUIQK JVQALZA.

—GUKK JLXVJA

The answer is:

I love a dog. He does nothing for political reasons.

—Will Rogers

Cryptoquote 1

XWFSOPL IZZUJ SOLMVC YWJC NMYP CZKF TIZN OJ W TYPHOI WPR CZK'FY W VMZKJWPR SOIYJ XFZS VMY HZFP XOYIR.

—RNOLMV YOJYPMZNYF

Cryptoquote 2

OFTDHYTDO NFGI KFN YO HWD OFGIBD FC NFGI OTYUD, EGH OFTDHYTDO NFGI OTYUD BZX ED HWD OFGIBD FC NFGI KFN.

—HWYBW XWZH WZXW

Cryptoquote 3

DGTL LURLQT VUX TG IVJXF LQVL AXGAMX KXXM TGUUW KGU LQXD VIF OGHXU LQXD RA, VL MXVTL V MZLLMX EZL.

—XFYVUF U. DRUUGY

Solution on page 284

Cryptoquote 4

DC PHFUTTH UTJ QEEFNBBDQT GQYN PQ PZDB IUTJ, DP ADII ON DT PZN KRDBN QC CDKZPDTK U CQFNDKT NTNYH.

—MUYNB YUJDBQT

Cryptoquote 5

X ZXBOGMV BN X PXO HAT ZXBOGN HAXG AM NMRRN. XO XVGBNG, ATHMUMV, BN X PXO GAXG NMRRN HAXG AM ZXBOGN.

—ZXCRT ZBSXNNT

Cryptoquote 6

OXI FYUGV IZZIGOLUDZ EK XUMMLGIZZ UYI: ZEHIOXLGF OE VE, ZEHIOXLGF OE DEBI, UGV ZEHIOXLGF OE XEMI KEY.

—UDDUG R. JXUDHIYZ

Solution on page 284

Cryptoquote 7

UH YWOIWN IWVY UX IW EIWR GMFSQD SQISUMIX YSQQXNE BWN BWCN. CQVXEE IGXNX MNX IGNXX WIGXN RXWRVX.

—WNEWQ LXVVXE

Cryptoquote 8

LET LTDL BI NXLTKRLVKT XD, X DVWWBDT, HETLETK HT BVKDTNUTD NXUT ABKT XOLTODTNZ IBK LET KTRGXOC BI XL.

—TNXFRSTLE GKTH

Cryptoquote 9

F LXMFQL OK FDJFXK KLOMMOQI CR KBYV JFM BM BLAVM, OQ BMNVM LAFL LAV RVBRDV YFX MVWCOMV F DVFNVM.

—RDFLB

Solution on page 284

Cryptoquote 10

X HRD'F MUDF FR ULJXOWO XEERZFUNXFA FJZRBTJ EA MRZP; X MUDF FR ULJXOWO XEERZFUNXFA FJZRBTJ DRF HAXDT.

—MRRHA UNNOD

Cryptoquote 11

Q RYKO XYQX CJXR KUO VOFRKU VJUGYOR QUKXYOF; XYOFO JR UK FOGJVO CKF AJEJUN XYQX RBJXR QAA GQROR.

—GQFA PBUN

Cryptoquote 12

UVMTM KZPT WMYWDM TMMG GRYHDMKNM, RYU HOTKYL. GRYHDMKNM OT YA UVM WZTU, HOTKYL OT YA UVM ACUCFM.

—BMFRYR XYYWMF

Solution on page 285

Cryptoquote 13

CI UDQ OXKOHP DX MHXI. CIMHIGI QFOQ MHXI HR ADKQF MHGHUY, OUP EDJK CIMHIX AHMM FIMS BKIOQI QFI XOBQ.

—FIUKE WONIR

Cryptoquote 14

IQU DF DG GIHG RDGGRZ SIDRJKZP HKZ FQ DPGZRRDWZPG HPJ NZP FQ FGAYDJ? DG NAFG TZ ZJASHGDQP GIHG JQZF DG.

—HRZBHPJKZ JANHF

Cryptoquote 15

Y BH ZHX NKZX XOP TPKEP XOKX TKMMPXO AZBPCMXKZBYZF. Y NKZX XOP AZBPCMXKZBYZF NOYEO VCYZFPXO TPKEP.

—OPUPZ WPUUPC

Solution on page 285

Cryptoquote 16

QAPBP VBP IPBAVIT FZ WVNT ZE ZXB HAJDWAZZW CP DJMPW TZ EXDDN VT QAZTP CP TIPFQ CJQA V EVMZBJQP GZZY.

—RVBHPD IBZXTQ

Cryptoquote 17

XV LS GQERQY RQAG LP X OJG QFAS WXH LXFIRPW RQ AXUP, X NQIAGF'R KYQQG X'G RSDP J AXRRAP VJWRPY.

—XWJJE JWXLQU

Cryptoquote 18

TCVRZQVXCU VIX LDOS DB QCC EDZNQORDOYIRN, MIXVIXJ RO ZQJJRQKX DJ RO BJRXOSYIRN, RY EDOAXJYQVRDO.

—DYEQJ MRCSX

Solution on page 285

Cryptoquote 19

S KJSCT SK'Q KJA HGKI ZP KJA BZVAHSXC KZ PSCH ZGK FJADA KJA YSCA SQ HDXFC XCH BDZQQ SK HAYSUADXKAYI.

—NAZDNA BXDYSC

Cryptoquote 20

QZM OPH NZF IMPBD HFQZGHJ PQ PXX GD VMQQMI MBERPQMB QZPH QZM OPH NZF IMPBD HFQZGHJ VEQ HMNDLPLMID.

—QZFOPD KMSSMIDFH

Cryptoquote 21

ORFSZJ FZZ IRO PFO NYFOM FMERSNWYJ, HXY WB JCX QFOY YC YRNY F IFO'N PTFSFPYRS, KWER TWI GCQRS.

—FHSFTFI ZWOPCZO

Solution on page 286

Cryptoquote 22

D XFZY IMVOT WXY GFCFTMR WXFW DI D JMZY VOWDJ DW XVCWP, WXYO WXYCY DP OM XVCW, QVW MOJN KMCY JMZY.

—KMWXYC WYCYPF

Cryptoquote 23

ZTLDL XDL ZHP RCMNI PA AXCWYDLI: ZTPIL HTP ZTPYJTZ XMN MLOLD NCN, XMN ZTPIL HTP NCN XMN MLOLD ZTPYJTZ.

—WXYDLMFL VLZLD

Cryptoquote 24

CL SQTJB MC SIQ UJMSQJ, CL SQTJB MC SIQ JQTEQJ. CL BNJWJMBQ MC SIQ UJMSQJ, CL BNJWJMBQ MC SIQ JQTEQJ.

—JLDQJS ZJLBS

Solution on page 286

Cryptoquote 25

SG ZGP SVMAA YZ PWM TXRP, SG ZGP SOMXJ GC PWM CFPFOM, EGZEMZPOXPM PWM JYZS GZ PWM TOMRMZP JGJMZP.

—UFSSWX

Cryptoquote 26

CJALAFOO JO VHDF JVIHDXZAX XGZA BJOLHV, ZAL XGF DFSHNAJXJHA HE XGJO JO XGF UFNJAAJAN HE BJOLHV.

—XGFHLHDF DPUJA

Cryptoquote 27

DSKJUXYXUH XO J UHTK MA QKJSVXVN TSMDKOO BZKSK UZK UKJDZKS JVR TFTXQ JSK QMDJUKR XV UZK OJGK XVRXYXRFJQ.

—JSUZFS WMKOUQKS

Solution on page 286

Cryptoquote 28

UBRZKZFI SV UBJFRCWDZR JWGFCZDV NFDB ZK W HZIB HFCJ FH XFNBCIJBID, SLD ZD'K W KDZIAZIX MWV DF RCBWDB.

—EZEEZWI OBEEJWI

Cryptoquote 29

AGCB GBHOEOPV OJ GBQH HODOVE; HODOVE FOAW QHH PVB'J JPCH, FOAW QHH PVB'J EPPNVBJJ QVN GOEWABPCJVBJJ.

—QHUBGA BOVJABOV

Cryptoquote 30

BGU SZG FNZU OWLA LON GJGT, FIL NUPJ NUG LNUCIG, WU NZXGZ LASL LAGJ TANIPX TGG LOWKG ST BIKA ST LAGJ TSJ.

—KASZPG TKSPG FKNPLNU

Solution on pages 286–287

Cryptoquote 31

GH EAV NODL ALXQFZ LA MQ XOYYE, YFOKLGKQ KAWYOZZGAD. GH EAV NODL LA MQ XOYYE, YFOKLGKQ KAWYOZZGAD.

—COBOG BOWO

Cryptoquote 32

AKQ AY VBQ GUEGKVGHQJ AY FQNKH UNJALUQLMP NJ VBGV AKQ NJ WAKJVGKVMP CGXNKH QDWNVNKH UNJWAEQLNQJ.

—G. G. CNMKQ

Cryptoquote 33

NQOF KZD QEIO ZFHK LNZ WOFFXOJ HOCL XF LQO NZGHR, MDK E HZEC ZC MGOER NXLQ ZFO, EFR E HXHK NXLQ LQO ZLQOG.

—YQXFOJO WGZIOGM

Solution on page 287

Cryptoquote 34

D'U BOO DQ GBXTV TG CAAYDQE WBQEAVTZM PABYTQM TZN TG NRA RBQWM TG GTTOM. OAN'M MNBVN PDNR NKYAPVDNAVM.

—GVBQC OOTKWP VDERN

Cryptoquote 35

U QHNJ VJHGCJE BUVJCYJ IGZO LQJ LHVPHLUNJ, LZVJGHCYJ IGZO LQJ UCLZVJGHCL HCE PUCECJBB IGZO LQJ SCPUCE.

—PHQVUV FUMGHC

Cryptoquote 36

JOIG WSGB XSQ DGLBG QS TG IMXXV RKGX CGSCJG WOG LXV FSPG QKLX OQ DGLBGB QS TG BGPOSMB RKGX CGSCJG JLMHK.

—HGSPHG TGPXLPW BKLR

Solution on page 287

Hints

Cryptoquote 1: The word "thousand" is found in the quote.

Cryptoquote 2: The word "sometimes" is found in the quote.

Cryptoquote 3: The word "truths" is found in the quote.

Cryptoquote 4: The word "foreign" is found in the quote.

Cryptoquote 5: The word "artist" is found in the quote.

Cryptoquote 6: The word "happiness" is found in the quote.

Cryptoquote 7: The word "dinners" is found in the quote.

Cryptoquote 8: The word "intensely" is found in the quote.

Cryptoquote 9: The word "stirring" is found in the quote.

Cryptoquote 10: The word "achieve" is found in the quote.

Cryptoquote 11: The word "pinches" is found in the quote.

Cryptoquote 12: The word "future" is found in the quote.

Cryptoquote 13: The word "create" is found in the quote.

Cryptoquote 14: The word "children" is found in the quote.

Cryptoquote 15: The word "peace" is found in the quote.

Cryptoquote 16: The word "favorite" is found in the quote.

Cryptoquote 17: The word "minutes" is found in the quote.

Cryptoquote 18: The word "marriage" is found in the quote.

Cryptoquote 19: The word "comedian" is found in the quote.

Cryptoquote 20: The word "educated" is found in the quote.

Cryptoquote 21: The word "adversity" is found in the quote.

Cryptoquote 22: The word "paradox" is found in the quote.

Cryptoquote 23: The word "thought" is found in the quote.

Cryptoquote 24: The word "surprise" is found in the quote.

Cryptoquote 25: The word "concentrate" is found in the quote.

Cryptoquote 26: The word "important" is found in the quote.

Cryptoquote 27: The word "teacher" is found in the quote.

Cryptoquote 28: The word "government" is found in the quote.

Cryptoquote 29: The word "goodness" is found in the quote.

Cryptoquote 30: The word "tongue" is found in the quote.

Cryptoquote 31: The word "practice" is found in the quote.

Cryptoquote 32: The word "disorderly" is found in the quote.

Cryptoquote 33: The word "pennies" is found in the quote.

Cryptoquote 34: The word "dangerous" is found in the quote.

Cryptoquote 35: The word "tolerance" is found in the quote.

Cryptoquote 36: The word "serious" is found in the quote.

Answers

ASDFGHJKL

Chapter 1: Quotagrams

Robert Frost

Half the world is composed of people who have something to say and can't, and the other half who have nothing to say and keep on saying it.

A. SHADOW
B. NETWORTH
C. SHOVEL
D. GANGPLANK
E. HOOD
F. FLAMINGO
G. HELMET
H. TRADE
I. PISTACHIO
J. NACHOS
K. HONEY
L. FAITH
M. POISON
N. OVEN
O. STONE
P. HEFTY
Q. TAPED
R. HEADWAY

Dwight Eisenhower

Though force can protect in emergency, only justice, fairness, consideration and cooperation can finally lead men to the dawn of eternal peace.

A. ANNOUNCE
B. PONTIAC
C. FENCE
D. ROMANCE
E. CANCEL
F. TEFLON
G. LAUNDRY
H. OSTRICH
I. POSTAGE
J. NEWLEAF
K. GROCERY
L. DISTANT
M. PIONEER
N. DECAF
O. LOOM
P. THRASH
Q. ENJOYED
R. INITIATE

Steve Martin

Kids like my act because I'm wearing nose glasses. Adults like my act because there's a guy who thinks putting on nose glasses is funny.

A. SESAME
B. HAWKS
C. MILKY
D. SIGNAL
E. BISCUIT
F. TISSUE
G. TUGBOAT
H. SOURGRAPES
I. NONSENSE
J. STILL
K. ITALY
L. KENYA
M. DOUGH
N. SWUNG
O. CHEESECAKE
P. SEDIMENT
Q. FANCY

Albert Camus

You will never be happy if you continue to search for what happiness consists of. You will never live if you are looking for the meaning of life.

A. VIOLIN
B. YOHOHO
C. RIPE
D. KNIFE
E. COCOON
F. WHOOPI
G. STUFF
H. VIEW
I. NURSERY
J. YOGURT
K. LASVEGAS
L. PRINCE
M. EIEIO
N. FLUFF
O. INHALE
P. PENNY
Q. UTENSIL
R. BETSY
S. MEATLOAF
T. WARHOL

Stanley Kubrick

People can misinterpret almost anything so that it coincides with views they already hold. They take from art what they already believe.

A. EARTHWORM
B. TRY
C. WHY
D. ALPHABET
E. DETAIL

F. SALTINE
G. STATEROOM
H. YOSEMITE
I. EIGHTY
J. YACHT
K. HEAVEN
L. WITNESS
M. HAYRIDE
N. DVD
O. ANTELOPE
P. ARTICHOKE
Q. CLIP
R. FLINT

Mary Calderone

I truly feel that there are as many ways of loving as there are people in the world and as there are days in the life of those people.

A. GASOLINE
B. TOOTH
C. FIELD
D. FATHER
E. PASADENA
F. SHOW
G. FAIRY
H. YELLOW
I. HEIFER
J. HOUSE
K. PASTE
L. ELEMENTARY
M. TRIP
N. TREE
O. NEVER
P. LAND
Q. TELEPATHY
R. HOARSE

Barbara De Angelis

Love and kindness are never wasted. They always make a difference. They bless the one who receives them, and they bless you, the giver.

A. DEGREE
B. BEEHIVE
C. BOWL
D. SENTENCE
E. THRIVE
F. STAFF
G. CHELSEA
H. HOSTEL
I. DISASTER
J. YANKEE
K. DRAW
L. MYTH
M. HONEYDEW
N. SAKE
O. NAVY
P. SHADY
Q. SOUVENIR
R. ELEMENT

Austin Dacey

Guts are important. Your guts are what digest things. But it is your brains that tell you which things to swallow and which not to swallow.

A. ATHEIST
B. SHORTSTOP
C. TAILGATE
D. TURTLE
E. WALRUS
F. MANILOW
G. STAIRWAY
H. BOGART
I. WEIGHT
J. LAUGH
K. SWING
L. SHIRT
M. LOTION
N. SUSHI
O. NBC
P. TOWN
Q. YOUTH
R. DOWNY
S. DUTCH

Mahatma Gandhi

It is easy enough to be friendly to one's friends. But to befriend the one who regards himself as your enemy is the quintessence of true religion.

A. FRISBEE
B. TREASON
C. FRESNO
D. SQUIRTGUN
E. EMBASSY
F. FANLETTER
G. NINETY
H. OBEDIENT
I. SIDEORDER
J. HEROIC
K. SHIELD
L. GYMSHOE
M. UNION
N. FIFE
O. EYES
P. HOTEL
Q. OUTWIT
R. ENOUGH

Martin Luther King Jr.

The ultimate measure of a man is not where he stands in moments of comfort, but where he stands at times of challenge and controversy.

A. TEENAGER
B. HOSTESS
C. CREAM
D. HUMAN
E. FILM
F. SHAVEN
G. FLAWED
H. FIFTH
I. TOMORROW
J. CHESTNUT
K. NOTE
L. SMOOTH
M. AMENDMENT
N. CARE
O. SOLITAIRE
P. SOYBEAN
Q. STUDENT

Mark Twain

There was never yet an uninteresting life. Such a thing is an impossibility. Inside of the dullest exterior there is a drama, a comedy and a tragedy.

A. MANDARIN
B. THIRD
C. DESMOINES
D. HALL
E. WEAVE
F. SUE
G. REPAIRMAN
H. CITY
I. BIG
J. OXIDE
K. GADGET
L. SHOUT
M. ANNOY
N. SISTER
O. INFLATE
P. FEET
Q. TIS
R. ITINERARY
S. CELERY
T. HAUNTED
U. THESIS

Amy Bloom

Love at first sight is easy to understand; it's when two people have been looking at each other for a lifetime that it becomes a miracle.

A. PROFIT
B. LAUGH
C. METHOD
D. AGAIN
E. CHOOSE
F. BROWSE
G. BLACKTIE
H. SHELF
I. ELEVATOR
J. EASY
K. IDIOT
L. STREETCAR
M. MITTEN
N. MOVIE
O. HOSPITAL
P. ANTENNA
Q. SWEET
R. THIEF

Carl Jung

Even a happy life cannot be without a measure of darkness, and the word happy would lose its meaning if it were not balanced by sadness.

A. MEADOW
B. SEASON
C. TEAPOT
D. DESTINY
E. THOUSAND
F. SUNSET
G. FLOAT
H. NIECE
I. ANSWER
J. PELICAN
K. DOVE
L. HAMBURGER
M. ELEPHANT
N. SARDINE
O. KNOB
P. WHIFF
Q. BYWAY
R. PLAID

Buddha

What we are today comes from our thoughts of yesterday, and our present thoughts build our life tomorrow. Our life is the creation of our mind.

A. SOURDOUGH
B. SHOWER
C. HOLLY
D. GOURMET
E. NEUTRAL
F. AFRICA
G. EDIT

H. UNICEF
I. FROSTY
J. FORFEIT
K. TUESDAY
L. WISEMEN
M. THROAT
N. OUT
O. ROBINHOOD
P. ODOMETER
Q. SPARROW
R. MOUTH

Erich Fromm

Conditions for creativity are to be puzzled; to concentrate; to accept conflict and tension; to be born everyday; to feel a sense of self.

A. ELECTION
B. CROUTON
C. COTTON
D. FRANCE
E. OBSTACLE
F. LIBERTY
G. FRONTIER
H. DOZEN
I. BENEFIT
J. SECOND
K. PLAZA
L. TORTOISE
M. ENVY
N. FACE
O. FACT
P. TODAY
Q. SEVEN
R. DEPOSIT

Henry Wadsworth Longfellow

Perseverance is a great element of success. If you only knock long enough and loud enough at the gate, you are sure to wake up somebody.

A. SHRINK
B. NUDGE
C. SMOKE
D. CANYON
E. CAKE
F. TREEHOUSE
G. YAHOO
H. SUGGEST
I. BUDDY
J. FOULPLAY
K. CONCRETE
L. SOULMATE
M. ORANGE
N. TOUPEE
O. ELEANOR
P. STING
Q. WEAVE
R. UFO

Chapter 2: Dropouts

Mahatma Gandhi

Live as if you were to die tomorrow. Learn as if you were to live forever.

Groucho Marx

A child of five would understand this. Send someone to fetch a child of five.

Anne Frank

Think of all the beauty that's still left in and around you, and be happy.

George Bernard Shaw

If you cannot get rid of the family skeleton, you may as well make it dance.

Victor Hugo

An invasion of armies can be resisted, but not an idea whose time has come.

Kurt Vonnegut

The practice of art isn't to make a living. It's to make your soul grow.

Ella Wheeler Wilcox

The truest greatness lies in being kind, the truest wisdom in a happy mind.

Abraham Lincoln

The best thing about the future is that it comes only one day at a time.

Benjamin Disraeli

Read no history: nothing but biography, for that is life without theory.

Claude Monet

The richness I achieve comes from Nature, the source of my inspiration.

Steve Martin

Chaos in the midst of chaos isn't funny, but chaos in the midst of order is.

Martin Fischer

Knowledge is a process of piling up facts; wisdom lies in their simplification.

Jimi Hendrix

When the power of love overcomes the love of power the world will know peace.

C.S. Lewis

Everyone feels benevolent if nothing happens to be annoying him at the moment.

George Santayana

Almost every wise saying has an opposite one, no less wise, to balance it.

William James

Genius means little more than the faculty of perceiving in an unhabitual way.

Harry Truman

It is amazing what you can accomplish if you do not care who gets the credit.

Anaïs Nin

The personal life deeply lived always expands into truths beyond itself.

Robert Frost

In three words I can sum up everything I've learned about life: it goes on.

Buckminster Fuller

There is nothing in a caterpillar that tells you it's going to be a butterfly.

Ring Lardner

The family you come from isn't as important as the family you're going to have.

Andy Warhol

Making money is art and working is art and good business is the best art.

Mark Twain

Kindness is the language which the deaf can hear and the blind can see.

Elbert Hubbard

The object of teaching a child is to enable him to get along without a teacher.

Mel Brooks

Hope for the best. Expect the worst. Life is a play. We're unrehearsed.

Baltasar Gracian

A wise man gets more use from his enemies than a fool from his friends.

Confucius

Choose a job you love, and you will never have to work a day in your life.

Mother Teresa

There is more hunger in the world for love and appreciation than for bread.

Alan Bennett

Life is rather like a tin of sardines—we're all of us looking for the key.

Mary Oliver

Tell me, what is it you plan to do with your one wild and precious life?

Oscar Wilde

To live is the rarest thing in the world. Most people exist, that is all.

Blaise Pascal

Man's nature is not always to advance; it has its advances and retreats.

Buddha

Happiness comes when your work and words are of benefit to yourself and others.

Lord Byron

The great art of life is sensation, to feel that we exist, even in pain.

Napoleon Bonaparte

Four hostile newspapers are more to be feared than a thousand bayonets.

Oscar Levant

There's a fine line between genius and insanity. I have erased this line.

Bill Cosby

Parents are not interested in justice, they're interested in peace and quiet.

T.S. Eliot

Our high respect for a well read person is praise enough for literature.

John Barrymore

Happiness often sneaks in through a door you didn't know you left open.

John D. Rockefeller

I can think of nothing less pleasurable than a life devoted to pleasure.

George Burns

Happiness is having a large, loving, caring, close-knit family in another city.

Rita Rudner

Have children while your parents are still young enough to take care of them.

Helen Keller

Walking with a friend in the dark is better than walking alone in the light.

Benjamin Franklin

The doorstep to the temple of wisdom is a knowledge of our own ignorance.

Albert Schweitzer

There are two means of refuge from the miseries of life: music and cats.

Woody Allen

I'm not afraid of death, I just don't want to be there when it happens.

Rumi

Let yourself be silently drawn by the stronger pull of what you really love.

George Eliot

What do we live for, if it is not to make life less difficult for each other?

Chapter 3: Fill-ins

Fill-in 1

										U				
							A	M	E	N	D	S		
	M	U	M	M	Y		B			S				
	O						O		M	U	S	I	C	
A	M	O	E	B	A		D			N			R	
	E						E			G			O	
	N			A							L		N	
	T	H	I	N	G			J	A	L	O	P	Y	
				N				A			C			
		A		U				R		T	A	B	L	E
Q	U	E	L	L		G		G			L			U
U		R				A		O						R
A		A		H	U	M	A	N						O
C		T				U								P
K		E	I	G	H	T				M	O	N	T	E

Fill-in 2

				F								B		
	A	M	B	L	E				A	V	A	I	L	
				O					P			G		
		G	R	O	U	P	S		P			O		
				Z			E		A			T		Q
	R			Y		B	E	D	L	A	M			U
	O						M		L		E			A
	S		S	H	O	W	E	D			D			I
	A		T				D				D			N
T	R	U	A	N	T				R	E	L	E	N	T
	Y		N		R				E		E			
			D		I				F					
					T		S	Q	U	A	R	E		
	A	C	U	T	E				S					
									E					

Fill-in 3

F	O	R	M	S				F						W
				E			M	O	D	E	R	N		I
	A	V	E	R	S	E		R				E		D
	N			I				C				A		O
	N		R	E	C	E	D	E		S	H	R	E	W
	E			S						O		L		
	A						N			U		Y		
	L	Y	N	C	H		E			T				
						B	E	R	T	H				S
	D						D					P		P
	O		A		O	P	E	N	E	D		L		I
	G		O		P		D			I		A		R
	M		R		E					G		C		I
	A	S	T	E	R	N			D	I	G	E	S	T
			A		A					T		D		

Fill-in 4

		S									B		R	
	S	C	R	I	M	P				R	A	J	A	H
		O				R					Z		N	
U	L	T	R	A		E		S			A		C	
S		C		B		S		O			A		I	
I		H		D		S	U	M	M	E	R		D	
N				U				B				A		
G		M	O	C	H	A		E				S		
		O		T		C		R		T	O	P	I	C
		B				T			F			E		O
T	R	I	A	D		I			I			N		U
O		L			R	O	M	A	N	O				N
T		E				N			A					T
A									L	I	K	E	L	Y
L	A	R	G	E	R									

Fill-in 5

G	A	I	N	E	R				A	R	A	B	L	E
I									G					
R						T	R	I	A	G	E			
L			T			W			T		A			
S	T	O	O	D		E			E		R			
			A			N		S		A	L	P	H	A
			S			T		O			Y			L
	A	R	T	E	R	Y		R		S				L
	D		Y				A	B	A	C	U	S		I
	A			C				E		H				E
	G		B	A	S	A	L	T		O		B		D
	I			N						O		A		
	O	P	I	N	E					L	O	W	E	R
				O								D		
T	E	N	E	T				R	E	A	D	Y		

Fill-in 6

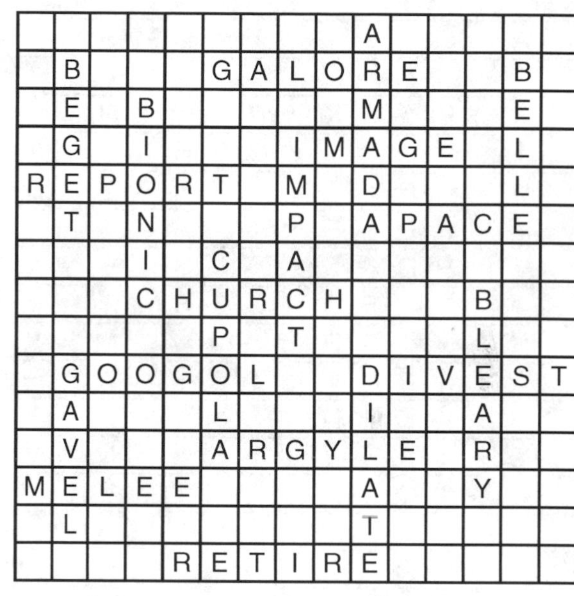

Fill-in 7

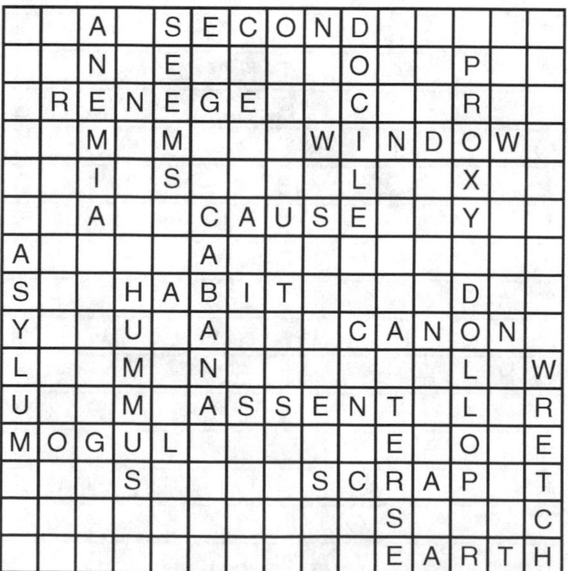

Fill-in 8

			W	I	T	H	I	N		S				
			H							A				
			O			R		C	A	L	L	E	D	
C	H	I	L	D		E				E			I	
A			E		E	G	R	E	S	S			C	
U						A							K	
C		A	C	C	O	R	D			M	O	V	E	D
U		D				D				I			R	
S	H	O	A	L				B	A	L	S	A		
		R								E			P	
		N	O	R	M	A	L			S	C	O	R	N
							A						I	
							T			T	R	Y	S	T
			C	E	N	T	E	R					S	
							R		B	A	L	M	Y	

Fill-in 9

	A						S	T	A	T	E	S		
	T			D								E		
	R		B	A	R	K	E	R				N		
	I			M						C	O	S	T	S
	U			P						R		E		C
	M	Y	S	E	L	F				A				A
				R		L				S				N
					F	O	R	C	E	S				T
	H					R						M		Y
	A			P	O	I	N	T	S			A		
	R			E		D			Y			N		
	L			A				I	S	L	A	N	D	
P	O	L	I	C	E				T			E		
	T			E					E			R		
					A	X	I	O	M					

Fill-in 10

B														
R		S	P	R	I	N	G		S	T	E	P	S	
O		O					R						O	
W		O		R			O			C	O	U	R	T
N	A	T	I	O	N		U						D	
		H		T			P			A	G	A	I	N
		E		G				G		S			D	
	Q			U		M	O	U	S	S	E			
B	U	I	L	T				M		E				
	A							B		S			A	
	V			A	M	I	G	O		S	T	U	D	Y
	E			R									R	
	R	E	V	E	R	E			T	O	M	B	O	Y
				A									I	
I	D	E	A	S				B	E	R	E	F	T	

Fill-in 11

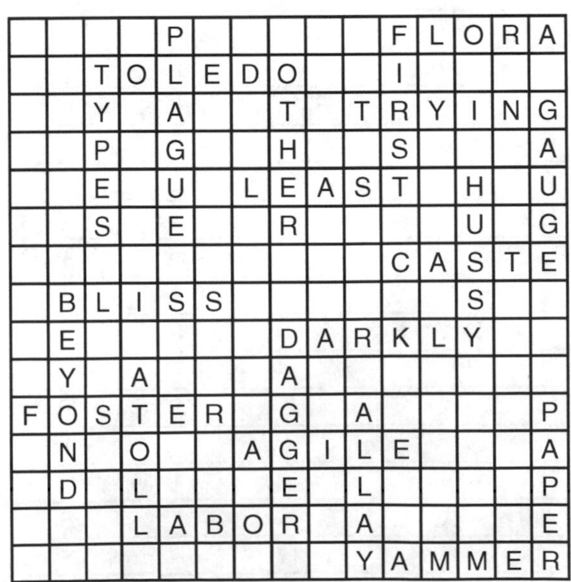

Fill-in 12

C	O	L	O	R										B
A				A			T	R	A	U	M	A		A
J				D			R					M		S
O			Z	I	N	G	E	R		C		O		E
L				O			B		S	H	O	U	L	D
E							L			O		R		
		R	E	F	U	G	E			I				
		E						C		C				
		C			C	H	A	R	G	E				M
W	R	O	T	E				E						A
O		I			B		I	T	S	E	L	F		Y
R		L	E	V	E	L		I				L		B
K					L			N		F	L	U	M	E
E					O							K		
D					W	A	N	T	E	D		E		

Fill-in 13

						R	E	B	U	K	E			
		S									B			
A	T	T	E	S	T						O			
		R					S	T	R	O	N	G		
P	I	E	C	E			T				Y			
U		E			A	D	O	N	I	S				
B		T			M		C			H				
L					O		K			A				
I			A		N					L		C		
C	O	M	I	N	G			T		O		A		
			K					O		M	O	D	E	M
			I					N				D		U
	A	L	D	E	R		B	I	G	A	M	Y		R
			O					C						K
									S	H	A	N	T	Y

Fill-in 14

												R		
G	A	R	N	E	R			M	E	T	H	O	D	
					E							T		
		B			B							U		
	B	A	R	I	U	M			B	E	I	N	G	
		N			F		B		E			D		D
		Y			F	L	E	E	C	E				E
M		A					H		A					A
O		N					I		M		T			T
N							N		E	N	O	U	G	H
T			A	C	R	I	D				N			
H			L								G			
S	T	A	T	E				S	C	R	U	F	F	
			A								E			
			R	E	J	E	C	T						

Fill-in 15

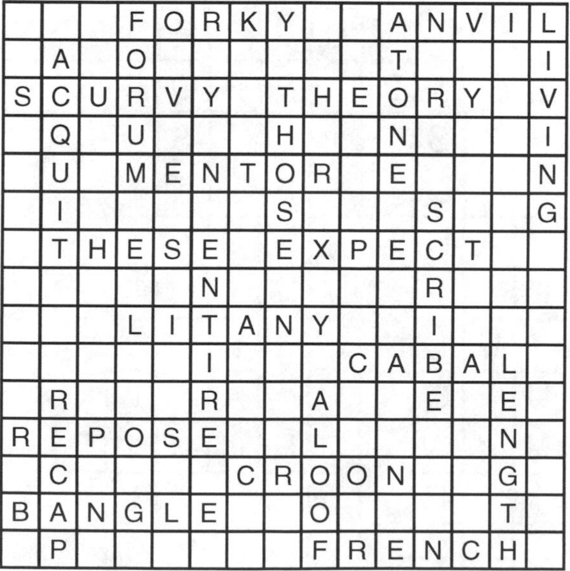

			F	O	R	K	Y			A	N	V	I	L
	A		O							T				I
S	C	U	R	V	Y		T	H	E	O	R	Y		V
	Q		U				H			N				I
	U		M	E	N	T	O	R		E				N
	I						S				S			G
	T	H	E	S	E		E	X	P	E	C	T		
					N						R			
			L	I	T	A	N	Y			I			
					I				C	A	B	A	L	
	R				R			A			E		E	
R	E	P	O	S	E			L					N	
	C					C	R	O	O	N			G	
B	A	N	G	L	E			O					T	
	P							F	R	E	N	C	H	

Fill-in 16

			R	E	V	A	M	P						
			A					R						
			N			C	O	U	L	D				
S	T	A	G	E		A		D		A			D	
I			E			R		E		P			A	
M				M		E				P			P	
P		T	H	E	R	E	S			E			P	
L				D		N				R	E	A	L	M
E		E		I				S					E	
		I		A				T						S
B	A	T	O	N		P	R	I	M	P		T		H
		H				R		L		R		O		A
		E				A		L		U		O		R
		R	E	N	O	W	N		U	N	I	T	E	D
						N				E		H		

Chapter 4: Groupies

Groupie 1

Groupie 2

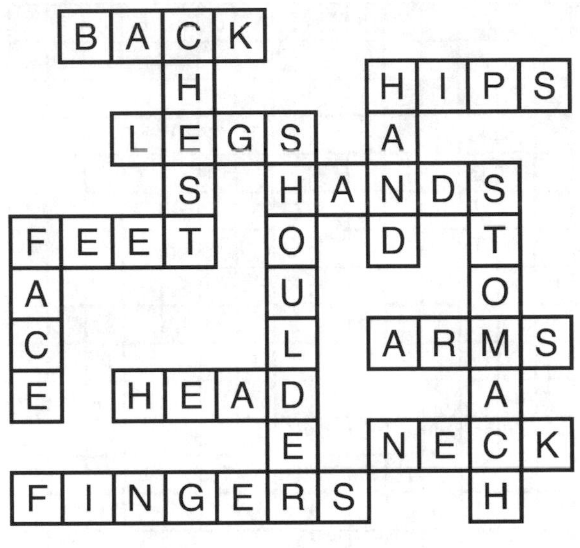

Groupie 3

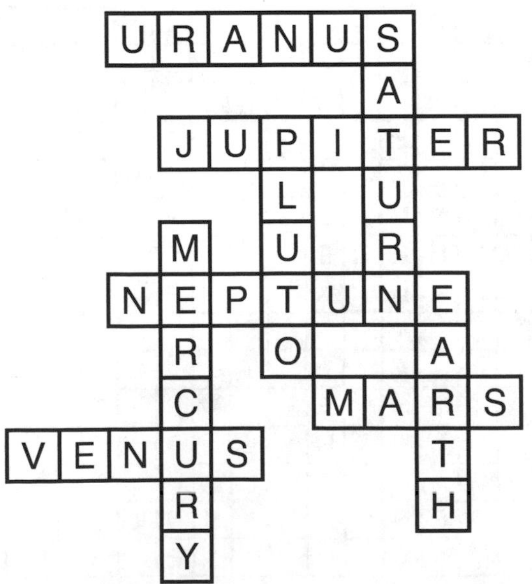

Groupie 4

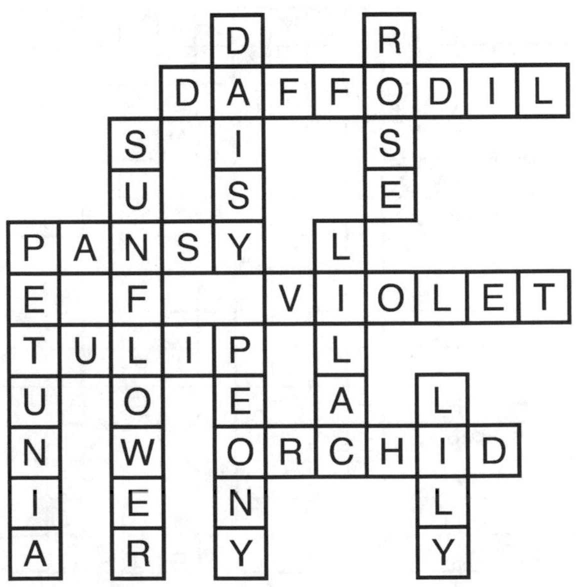

Groupie 5

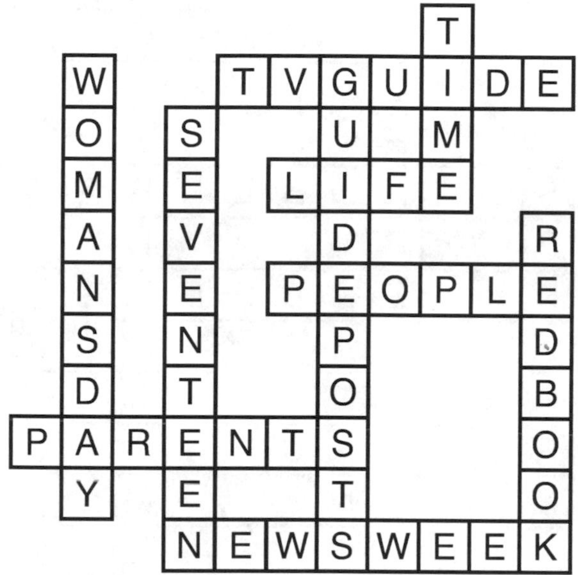

Groupie 6

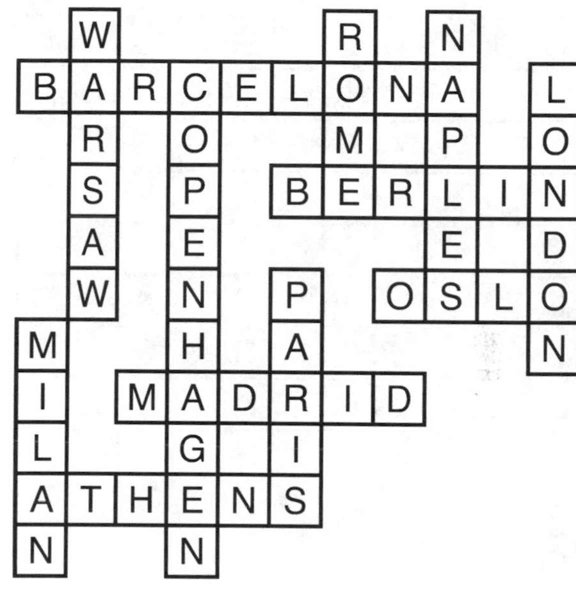

Groupie 7

Groupie 8

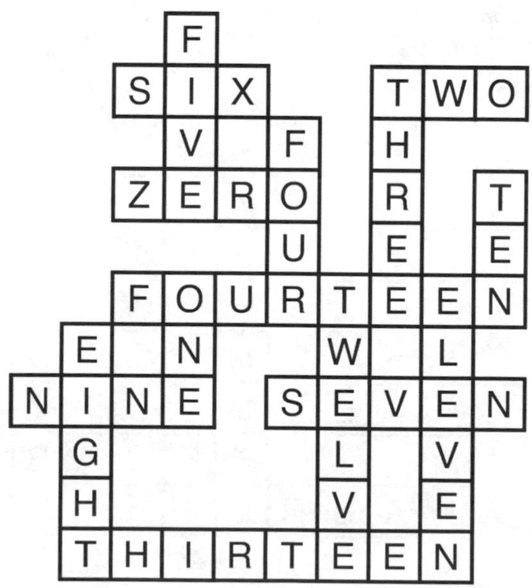

Groupie 9

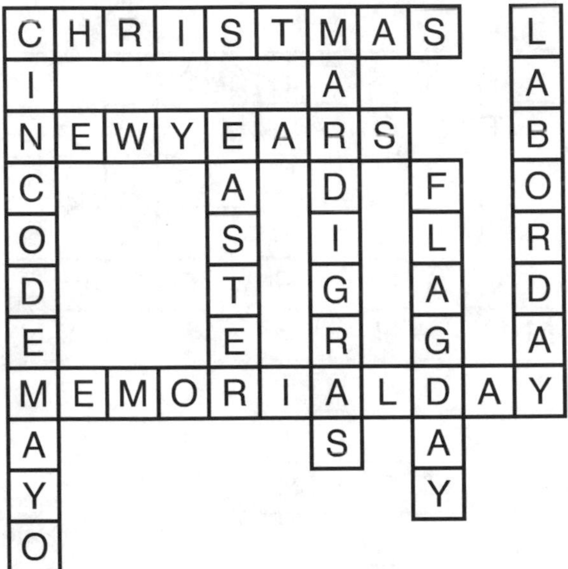

Groupie 10

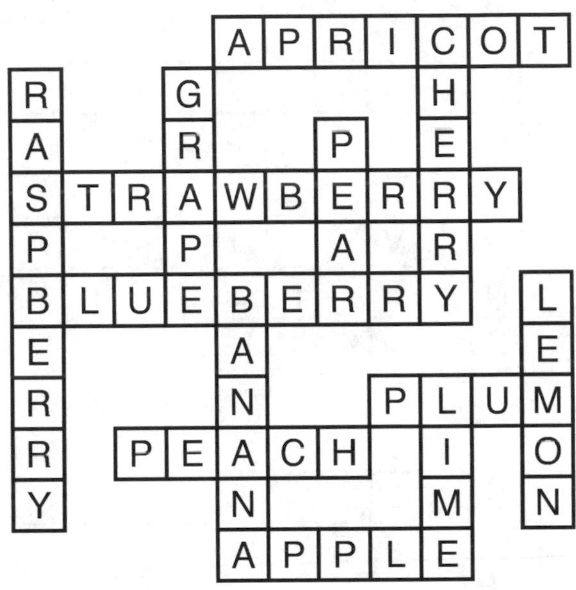

Groupie 11

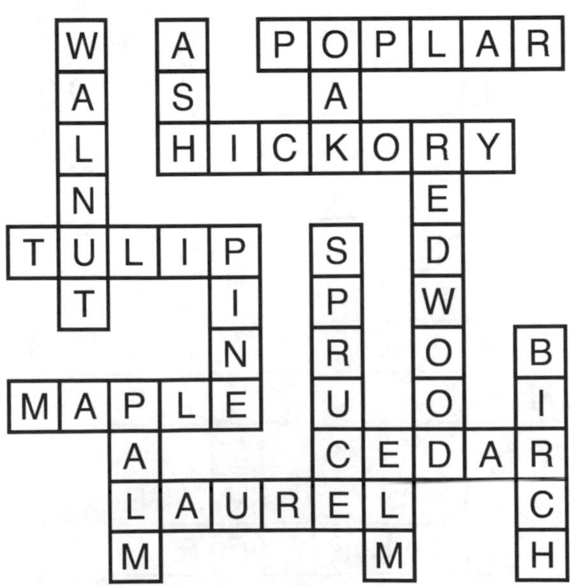

Groupie 12

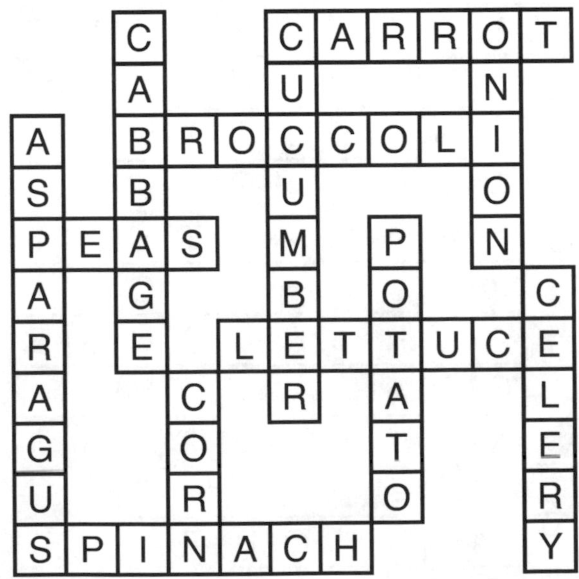

Groupie 13

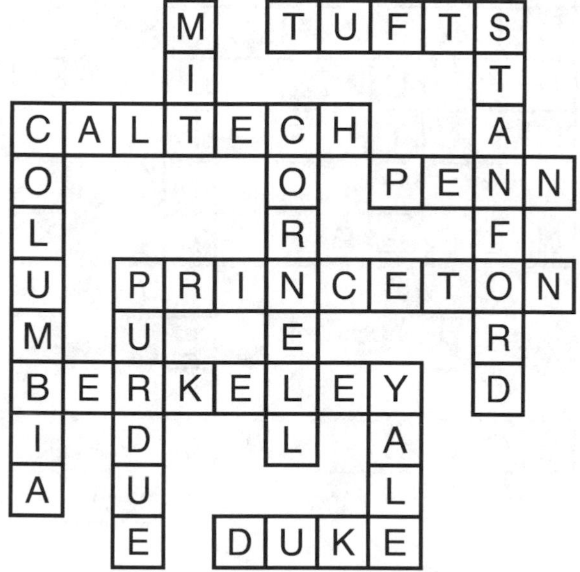

Groupie 14

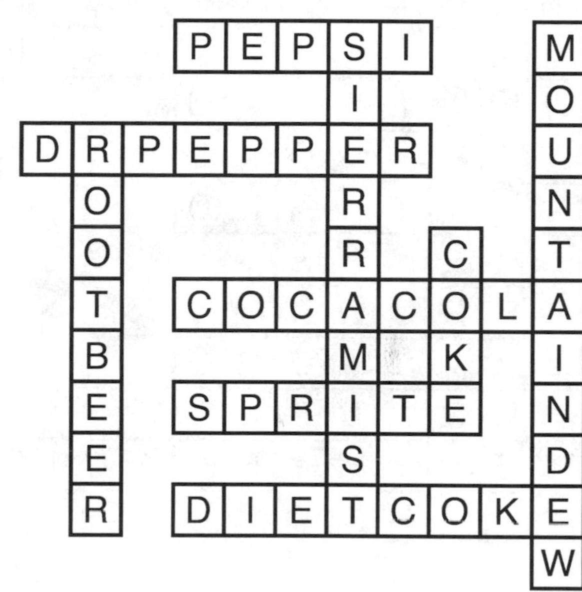

Groupie 15

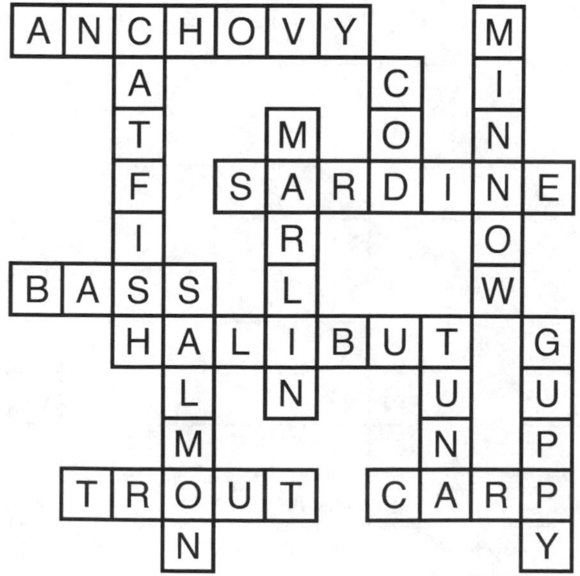

Groupie 16

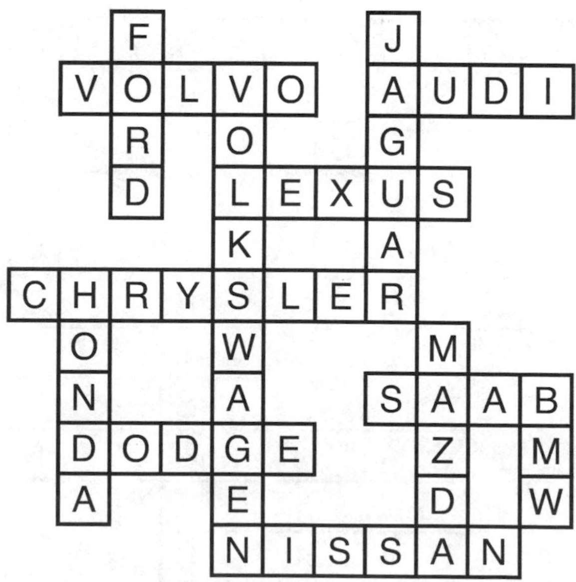

Groupie 17

Groupie 18

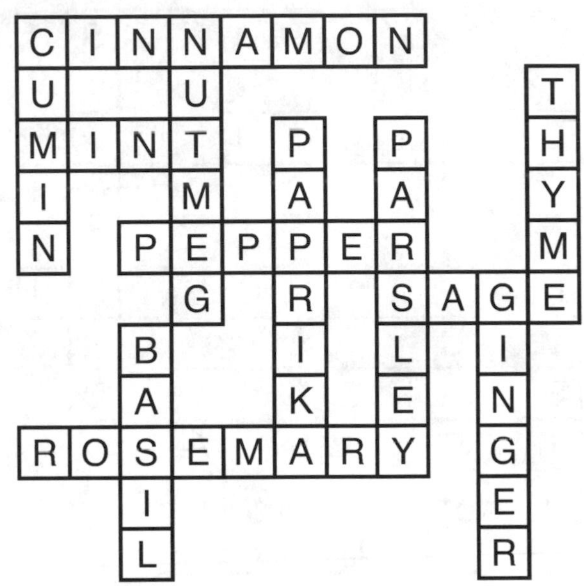

Groupie 19

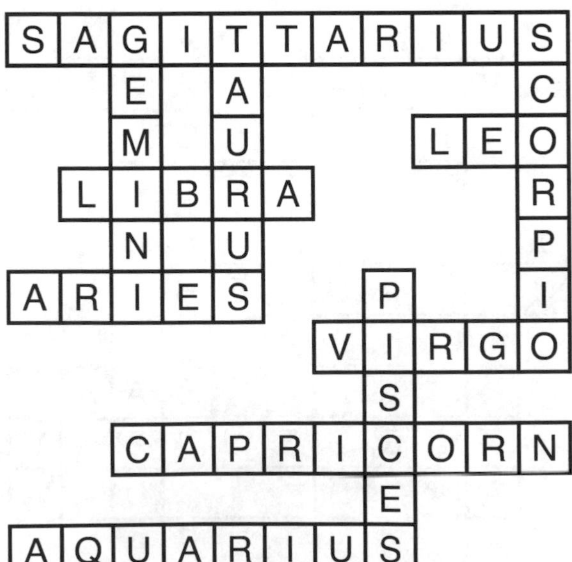

Groupie 20

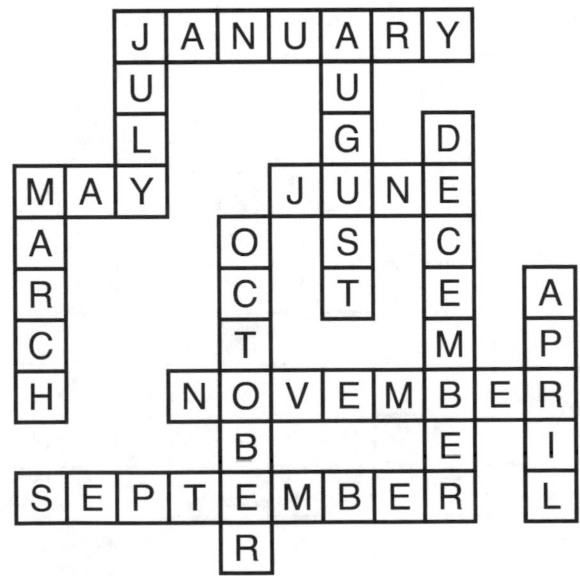

Groupie 21

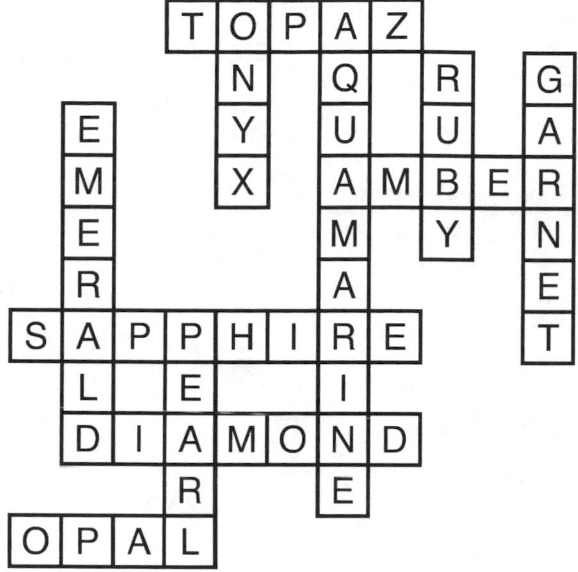

Groupie 22

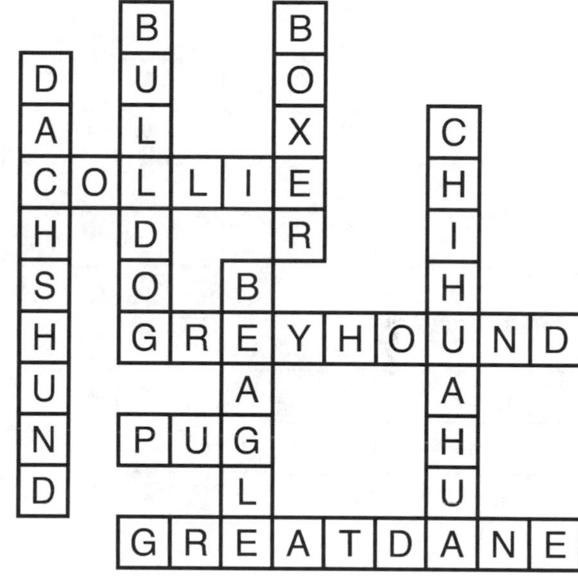

Groupie 23

Groupie 24

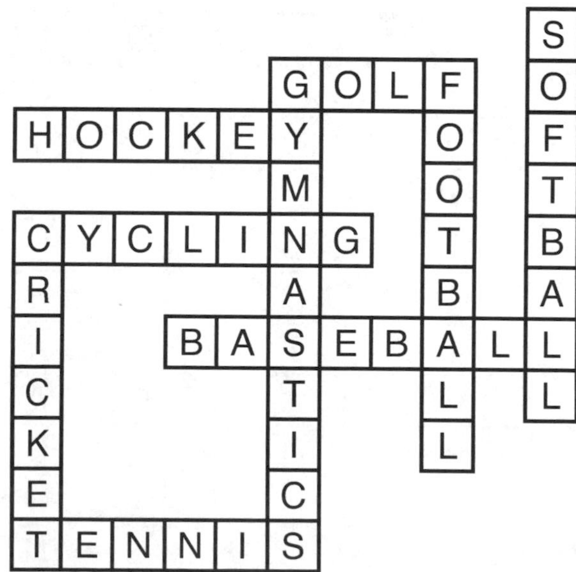

Groupie 25

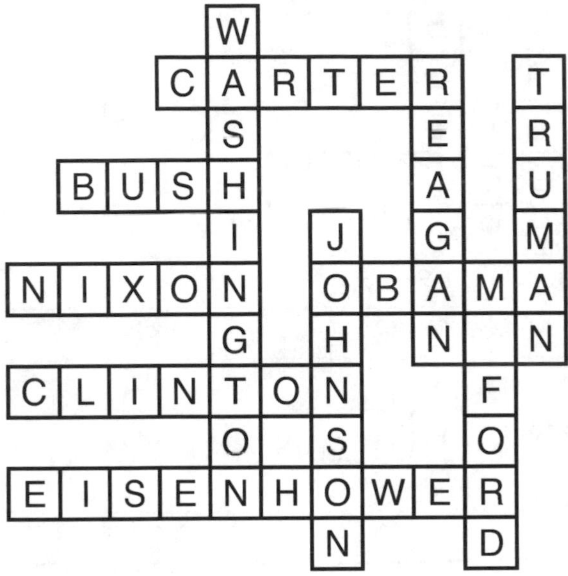

Groupie 26

Groupie 27

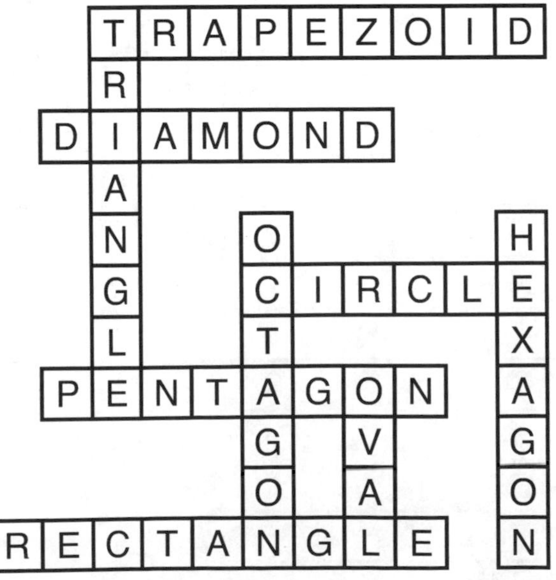

Groupie 28

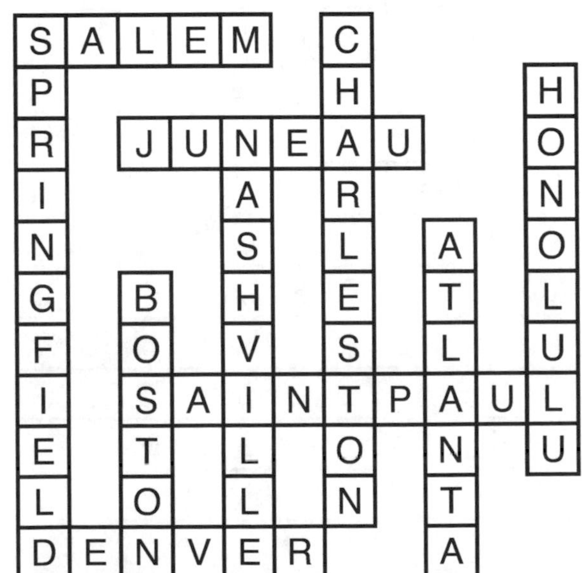

Groupie 29

Groupie 30

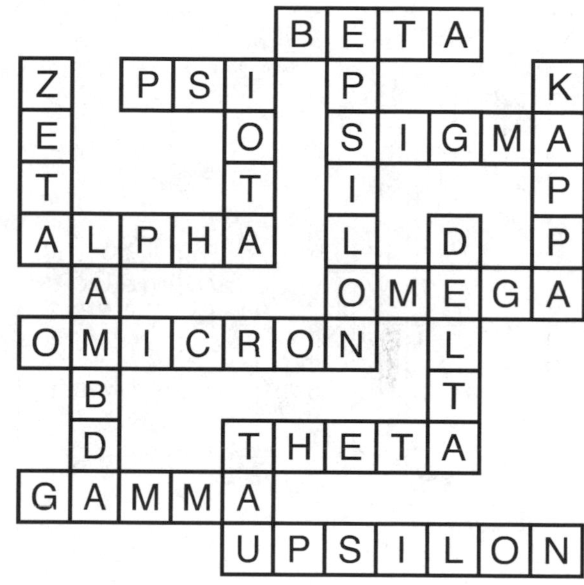

Groupie 31

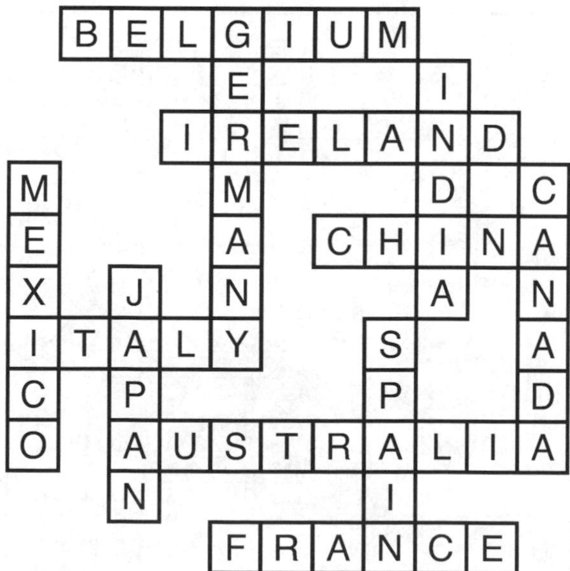

Groupie 32

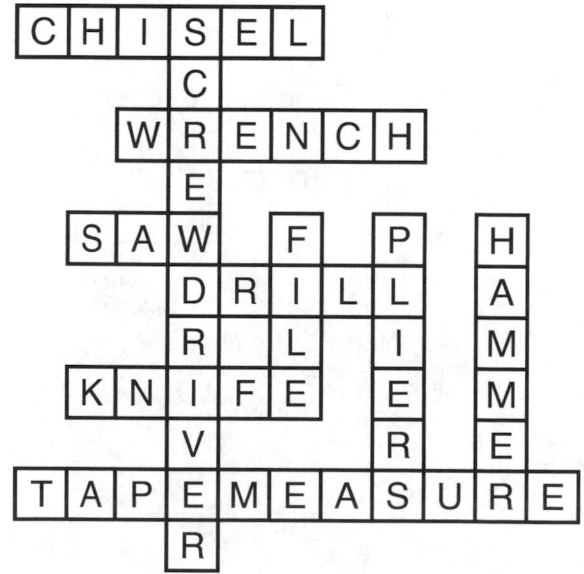

Chapter 5: Word Search

Tree Forest

Let's Go Shopping

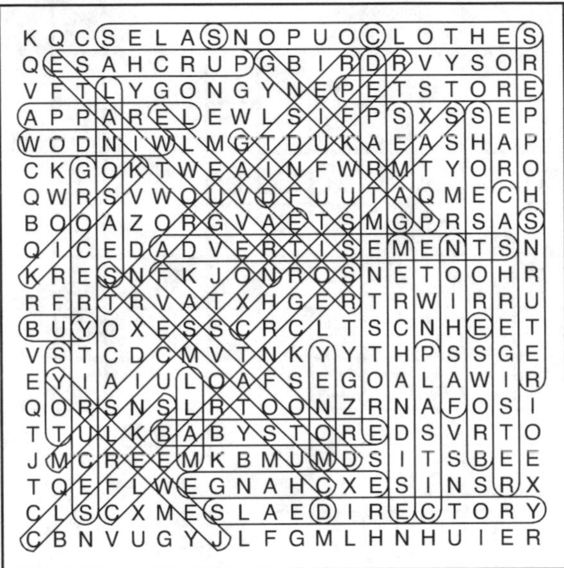

Scientifically Speaking

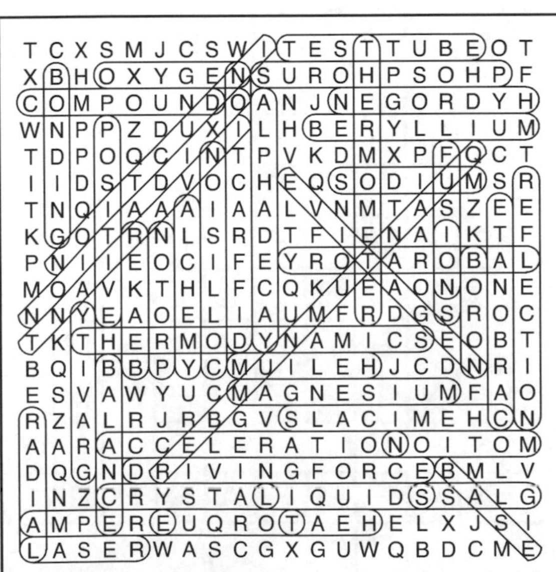

Have a Drink

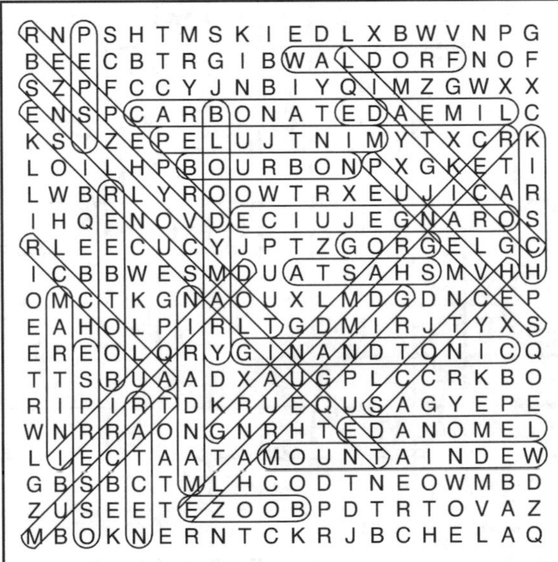

Raining Cats and Dogs

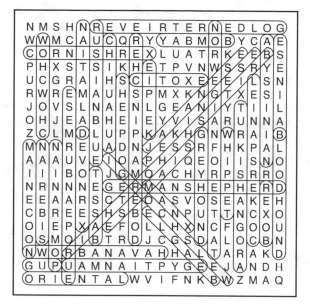

N M S H N R E V E I R T E R N E D L O G
W W M C A U C Q R Y Y A B M O B Y C A E
C O R N I S H R E X L U A T R K E E B S
P H X S T S I K H E T P V N W S S R Y E
U C G R A I H S C I T O X E E E I L S N
R W R E M A U H S P M X K N G T X E S I
J O V S L N A E N L G E A N I Y T I I L
O H J E A B H E I E Y V I S A R U N N A
Z C L M D L U P P K A K H G N W R A I B
M N N R E U A D N J E S S R F H K P A L
A A A U V E I O A P H I Q E O I I S N O
I I I B O T J G M O A C H Y R P S R R O
N R N N N E G E R M A N S H E P H E R D
E E A A R S C T E O A S V O S E A K E H
C B R E E S H S B E C N P U T T N C X O
O I E P X A E F O L L H X N C F G O O U
O S M O I B T R D J C G S D A L O C B N
N W O R B A N A V A H H A L T A R A K D
G U P U A M N A I T P Y G E E J A N D H
O R I E N T A L W V I F N K B W Z M A Q

Making Music

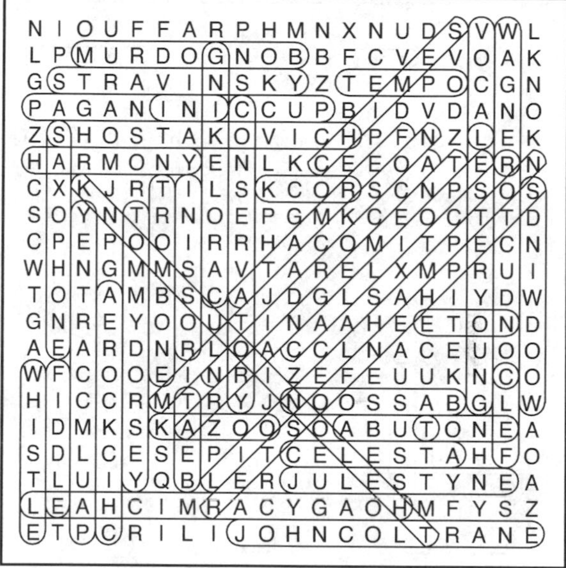

Animal Kingdom

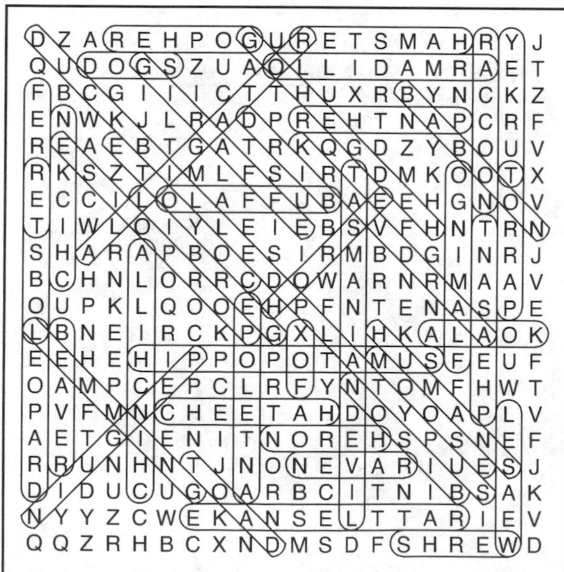

Bookish

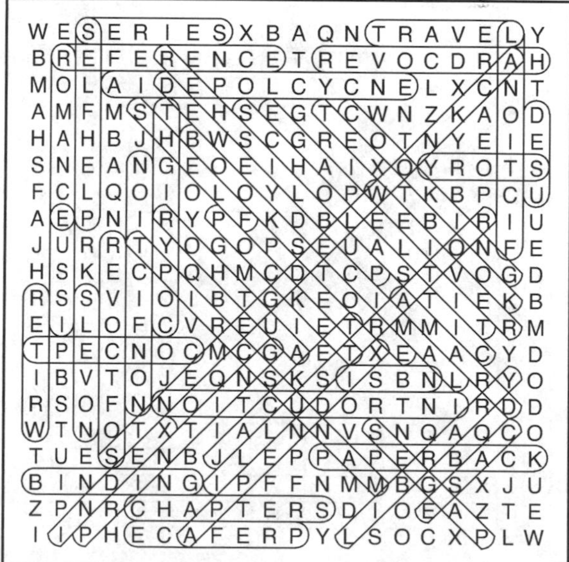

Play Sports

Back to Business

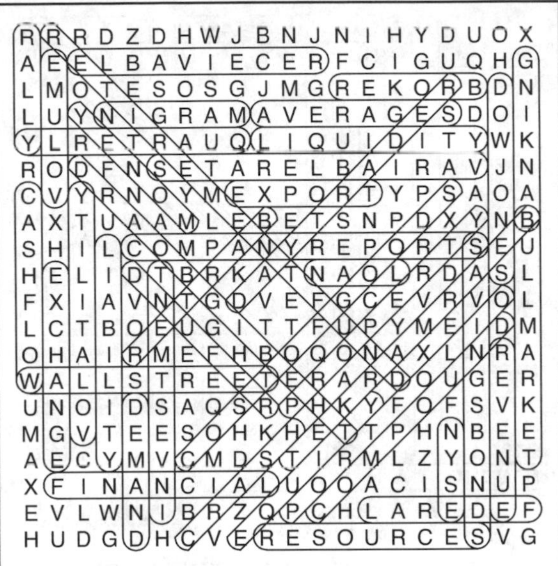

Turn on the TV

Treat Yourself

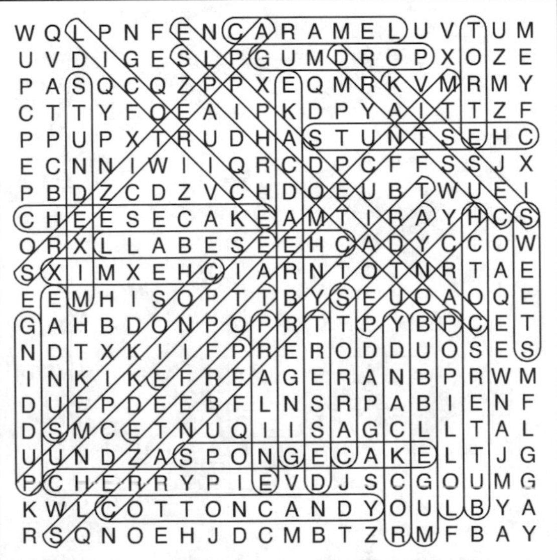

Dive In

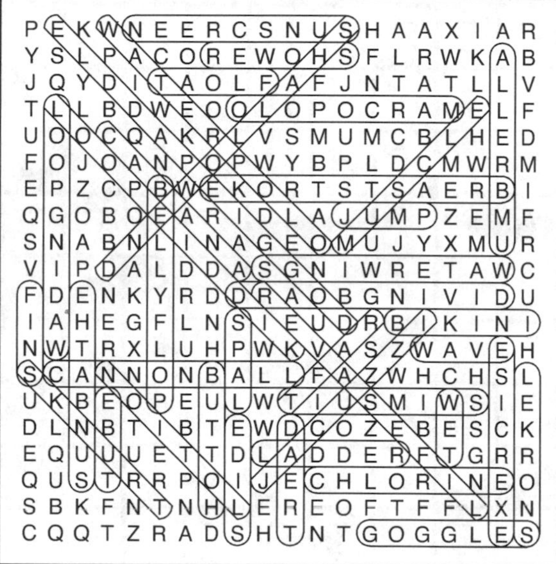

Car Crazy

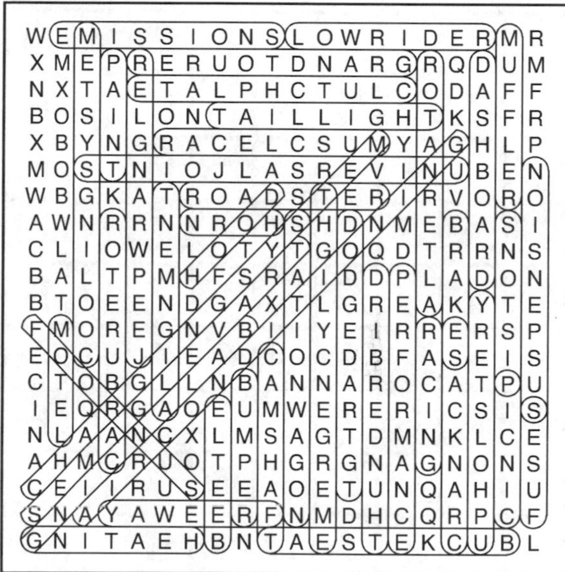

Wild Adventure

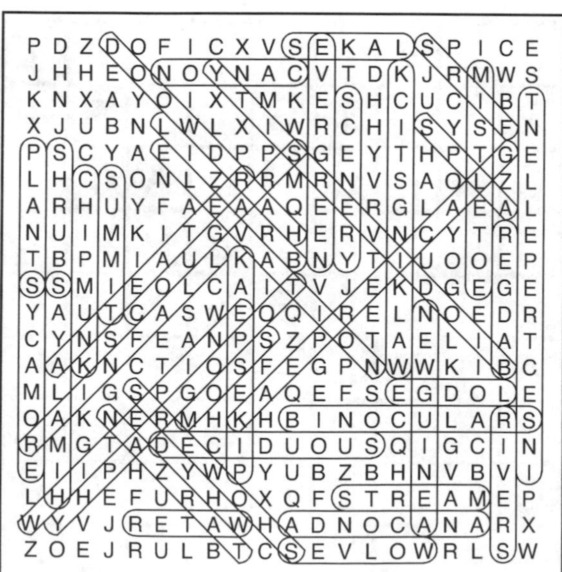

Home Construction

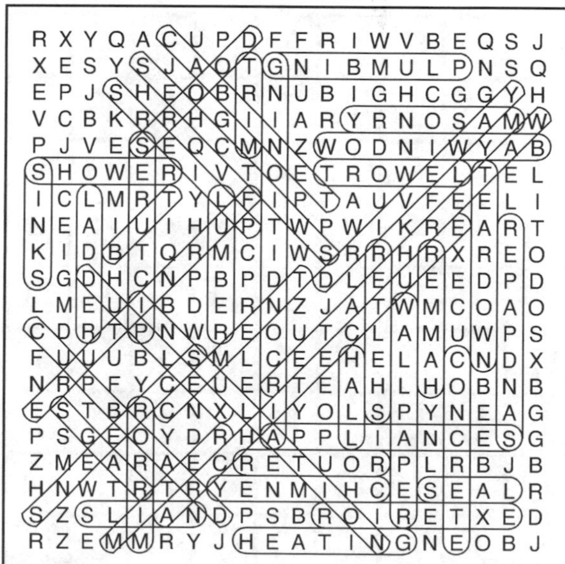

Chapter 6: Lost and Found

Lost and Found 1

I		C		O	F	F		O
N	Y	L	O	N		E	A	R
C		I		C		D		E
H	A	P	P	E	N	E	D	
	T		O			R	U	B
	T		S	U	G	A	R	
L	A	S	T	S		L	I	E
	C		S	E	W		N	
S	K	Y		D		E	G	G

Lost and Found 2

D	E	P	T	H		O	I	L
I		O		A				E
S		T	H	U	M	B		N
A				L		A	P	T
S	E	T				S		
T		H		S	L	I	C	E
E	L	A	S	T	I	C		N
R	E	T	A	I	N			V
	T		T	R	E	A	T	Y

Lost and Found 3

B	U	D		S	P	E	L	T
E		R	A	T			E	
A		E		A	C	I	D	
U		S	T	R	A	N	G	E
T		S		T	R	I	E	D
I			F	E	E	T		I
F	L	U	I	D		I		T
U			G			A		O
L	A	W		C	O	L	O	R

Lost and Found 4

A	L	L			P	R	A	Y
R		I	T	S			R	
C	A	K	E		H	A	T	
H		E	N	T	E	R		
	E	L	D	E	S	T		
A		Y	E	A		I	L	L
R			N			S		A
C	O	N	C	E	P	T		V
			Y			S	E	A

Lost and Found 5

E			A	F	F	A	I	R
X		M		O				A
A	G	I	N	G		W		I
M		X			M	I	N	D
I				C	A	N	E	
N		P		L	I	K	E	S
E	A	R	N	E	D		D	
		E		A		P	E	G
A	N	Y	O	N	E		D	

Lost and Found 6

K	N	O	B		L	I	P	S
	O		I		A		I	
P	O	S	S	I	B	L	E	
	N		C		E	A	S	E
A			U	G	L	Y		A
L			I		S	E	W	S
L	I	F	T			R		I
O		O		P	A	S	T	E
W	A	X						R

Lost and Found 7

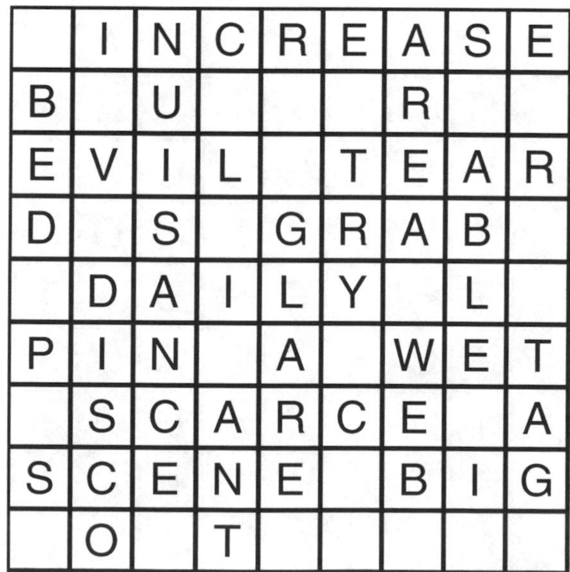

	I	N	C	R	E	A	S	E
B	U				R			
E	V	I	L		T	E	A	R
D		S		G	R	A	B	
	D	A	I	L	Y		L	
P	I	N		A		W	E	T
	S	C	A	R	C	E		A
S	C	E	N	E		B	I	G
	O		T					

Lost and Found 8

M			C		T	U	B	
O		M	U	M			A	
D	R	I	P		C	A	S	H
E		R		W	O	R	E	
R		A	P	A	R	T		
A	C	C	O	R	D	I	N	G
T	A	L	E			S		O
E	L	E	M	E	N	T		E
	L							S

Lost and Found 9

O	W	L					L	
	H	O	P		L	E	A	F
N	O	W	A	D	A	Y	S	
A			J		N	E	T	
T		B	A	N	G		E	
U			M	O	U	N	D	
R		D	A	T	A			T
E	Y	E	S		G			W
		W		T	E	M	P	O

Lost and Found 10

	S		B	O	M	B		C
S	P	Y				E		A
	E			R		N	A	P
A	C	H	I	E	V	E		
	I			A		F		S
E	F	F	E	C	T	I	V	E
A	I	R		H	I	T		E
S	C	O	R	E	D			M
Y		G		D	E	A	L	S

Lost and Found 11

B	U	I	L	D	S		E	
U			O			C	R	Y
L	E	S	S		D		O	
B	L	O	S	S	O	M	S	
	S	M	E	L	T		I	
G	E	E	S	E		T	O	Y
		D		E	A	R	N	
G	R	A	S	P		E		
		Y		Y	I	E	L	D

Lost and Found 12

A	C	T		H			W	
	H			I		P	E	N
P	R	E	S	S	U	R	E	
	I		A			O	D	D
	S		V	E	R	B		I
	T	O	E			A	G	E
	I			O		B	U	S
F	A	R	E	W	E	L	L	
	N			N		E	L	F

Lost and Found 13

	H	E	R	O	I	N	E	S
	E					E		E
O	R	G	A	N		W	O	N
	I		G	U	Y			D
S	T	I	R	R	E	D		S
	A		E	S	S	A	Y	
A	G	R	E	E		M	A	T
	E		D	R	Y		R	
				Y		E	N	D

Lost and Found 14

H	O	T	E	L		Z	I	P
E				A	R	E		E
R		A		P	E	R		A
O		B			S	O	N	
E		S	I	T	E		A	
S	E	E			M	I	S	S
	A	N	D		B		T	
A	C	T	U	A	L	L	Y	
	H		E		E			

Lost and Found 15

C	H	I	N	A		C	U	T
A				N		I		O
R		B		A	N	G	R	Y
	H	O	W	L		A		S
G	O	D		Y	A	R	D	
	R	I	B	S			R	
	R	E	L	I	G	I	O	N
N	O	S	E	S			W	
	R		W		F	A	N	

Lost and Found 16

M	A	R	S			S		
I		U		G	L	A	D	
D	I	G		R		C		
D				E		R		
A	L	P	H	A	B	E	T	
Y		H	A	T	E	D		S
	J	O	B		A			I
		T	I	C	K			Z
	H	O	T		S	A	K	E

Lost and Found 17

S	H	R	I	L	L		P	
	I			O			L	
	S	O	F	T		J	A	W
	T		E		P	E	T	
	O	P	E	R	A	T	E	D
	R	E	L	A	Y		A	
D	Y	E		I	S	S	U	E
		L		L		I		
F	I	S	H		O	X	E	N

Lost and Found 18

	D		E	F	F	O	R	T
D	I	D		O			I	
R	A	I	L	R	O	A	D	
A	L	S	O					C
G		T	O	R	C	H		R
	G	A	S	O	L	I	N	E
R		N	E	W	E	R		W
I		C			R	E	D	S
M	E	E	T		K			

Lost and Found 19

	G	A	P				R	
R	A	G		M	A	K	E	S
	S	O	L	O			A	
			A	V	O	I	D	
	H	I	K	E		V	E	T
R	E	M	E	M	B	E	R	
E	R	A		E				
L	E	G		N				
Y		E	I	T	H	E	R	

Lost and Found 20

H	A	D		U		A	D	D
E			U	S	E		E	
L				U		O	N	E
P	R	O	B	A	B	L	Y	
	A			L	E	D		
	F		F	L	Y		S	
A	T	E		Y	O	L	K	
N		A			N		I	
Y	E	T			D	U	M	P

Lost and Found 21

H					R		O	
I		A	P	P	E	A	R	S
M	O	M			L	I	D	
		E		A	I	M	E	D
	W	R	O	N	G		R	
S		I		K	I	T		A
O		C		L	O	A	D	S
A	M	A	T	E	U	R		K
K		N			S			S

Lost and Found 22

		B		D		P		H
T	H	E	R	E	F	O	R	E
E		L		V	A	P	O	R
X		O	M	I	T		B	
T	O	W		L	A	B	O	R
B			T		L	A	T	E
O	A	S	I	S		I		D
O			L	I	S	T	S	
K	N	E	L	T				

Lost and Found 23

O	U	T	P	U	T		G	
U					H	A	L	L
N	I	B			R		U	
C		E	X	C	U	S	E	
E		G		A	S	K		E
	F	U	N	C	T	I	O	N
		N	U	T				D
			T	U	R	T	L	E
	B	O	S	S				D

Lost and Found 24

			L		B		D	
	I	S	O	L	A	T	E	D
M		O	V	E	R		C	
I		M	E	T		B	I	T
S	H	E		S			S	
T		T			A	X	I	S
S	A	I	L	O	R		O	
		M		A	M	O	N	G
	L	E	A	K				

Lost and Found 25

A	S	H		C	U	B		O
	E		U			O	U	R
E	V	E	N			R		A
	E	X	T	E	R	N	A	L
I	N	C	O	M	E		P	
C		E		P	A	I	R	S
E		S	E	T	S		O	
		S		Y	O	U	N	G
					N		S	

Lost and Found 26

	R			C	R	E	P	T
H	E	M					L	
	S				F	O	U	R
S	U	N	S		U		M	
	L		E	U	R	O	P	E
O	T	H	E	R	S			A
U	S	I	N	G		D		G
R		P		E	Q	U	A	L
S		S				G		E

Lost and Found 27

C	O	N	C	E	P	T	S	
	A		O		R		C	
	T		P	O	O	R	E	R
	H	A	Y		G	O	N	E
C		C			R	A	T	S
R		C		B	A	D		P
I	D	E	A		M			O
E		S			S	O	O	N
D	U	S	T	Y				D

Lost and Found 28

E					P	L	O	T
C	U	B	I	C		I		O
H		A		O		P	A	W
O	C	C	U	R	S			E
	H	O	S	P	I	T	A	L
H	O	N	E	S	T		W	
	I		F		S	E	A	S
G	R	O	U	P			R	
			L		H	I	D	

Lost and Found 29

				C				
A		N	E	E	D	L	E	S
U		E		R				O
G	U	I	D	E		C		N
U		T		A	T	O	M	S
S	C	H	O	L	A	R		
T	I	E	D		S	K	I	P
	T	R	O	U	T			A
	Y		R		E	X	I	T

Lost and Found 30

S				U	P	S	E	T
C	O	I	L			T		U
A		N		S	A	I	L	S
R		T	O	O		T		K
		E		F	O	C	U	S
B	E	N	E	A	T	H		
A		D			H	E	A	D
L		E	D	G	E	S		A
L	A	D			R			D

Lost and Found 31

H	A	S				R	A	N
		E		W		U		O
C	E	R	T	A	I	N		W
		V	A	S	T		E	
	G	I	N		S	O	X	
H		C			E		A	
A	G	E	S		L	A	C	K
M	Y	S	E	L	F		T	
	M		X					

Lost and Found 32

J	A	Z	Z		K	I	L	L
			I	N	N		A	
S	I	G	N		E		W	
	D	E	C	R	E	A	S	E
B	E	T				I		V
	A		A		E	D	G	E
B	L	O	W		A			N
	S	W	E	E	T	E	S	T
		E			S			

Chapter 7: Providers

Provider 1

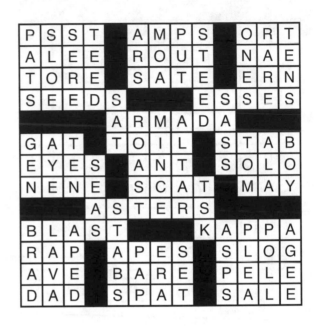

Provider 2

P	S	S	T	■	A	M	P	S	■	O	R	T
A	L	E	E	■	R	O	U	T	■	N	A	E
T	O	R	E	■	S	A	T	E	■	E	R	N
S	E	E	D	S	■	■	■	E	S	S	E	S
■	■	■	■	A	R	M	A	D	A	■	■	■
G	A	T	■	T	O	I	L	■	S	T	A	B
E	Y	E	S	■	A	N	T	■	S	O	L	O
N	E	N	E	■	S	C	A	T	■	M	A	Y
■	■	■	A	S	T	E	R	S	■	■	■	■
B	L	A	S	T	■	■	■	K	A	P	P	A
R	A	P	■	A	P	E	S	■	S	L	O	G
A	V	E	■	B	A	R	E	■	P	E	L	E
D	A	D	■	S	P	A	T	■	S	A	L	E

Provider 3

O	W	E	D	■	M	A	D	■	C	A	R	D
T	O	P	E	■	O	R	E	■	A	G	I	O
T	E	E	N	■	B	R	A	■	M	A	G	S
O	S	E	S	■	■	E	L	S	E	■	■	■
■	■	■	E	R	G	S	■	T	R	E	S	S
O	D	S	■	O	A	T	■	R	A	V	E	N
A	R	E	N	A	S	■	P	E	S	E	T	A
R	A	G	E	S	■	T	O	E	■	S	A	G
S	T	O	A	T	■	H	I	T	S	■	■	■
■	■	■	T	S	A	R	■	■	T	H	A	T
T	Y	N	E	■	M	O	P	■	A	E	R	O
A	E	O	N	■	A	N	A	■	T	R	I	M
T	A	R	S	■	H	E	S	■	S	O	D	S

Provider 4

L	A	B	■	■	B	R	A	G	■	M	A	T
A	G	A	R	■	R	O	T	E	■	A	G	E
S	O	M	A	■	O	D	E	S	■	N	U	N
■	■	■	T	A	S	■	■	T	R	E	E	D
S	A	V	E	R	■	G	L	E	E	■	■	■
O	B	I	■	B	R	A	E	■	S	O	T	S
A	L	S	■	S	A	T	E	S	■	A	H	A
K	E	E	L	■	C	O	R	E	■	S	E	N
■	■	■	A	P	E	R	■	M	A	T	E	S
S	L	A	T	S	■	■	M	I	L	■	■	■
E	O	N	■	A	C	H	E	■	B	R	A	S
A	C	T	■	L	O	O	T	■	S	A	S	H
L	I	E	■	M	O	P	E	■	■	S	P	Y

Provider 5

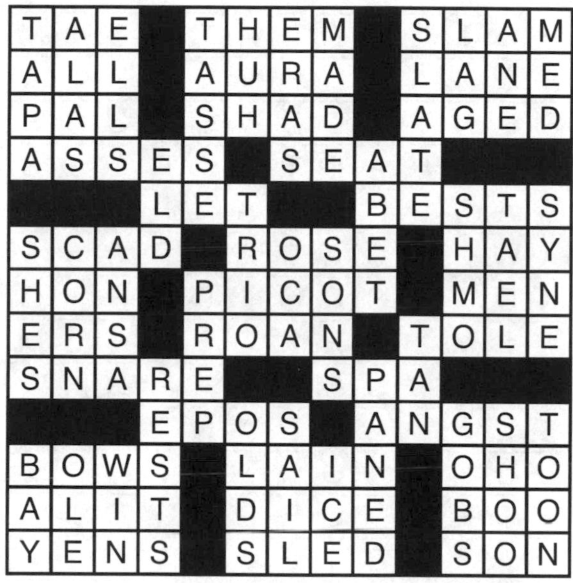

Provider 6

Provider 7

Provider 8

SLAT WAG SLAW
TARE EYE PAPA
ACES BEN AWED
REST SETT
YES REAPS
ARC MOCHA RAH
WOO BROOD FRO
LUV RESEE SAW
SEEPY SRI
OOPS MORT
TODS FIB AMIE
HOOT FLU MILS
OHMS TOY STET

Provider 9

C	A	P		P	E	P	S		S	H	A	G
H	I	E		A	L	S	O		H	O	B	O
I	D	S		S	K	I	P		R	E	A	D
S	E	T	A	E			S	H	E			
			L	O	S	S		A	D	A	P	T
B	Y	T	E		T	O	G	S		F	O	E
R	U	E	S		O	A	R		M	A	L	E
I	L	L		S	A	K	E		I	R	E	S
T	E	E	T	H		S	W	A	T			
			A	A	S			R	E	C	A	P
A	L	L	S		E	A	V	E		O	V	A
N	E	A	T		I	L	I	A		N	O	T
D	I	M	E		S	P	A	S		E	W	E

Provider 10

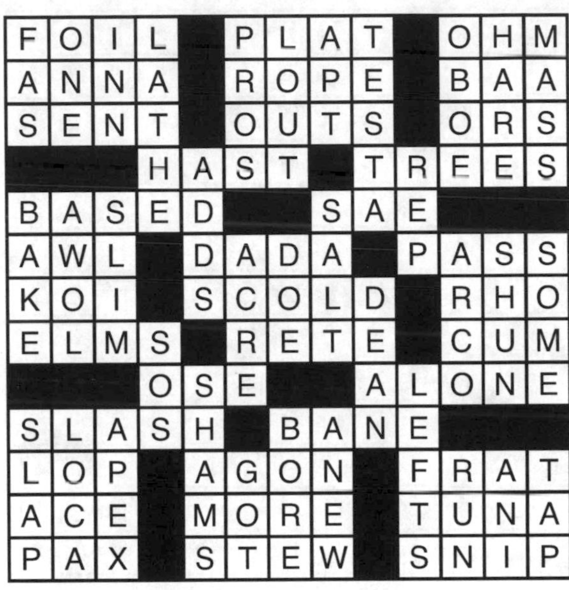

F	O	I	L		P	L	A	T		O	H	M
A	N	N	A		R	O	P	E		B	A	A
S	E	N	T		O	U	T	S		O	R	S
			H	A	S	T		T	R	E	E	S
B	A	S	E	D			S	A	E			
A	W	L		D	A	D	A		P	A	S	S
K	O	I		S	C	O	L	D		R	H	O
E	L	M	S		R	E	T	E		C	U	M
			O	S	E			A	L	O	N	E
S	L	A	S	H		B	A	N	E			
L	O	P		A	G	O	N		F	R	A	T
A	C	E		M	O	R	E		T	U	N	A
P	A	X		S	T	E	W		S	N	I	P

Provider 11

F	A	R		A	M	E	N		M	E	L	D
O	D	E		V	A	N	E		O	Y	E	R
B	O	S		E	R	S	T		D	R	A	Y
		T	O	R	S	I		T	E	E	N	S
S	L	A	M	S		L	E	A	S			
C	I	T	E		P	E	R	T		T	A	B
A	M	E	R	C	E		R	E	D	O	N	E
B	A	D		L	A	W	S		R	O	T	A
			S	O	L	I		S	O	L	A	R
A	R	C	E	D		S	L	A	P	S		
L	I	L	T		P	E	A	S		H	A	H
F	E	A	T		I	S	M	S		E	V	E
A	L	M	S		S	T	A	Y		D	A	P

Provider 12

H	M	M		B	E	S	T		B	A	T	E
E	A	U		A	M	A	S		A	L	E	F
H	I	T		S	U	L	K		S	T	A	T
	D	E	L	E			S	O	T			
			A	R	M	S		R	E	M	A	P
A	B	E	D		A	L	B	A		A	X	E
W	I	G		O	R	E	A	D		M	O	N
E	K	E		R	E	E	S		S	A	N	D
S	E	R	A	C		P	E	S	O			
			N	A	N			T	U	B	S	
B	R	A	T		A	S	H	Y		L	A	C
R	O	L	E		M	O	U	E		O	K	A
R	E	B	S		E	W	E	S		B	I	D

Provider 13

T	W	O		P	I	E	D		A	N	I	L
R	I	D		A	C	T	A		C	O	D	E
A	D	D		S	H	A	Y		T	E	L	S
M	E	S	A	S				A	S	S	E	T
			S	E	A	M	E	N				
P	O	R	K		T	O	G	A		P	O	P
O	X	Y		O	R	L	E	S		R	U	E
W	O	E		R	I	D	S		P	O	R	N
				C	A	S	T	L	E			
S	C	A	B	S				O	R	C	A	S
P	A	L	E		P	L	U	S		O	R	C
U	R	G	E		H	I	R	E		P	I	A
D	E	A	R		I	N	N	S		E	L	M

Provider 14

R	U	S	E		B	E	G	S		C	H	I
U	S	E	S		A	G	H	A		Y	A	R
T	E	X	T		L	O	I	N		S	K	I
			E	L	L			T	A	T	E	S
M	A	D	R	E		I	D	O	L			
I	V	Y		D	O	O	R		T	O	Y	S
L	E	N	T		G	N	U		O	R	A	L
T	R	E	E		L	I	M	B		T	W	A
			A	L	E	C		R	A	S	P	Y
S	A	B	R	A			S	O	L			
C	U	E		M	Y	N	A		P	H	E	W
U	T	A		B	O	I	L		H	E	A	R
M	O	M		S	U	P	S		A	W	R	Y

Provider 15

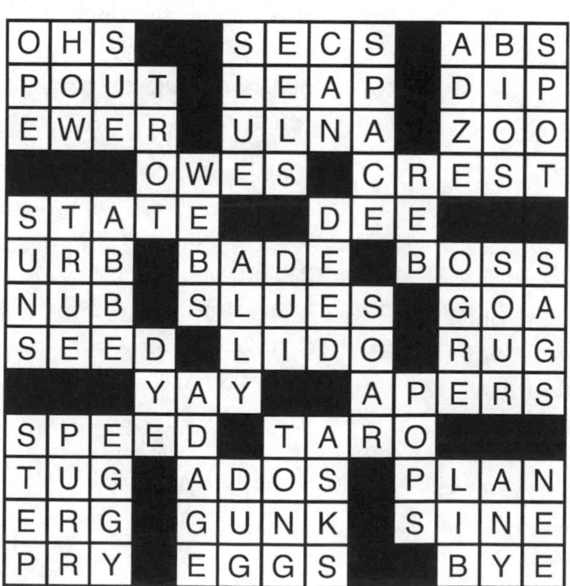

O	H	S			S	E	C	S		A	B	S
P	O	U	T		L	E	A	P		D	I	P
E	W	E	R		U	L	N	A		Z	O	O
			O	W	E	S		C	R	E	S	T
S	T	A	T	E			D	E	E			
U	R	B		B	A	D	E		B	O	S	S
N	U	B		S	L	U	E	S		G	O	A
S	E	E	D		L	I	D	O		R	U	G
			Y	A	Y			A	P	E	R	S
S	P	E	E	D		T	A	R	O			
T	U	G		A	D	O	S		P	L	A	N
E	R	G		G	U	N	K		S	I	N	E
P	R	Y		E	G	G	S			B	Y	E

Provider 16

G	R	A	D		R	A	C	Y		W	H	A
L	O	N	E		E	U	R	O		Y	O	N
A	V	E	S		C	R	A	W		E	N	D
D	E	S	K	S		A	T	L	A	S	E	S
				A	P	T	E	S	T			
F	L	Y		M	A	E			O	P	E	D
E	Y	E	L	E	T		A	S	P	I	R	E
Y	E	T	I			S	I	P		T	R	Y
			N	E	S	T	L	E				
T	E	S	T	A	T	E		C	L	A	S	S
I	M	P		S	O	L	D		A	N	T	I
F	I	R		T	I	L	E		T	O	U	T
F	R	Y		S	C	A	N		E	N	D	S

Chapter 8: Words Within Words

BARRISTER

arts, bait, bare, bars, base, bats, bear, beat, best, bets, bite, bits, ears, east, eats, rare, rate, rats, rear, rest, ribs, rise, seat, site, star, stir, tear, teas, ties, tire, arise, bears, beast, bites, raise, rates, stair, stare, tears, tires, tribe, tries, arrest, breast, tribes, barrier

ABORIGINE

bang, bare, barn, bean, bear, bone, bore, born, earn, gain, gear, gone, grab, grin, iron, near, rage, rain, rang, ring, robe, anger, began, begin, being, bring, grain, negro, organ, range, reign, robin, ignore, orange, origin

ACCRETION

acre, cane, cant, care, cart, cent, coat, coin, cone, core, corn, earn, into, iron, near, neat, nice, note, once, race, rain, rate, rent, rice, tear, tire, tone, tore, torn, actor, canoe, crane, nicer, ocean, ratio, react, trace, accent, action, arctic, carton, nectar, retain, certain, reaction

TOROIDAL

dial, dirt, door, laid, load, lord, odor, oral, raid, rail, road, root, tail, toad, told, tool, radio, ratio, tidal, trail, trial, tailor

QUINQUAGENARIAN

area, earn, gain, gear, grin, near, nine, rage, rain, rang, ring, ruin, rung, urge, again, anger, argue, grain, inner, range, reign, inning, unique, running

PLANGENT

gale, gate, lane, late, lean, leap, lent, neat, page, pale, plan, tale, tape, agent, angel, angle, panel, plane, plant, plate, planet, tangle

DIADROMOUS

adds, aims, arms, dads, door, drum, maid, mars, mood, oars, odor, ours, raid, road, roam, rods, room, said, sour, doors, maids, moods, radio, roads, rooms, sodium

RECONDITE

cent, code, coin, cone, cord, core, corn, deer, dent, diet, dirt, done, into, iron, need, nice, note, once, reed, rent, rice, ride, tend, tide, tied, tire, tone, tore, torn, tree, cried, enter, nicer, noted, tired, trend, tried, center, credit, direct, editor, entire, recent, rented, tender

ANACHRONISM

aims, arch, arms, cams, cars, cash, chin, coin, corn, hair, harm, horn, inch, iron, main, mans, mars, moan, oars, rain, rich, roam, scar, chain, chair, charm, china, choir, coins, crash, hairs, harms, irons, march, marsh, minor, rains, ranch, roman, anchor, romans

TRAVESTY

arts, ears, east, easy, eats, rate, rats, rays, rest, save, seat, star, stay, tart, tear, teas, test, tray, tyre, vary, vase, vast, very, vets, year, rates, stare, start, state, stray, tarts, taste, tasty, tears, treat, years, starve, treaty

PROSCRIBE

bore, core, crop, ices, pies, ribs, rice, ripe, rise, robe, robs, rope, rose, sore, corps, cries, crisp, crops, price, robes, ropes, score

DACTYLOGRAM

army, atom, calm, card, cart, clam, clay, coal, coat, cold, colt, cord, data, drag, glad, goal, goat, gold, gray, lady, load, lord, mold, oral, road, roam, toad, told, tray, yard, yoga, actor, alarm, cargo, coral, drama, mayor, moral, royal, today

CANTILLATE

call, cane, cant, cell, cent, lace, lane, late, lean, lent, line, nail, neat, nice, tail, tale, tall, tell, tent, tile, till, tilt, alien, attic, canal, clean, title, cattle, little, talent

SHEEPSHANK

asks, ease, heap, hens, keen, keep, knee, pans, pass, peak, peas, pens, sake, sank, seas, seek, seen, sees, snap, span, ashes, keeps, knees, phase, sense, shape, sheep, snake, snaps, sneak, speak, speaks

REFULGENT

feel, feet, felt, fern, free, fuel, glue, gulf, left, lent, lung, rent, rule, rung, tree, true, tune, turn, urge, enter, fleet, flute, green, refuge

SORTILEGE

else, gets, girl, goes, legs, lets, lies, list, logs, lose, lost, lots, oils, rest, rise, role, rose, site, slit, slot, soil, sore, sort, stir, ties, tile, tire, toes, tore, tree, girls, liter, loser, steel, steer, stole, store, tiger, tiles, tires, trees, tries, liters, tigers

BLANCMANGE

able, bang, beam, bean, cage, calm, came, cane, clam, gale, game, lace, lamb, lame, lane, lean, male, mane, meal, mean, name, angel, angle, began, blame, cable, camel, canal, clean, glance, manage

ABSTRUSE

arts, bare, bars, base, bass, bats, bear, beat, best, bets, ears, east, eats, rate, rats, rest, rubs, rust, seas, seat, sets, star, sure, tear, teas, true, tube, uses, bases, bears, beast, brass, burst, rates, rests, seats, stare, stars, tears, tubes, assure, beasts, breast

TELAMON

atom, lame, lane, late, lean, lent, loan, lone, male, mane, mate, meal, mean, meat, melt, moan, mole, name, neat, note, tale, tame, team, tone, alone, lemon, metal

ATOMIZER

atom, item, mare, mate, meat, more, omit, rate, roam, tame, team, tear, term, time, tire, tore, trim, zero, ratio, timer

CALIGINOUS

also, coal, coil, coin, gain, goal, lion, loan, logs, long, lung, nail, oils, sail, sang, sign, sing, soil, song, soul, sung, along, cling, clung, coals, coins, gains, goals, lions, nails, snail, using, cousin, losing, signal, social

APIARIST

arts, pair, part, past, pats, pits, rats, spit, star, stir, taps, tips, trap, trip, apart, pairs, parts, stair, strap, strip, traps, spirit

BANDORE

band, bare, barn, bead, bean, bear, bend, bond, bone, bore, born, dare, dear, done, earn, near, read, road, robe, beard, board, bored, brand, bread, broad

CASTIGATE

acts, ages, cage, case, cast, cats, east, eats, gate, gets, ices, seat, site, teas, test, ties, attic, gates, stage, state, taste, static

GOSSAMER

ages, arms, ears, game, gear, germ, goes, mare, mars, mass, mess, more, moss, oars, rage, rags, roam, rose, same, seam, seas, some, sore, arose, games, gears, germs, grass, roses

SCOTOPIA

acts, caps, cast, cats, coat, cost, cots, oats, past, pats, pits, post, pots, soap, spit, spot, stop, taps, tips, tops, coast, coats, stoop, topic, topics

PLATITUDE

date, deal, dial, diet, idea, idle, laid, late, lead, leap, paid, pail, pale, pile, tail, tale, tape, tide, tied, tile, tilt, adult, ideal, pedal, piled, plait, plate, tidal, title, detail

PRESCIENCE

ices, nice, pens, pies, pine, pins, rice, ripe, rise, seen, spin, creep, cries, crisp, nicer, pence, piece, pines, price, reins, ripen, scene, since, spine, creeps, pieces, prince, recipe, screen, precise, science

SOLECISM

coil, come, ices, less, lies, lime, lose, mess, mice, mile, miss, mole, moss, oils, slim, soil, some, close, comes, loses, miles, moles, slice, smile, soils, closes

SHIITAKE

east, eats, hate, hats, heat, hike, hits, kite, sake, seat, site, take, task, teas, this, ties, haste, hates, heats, kites, skate, steak, takes

BLANDISH

band, dash, dial, dish, hail, hand, hind, laid, land, lids, nail, said, sail, sand, slid, bands, basin, hands, lands, nails, snail, island

ADUMBRATE

area, bare, bead, beam, bear, beat, dare, data, date, dear, debt, drum, dumb, made, mare, mate, meat, rate, read, rude, tame, team, tear, term, true, tube, armed, beard, bread, drama, dream, tamed, trade, amateur

ANGSTROM

ants, arms, arts, atom, goat, mans, mars, mast, mats, moan, most, oars, oats, rags, rang, rats, roam, sang, song, sort, star, tons, torn, among, atoms, goats, grant, organ, roast, roman, smart, storm, organs, romans, strong

PRECOCIOUS

core, crop, cups, cure, ices, ours, pies, poor, pour, pure, rice, ripe, rise, rope, rose, sore, soup, sour, sure, corps, cries, crisp, crops, occur, pours, price, purse, ropes, score, super, course, occurs, source

CAPRIOLE

acre, care, clap, clip, coal, coil, core, crop, lace, leap, oral, pace, pail, pair, pale, pear, pile, pole, race, rail, real, rice, ripe, role, rope, clear, coral, opera, pearl, place, polar, price, parcel, police

REPROBATE

bare, bear, beat, beer, boat, bore, part, pear, poet, port, rare, rate, rear, roar, robe, rope, tape, tear, tore, trap, tree, opera, parrot, repeat, report, operate

SOMMELIER

else, lies, lime, lose, mere, mile, mole, more, oils, rise, role, rose, seem, slim, soil, some, sore, loser, miles, mimes, moles, smile

PRODIGAL

dial, drag, drip, drop, girl, glad, goal, gold, grip, laid, load, lord, oral, paid, pail, pair, raid, rail, road, polar, radio, rapid

DILETTANTE

date, deal, dial, diet, idea, idle, laid, land, lane, late, lead, lean, lend, lent, line, nail, neat, need, tail, tale, tend, tent, tide, tied, tile, tilt, alien, eaten, ideal, lined, tidal, title, attend, dental, detail, leaned, nailed, netted, talent

MOUNTEBANK

atom, aunt, bake, bank, beak, beam, bean, beat, bent, boat, bone, bunk, knob, knot, make, mane, mate, mean, meat, moan, name, neat, none, note, noun, take, tame, tank, team, tone, tube, tune, unto, about, mount, taken, amount

CARMINE

acre, came, cane, care, earn, main, mane, mare, mean, mice, mine, name, near, nice, race, rain, rice, crane, cream, crime, nicer, cinema, marine, remain

APOSTASY

oats, pass, past, pats, pays, post, pots, says, soap, spot, stay, stop, taps, tops, toss, toys, posts, spots, stays, stops

AD HOMINEM

dome, done, hand, head, hide, hind, home, idea, made, maid, main, mane, mean, mend, mind, mine, moan, mode, name, aimed, mined, named

TELLURIAN

aunt, earn, lane, late, lean, lent, line, nail, near, neat, rail, rain, rate, real, rent, ruin, rule, tail, tale, tall, tear, tell, tile, till, tire, true, tune, turn, unit, alert, alien, later, learn, liter, lunar, trail, trial, untie, until, auntie, learnt, nature, retain, taller, neutral

PROPITIOUS

ours, pits, poor, pops, port, post, pots, pour, puts, root, rust, sort, soup, sour, spit, spot, stir, stop, suit, tips, tops, tour, trip, ports, pours, roots, sport, stoop, strip, spirit, support

REMUNERATE

aunt, earn, mane, mare, mate, mean, meat, meet, mere, name, near, neat, rare, rate, rear, rent, tame, team, tear, term, tree, true, tune, turn, eaten, enter, meter, metre, nature, nearer, return

CARABINEER

acre, area, bare, barn, bean, bear, been, beer, cane, care, crab, earn, near, nice, race, rain, rare, rear, rice, cabin, crane, nicer, career, nearer

RECENSION

coin, cone, core, corn, ices, iron, nice, nine, none, nose, once, ones, rice, rise, rose, seen, sore, coins, cones, cries, inner, irons, nicer, nines, noise, reins, scene, score, since, screen, senior

Chapter 9: Crosswords

Crossword 1

Crossword 2

Crossword 3

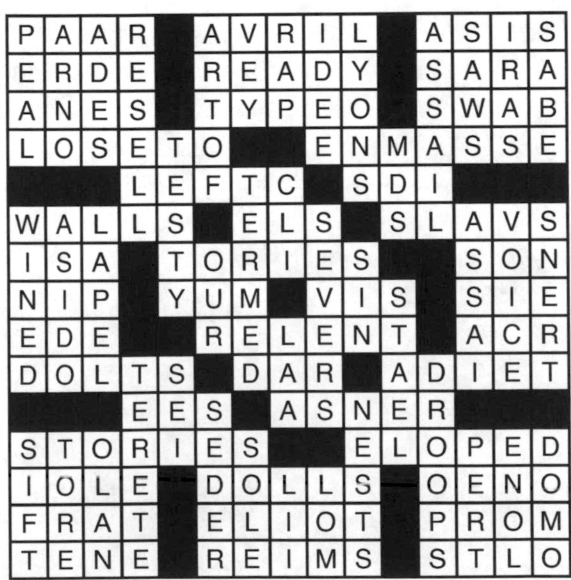

Crossword 4

E	T	A	S		L	O	C	K	E		A	R	A	M
L	Y	L	E		A	S	A	N	A		L	A	G	O
A	R	I	P		M	O	R	E	S		B	R	A	T
N	E	T	T	L	E		P	L	E	A	S	E	S	
			E	A	D	S		L	D	L				
M	A	L	T	S		N	E	S		E	K	E	S	
I	N	I		T	Y	R	A		A	G	O	R	A	E
S	I	M	P		A	S	R	E	D		I	N	N	S
S	L	A	T	E	R		L	U	M	P		I	K	E
	E	S	A	I		S	Y	R		A	N	E	A	R
				N	A	P		E	A	R	L			
	S	E	N	E	C	A	S		G	R	E	A	S	E
P	A	R	E		A	R	L	E	N		A	R	T	S
R	I	L	E		S	T	A	K	E		S	T	E	T
U	S	E	D		T	A	P	E	S		T	A	P	S

Crossword 5

L	O	O	S	E		F	A	S	T		H	A	M	A
E	N	R	O	N		A	N	N	A		I	D	A	S
D	I	D	N	T		R	I	A	L		A	D	O	S
S	T	O	N	E	H	E	N	G	E		W	E	R	E
			E	R	A	S			S	T	A	R	I	S
E	L	A	T	E	R		S	E	E	I	T			
V	I	N		D	E	T	E	R		C	H	A	S	E
A	N	T	H		S	E	N	N	A		A	T	O	N
N	O	S	E	D		A	D	A	M	E		L	O	L
			R	A	N	T	S		U	P	S	E	T	S
S	T	R	I	P	E			A	S	I	T			
P	O	E	T		W	H	I	T	E	S	A	N	D	S
A	R	P	A		T	E	N	T		T	R	A	I	T
S	T	A	G		O	S	A	Y		L	E	N	N	Y
M	E	D	E		N	A	T	S		E	R	O	S	E

Crossword 6

M	M	L				B	I	E	R		E	T	E	S
A	O	U	T		C	A	B	L	E		A	H	A	T
R	O	T	E		A	D	E	A	L		S	E	R	A
E	G	E	S	T	S			L	A	P	T	O	P	S
			T	O	T	E	S		Y	O	O			
C	R	I	E	D		M	E	M		U	N	L	E	T
H	I	N	D		D	E	C	A	N	T		A	F	R
A	C	U		F	I	E		L	A	Y		T	R	U
I	C	I		A	D	R	O	I	T		S	T	E	S
N	I	T	E	R		S	I	C		S	T	E	M	S
			A	G	A		D	E	A	R	E			
A	L	L	G	O	N	E			M	I	A	T	A	S
N	O	E	L		A	L	F	I	E		L	E	N	A
A	C	N	E		R	E	A	R	S		S	A	I	L
S	A	S	S		M	A	R	T				M	L	S

Crossword 7

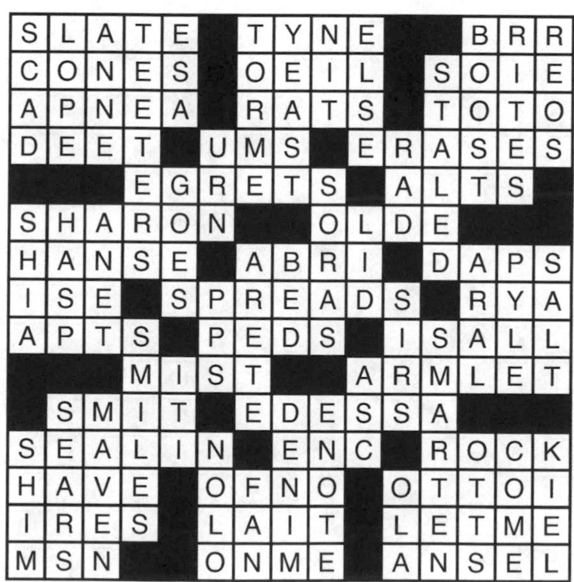

S	L	A	T	E		T	Y	N	E			B	R	R
C	O	N	E	S		O	E	I	L		S	O	I	E
A	P	N	E	A		R	A	T	S		T	O	T	O
D	E	E	T		U	M	S		E	R	A	S	E	S
			E	G	R	E	T	S		A	L	T	S	
S	H	A	R	O	N			O	L	D	E			
H	A	N	S	E		A	B	R	I		D	A	P	S
I	S	E		S	P	R	E	A	D	S		R	Y	A
A	P	T	S		P	E	D	S		I	S	A	L	L
			M	I	S	T			A	R	M	L	E	T
	S	M	I	T		E	D	E	S	S	A			
S	E	A	L	I	N		E	N	C		R	O	C	K
H	A	V	E		O	F	N	O		O	T	T	O	I
I	R	E	S		L	A	I	T		L	E	T	M	E
M	S	N			O	N	M	E		A	N	S	E	L

Crossword 8

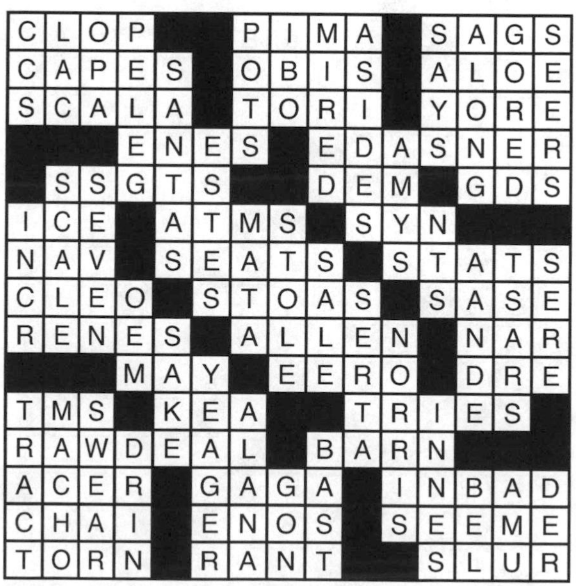

C	L	O	P			P	I	M	A		S	A	G	S
C	A	P	E	S		O	B	I	S		A	L	O	E
S	C	A	L	A		T	O	R	I		Y	O	R	E
			E	N	E	S		E	D	A	S	N	E	R
	S	S	G	T	S			D	E	M		G	D	S
I	C	E		A	T	M	S		S	Y	N			
N	A	V		S	E	A	T	S		S	T	A	T	S
C	L	E	O		S	T	O	A	S		S	A	S	E
R	E	N	E	S		A	L	L	E	N		N	A	R
			M	A	Y		E	E	R	O		D	R	E
T	M	S		K	E	A			T	R	I	E	S	
R	A	W	D	E	A	L		B	A	R	N			
A	C	E	R		G	A	G	A		I	N	B	A	D
C	H	A	I		E	N	O	S		S	E	E	M	E
T	O	R	N		R	A	N	T			S	L	U	R

Crossword 9

Crossword 10

Crossword 11

Crossword 12

SPCA STAGE SIAM
PAIL ERROL AVIA
ALTA RIDGE MERE
KEENEST NOOSES
EDDAS OSCARS
LEANTO CARBS
SADDLE ORBS HUP
UREA RHONE REDO
EMB SOIL ALEAST
TASSE TIPTOP
NASSER SLANT
TAMALE ELEANOR
OLOR AFAST COMA
NINE MOVER ELAM
GETS SPITS DENS

Crossword 13

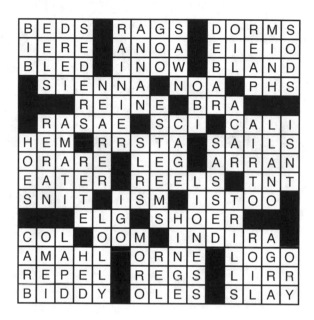

B	E	D	S		R	A	G	S		D	O	R	M	S
I	E	R	E		A	N	O	A		E	I	E	I	O
B	L	E	D		I	N	O	W		B	L	A	N	D
	S	I	E	N	N	A		N	O	A		P	H	S
			R	E	I	N	E		B	R	A			
	R	A	S	A	E		S	C	I		C	A	L	I
H	E	M		R	R	S	T	A		S	A	I	L	S
O	R	A	R	E		L	E	G		A	R	R	A	N
E	A	T	E	R		R	E	E	L	S		T	N	T
S	N	I	T		I	S	M		I	S	T	O	O	
			E	L	G		S	H	O	E	R			
C	O	L		O	O	M		I	N	D	I	R	A	
A	M	A	H	L		O	R	N	E		L	O	G	O
R	E	P	E	L		R	E	G	S		L	I	R	R
B	I	D	D	Y		O	L	E	S		S	L	A	Y

Crossword 14

M	A	T	C	H		A	P	O	C			M	C	D
A	T	R	I	A		W	A	N	E		S	O	L	I
C	O	O	E	R		O	R	T	S		T	O	O	N
K	I	N		A	L	L	T	O		P	A	S	T	E
			B	R	O	S		P	E	E	R	E	S	S
A	B	A	S	E	S				F	E	E			
I	A	M	S		S	C	A	M	S		S	O	P	S
M	I	I				T	W	I				M	I	C
S	O	N	S		P	A	L	O	S		P	O	G	O
			A	R	Y				A	L	M	O	S	T
C	O	A	R	S	E	N		E	D	A	S			
O	U	T	T	A		E	A	S	E	R		B	U	D
I	T	A	R		Y	A	M	S		O	B	O	L	E
N	I	L	E		A	L	E	E		S	A	L	E	M
S	E	E			M	E	N	S		A	N	T	E	S

Crossword 15

R	A	E	S		U	M	P	S				E	M	E
O	P	E	N		P	O	L	E	R		S	A	U	R
M	U	L	E		A	M	E	R	E		A	V	O	N
A	S	Y	E	T			D	I	I		L	E	N	E
			S	U	C	H		E	T	R	E			
A	P	B		G	R	O	S	S		A	R	R	A	S
N	A	E		S	E	N	T		D	I	N	E	R	O
I	T	S	O		M	E	I	E	R		O	D	E	S
T	E	E	P	E	E		L	E	A	R		O	C	A
A	S	T	A	R		S	L	O	M	O		S	A	D
			C	O	T	E		C	A	N	T			
A	L	A	I		A	N	I			S	A	A	B	S
L	E	S	T		S	A	S	H	A		B	R	A	E
O	A	T	Y		S	T	A	G	G		L	I	L	I
T	S	R				E	R	T	E		A	L	M	S

Crossword 16

D	I	V	A	S		N	Y	E	S		L	O	R	E
A	R	E	S	T		C	U	R	E		A	L	A	N
R	A	S	P	Y		O	R	R	A		X	E	N	O
E	N	T	E	R	S		T	E	T	S		I	A	L
			R	O	O	S		D	E	T	E	C	T	S
P	A	R	S	N	I	P	S		D	D	T			
O	B	O	E		L	E	E	S		S	C	A	T	S
N	O	U			S	A	L	A	S			L	A	R
T	O	E	R	R		R	E	N	I		E	L	L	A
			D	I	R		S	T	E	N	C	I	L	S
D	O	N	A	T	E	S		O	N	O	S			
U	N	E		T	A	T	A		A	N	T	E	E	D
M	E	A	L		L	O	C	H		C	A	R	G	O
P	A	T	E		M	O	T	A		O	S	I	E	R
S	L	O	W		S	L	E	Y		M	Y	E	R	S

Chapter 10: Diagramless

Diagramless 1

Diagramless 2

Diagramless 3

Diagramless 4

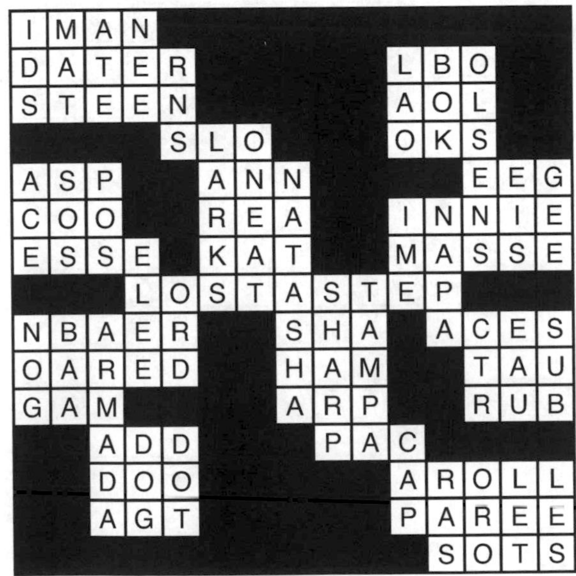

Diagramless 5

Diagramless 6

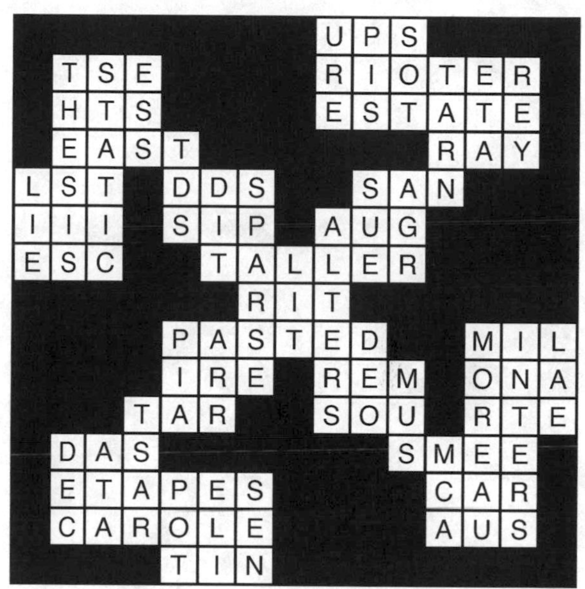

Diagramless 7

Diagramless 8

Diagramless 9

Diagramless 10

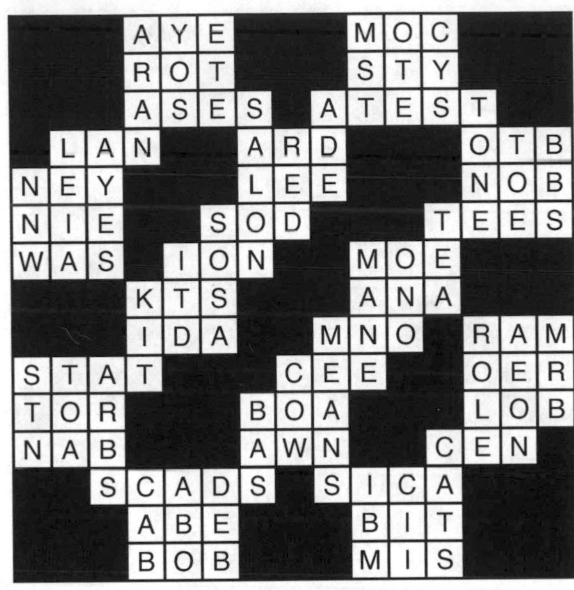

Diagramless 11

Diagramless 12

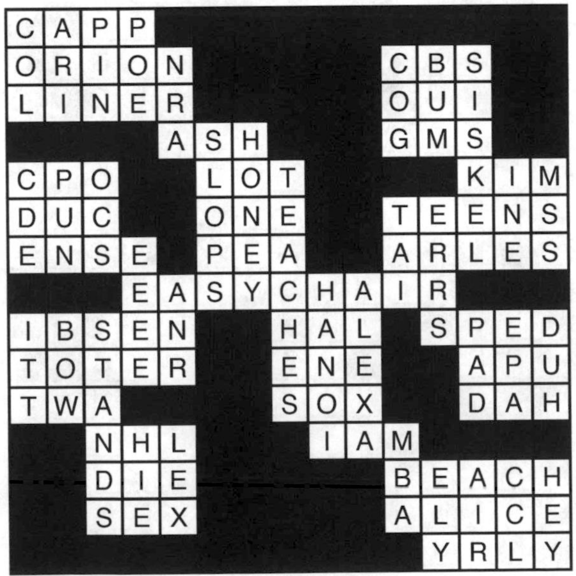

Diagramless 13

Diagramless 14

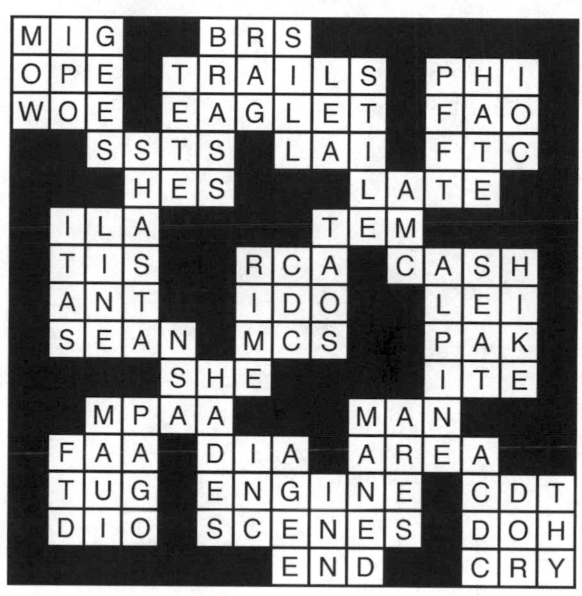

Diagramless 15

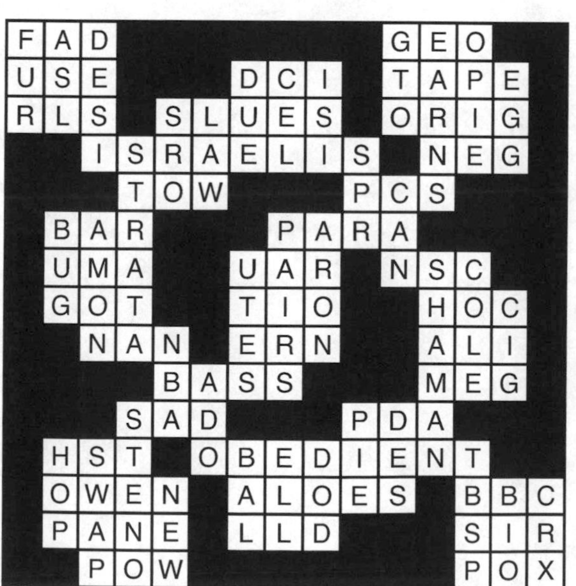

Diagramless 16

Chapter 11: Double Scrambles

Some Canines

- HOTEL
- THINK
- ENJOY
- THANK
- EAGLE

TEETH

Rosetta Stone Language

- GRACE
- EATEN
- KNIFE
- EIGHT
- ROMAN

GREEK

Worthless Wheels

- MERCY
- LAUGH
- EMPTY
- NERVE
- OASIS

LEMON

Conversation Starter

- LIGHT
- HANDY
- LEARN
- ENEMY
- OCEAN

HELLO

Diametrically Opposite

- ONION
- ALIVE
- LASSO
- PLANT
- RANCH

POLAR

Dining Room Staple

- TORCH
- LEVEL
- ESSAY
- BLEND
- ANKLE

TABLE

Uncle Sam Feature

- APRON
- BERRY
- DIRTY
- RADIO
- EQUAL

BEARD

Cheese Choice

- STAFF
- SCARE
- IMAGE
- WORRY
- STEAK

SWISS

'70S Hot Spot

- IDEAS
- SILKY
- DOLLY
- ORGAN
- CRAFT

DISCO

First Anniversary Gift

- PILOT
- ALOUD
- ROYAL
- PEACE
- ELDER

PAPER

One of the Deadly Sins

- RIGID
- DOZEN
- EVENT
- PULSE
- IDEAL

PRIDE

Out of Practice

- RAPID
- SIGHT
- TASTE
- YACHT
- UNION

RUSTY

Syrup Source

- LABOR
- ALARM
- EXACT
- PANIC
- MAGIC

MAPLE

Cold Covering

- SUPER
- RATIO
- TEMPO
- FLOOR
- ORBIT

FROST

Up on a Map

- NIGHT
- OUNCE
- TEACH
- HAPPY
- RELAX

NORTH

Give a Hoot

- SHAPE
- OLIVE
- TIGER
- USUAL
- HONEY

SHOUT

Tot Watcher

- ADDED
- NOVEL
- YIELD
- NOISE
- NEVER

NANNY

Prepare for Surgery

- RHYME
- UPPER
- COLOR
- BACON
- SEVEN

SCRUB

It's Stuck in the Corner

- MINOR
- ARRAY
- PANEL
- TEASE
- SPILL

STAMP

Three, They Say

- RAZOR
- DREAM
- WRECK
- COMIC
- OFTEN

CROWD

Pasta Topper

- UNTIL
- CHEEK
- SCORE
- AFTER
- ENTER

SAUCE

Classroom or Poolroom Item

- KNELT
- HAUNT
- LODGE
- ARISE
- CHOIR

CHALK

Grown-Up Kids

- GREAT
- ALIEN
- OTHER
- THIEF
- STEEP

GOATS

Fable Finale

- AGENT
- RIVER
- MOVIE
- OPERA
- LARGE

MORAL

Charlie Chaplin Persona

- PITCH
- ANGEL
- MAJOR
- REACH
- TIMID

TRAMP

Rocker Site

- READY
- OCCUR
- HOUSE
- POINT
- CHAIR

PORCH

Tie the Knot

- ROAST
- MAYBE
- YOUTH
- AGAIN
- ROBIN

MARRY

Surgeon's Assistant

- EARLY
- NOBLE
- RURAL
- UNCLE
- SLEEP

NURSE

Like Some Talk

- SLIDE
- LINEN
- LOCAL
- AWAKE
- MEDAL

SMALL

Sister's Attire

- HEAVY
- ISSUE
- AGREE
- BREAD
- THEME

HABIT

Weather Woe

- SNAIL
- MUMMY
- TENTH
- OILED
- ROUTE

STORM

One of the Senses

- MARCH
- EAGER
- LEGAL
- LIMIT
- SKATE

SMELL

Field's Partner

- KEEPS
- CAMEL
- TOWEL
- RADAR
- ALONE

TRACK

Pleasing to the Palate

- YOUNG
- ABOVE
- TENSE
- SPELL
- THICK

TASTY

Military Bigwigs

- BRIEF
- ANNOY
- SPADE
- SOLID
- RANGE

BRASS

Come Out of One's Shell

- HEART
- ARROW
- THUMB
- HOBBY
- CORAL

HATCH

Fuzzy Fruit

- EASEL
- PAINT
- HORSE
- ATLAS
- COUGH

PEACH

Bouquet Tosser

- RIVAL
- EDGES
- INNER
- DRINK
- BOARD

BRIDE

Political Group

- TOPIC
- RAISE
- YEARS
- PHONE
- ATTIC

PARTY

Funny Business

- ROBOT
- OFFER
- UTTER
- MONEY
- HEARD

HUMOR

It's a Fact

- TRIAL
- REPLY
- HUMAN
- TRAIL
- UPSET

TRUTH

Pulitzer Prize Category

- DOUBT
- APPLE
- AHEAD
- REACT
- METAL

DRAMA

Lighter Alternative

- ALERT
- TIMER
- MAYOR
- CANOE
- HONOR

MATCH

Get Rid Of

- HILLY
- DRIFT
- TAXES
- IRONS
- CHINA

DITCH

Rose Feature

- HERBS
- ORDER
- RELAY
- TODAY
- NOUNS

THORN

Not on Deck

- WHALE
- BASIN
- ELBOW
- LABEL
- OWNER

BELOW

Kind of Blockade

- LITER
- NOSEY
- VITAL
- ABOUT
- ANGER

NAVAL

Fire Starter

- SPEND
- ADULT
- KNOWN
- ROCKY
- POWER

SPARK

Sudoku 1

4	9	3	8	7	2	1	5	6
1	5	2	9	3	6	4	8	7
8	7	6	4	5	1	9	2	3
7	6	5	1	2	8	3	9	4
9	8	4	7	6	3	5	1	2
3	2	1	5	4	9	6	7	8
6	1	7	2	9	4	8	3	5
2	4	8	3	1	5	7	6	9
5	3	9	6	8	7	2	4	1

Sudoku 2

8	9	4	3	7	1	5	6	2
2	1	5	4	8	6	3	9	7
6	7	3	9	5	2	4	8	1
9	2	1	6	4	3	7	5	8
3	5	6	7	1	8	9	2	4
7	4	8	5	2	9	1	3	6
5	8	2	1	3	4	6	7	9
1	6	7	8	9	5	2	4	3
4	3	9	2	6	7	8	1	5

Sudoku 3

6	4	1	2	8	7	5	3	9
3	9	8	1	4	5	2	6	7
5	2	7	6	9	3	4	8	1
7	6	9	4	3	8	1	2	5
4	1	3	9	5	2	6	7	8
2	8	5	7	6	1	3	9	4
8	7	6	5	2	4	9	1	3
9	3	4	8	1	6	7	5	2
1	5	2	3	7	9	8	4	6

Sudoku 4

7	5	4	9	6	3	1	8	2
9	2	1	8	7	4	6	5	3
3	6	8	1	5	2	9	7	4
1	4	5	7	3	6	8	2	9
2	9	6	5	4	8	3	1	7
8	7	3	2	1	9	5	4	6
4	3	2	6	8	5	7	9	1
6	8	7	4	9	1	2	3	5
5	1	9	3	2	7	4	6	8

Sudoku 5

6	5	7	9	3	4	8	2	1
9	1	4	7	2	8	5	6	3
2	3	8	1	5	6	9	7	4
5	6	3	4	8	1	2	9	7
7	8	9	2	6	3	4	1	5
1	4	2	5	7	9	6	3	8
8	9	6	3	4	7	1	5	2
3	2	1	8	9	5	7	4	6
4	7	5	6	1	2	3	8	9

Sudoku 6

7	4	5	3	1	6	8	2	9
1	6	2	9	8	5	4	7	3
3	9	8	2	7	4	5	6	1
9	8	7	6	4	3	2	1	5
4	3	1	5	2	8	7	9	6
2	5	6	7	9	1	3	4	8
8	2	9	1	5	7	6	3	4
6	1	4	8	3	2	9	5	7
5	7	3	4	6	9	1	8	2

Sudoku 7

8	1	3	7	2	6	4	5	9
4	7	6	5	8	9	1	2	3
5	9	2	4	1	3	7	8	6
6	2	8	3	9	1	5	4	7
1	4	9	8	7	5	3	6	2
7	3	5	6	4	2	8	9	1
2	8	1	9	3	4	6	7	5
3	5	7	2	6	8	9	1	4
9	6	4	1	5	7	2	3	8

Sudoku 8

5	6	1	8	3	9	4	7	2
2	8	7	1	4	5	6	3	9
4	3	9	6	7	2	5	8	1
6	2	8	3	9	7	1	5	4
9	1	5	4	2	8	7	6	3
7	4	3	5	6	1	2	9	8
1	7	2	9	5	3	8	4	6
3	5	6	2	8	4	9	1	7
8	9	4	7	1	6	3	2	5

Sudoku 9

1	5	2	9	8	4	6	7	3
3	9	7	2	5	6	4	1	8
4	6	8	1	3	7	2	5	9
7	2	3	5	9	8	1	6	4
6	4	9	7	1	3	8	2	5
5	8	1	4	6	2	9	3	7
9	7	4	3	2	1	5	8	6
8	1	5	6	7	9	3	4	2
2	3	6	8	4	5	7	9	1

Sudoku 10

1	7	6	5	9	4	8	3	2
2	9	4	8	1	3	7	6	5
8	3	5	7	2	6	9	1	4
5	1	2	6	4	8	3	9	7
4	8	9	2	3	7	1	5	6
3	6	7	9	5	1	4	2	8
9	2	8	3	7	5	6	4	1
7	5	1	4	6	9	2	8	3
6	4	3	1	8	2	5	7	9

Sudoku 11

6	9	4	5	3	7	1	2	8
2	5	3	4	8	1	7	9	6
1	8	7	2	9	6	5	3	4
4	3	8	9	1	5	6	7	2
5	1	2	7	6	8	9	4	3
7	6	9	3	4	2	8	1	5
9	2	1	6	5	4	3	8	7
3	4	6	8	7	9	2	5	1
8	7	5	1	2	3	4	6	9

Sudoku 12

1	3	4	8	5	7	6	9	2
5	9	2	1	3	6	4	8	7
6	8	7	9	2	4	3	5	1
4	6	3	7	1	5	9	2	8
8	1	9	3	4	2	7	6	5
2	7	5	6	9	8	1	4	3
7	4	8	2	6	1	5	3	9
3	2	6	5	7	9	8	1	4
9	5	1	4	8	3	2	7	6

Sudoku 13

4	7	3	1	9	2	5	6	8
5	6	9	4	8	7	2	1	3
1	8	2	5	3	6	7	9	4
8	4	7	6	5	1	3	2	9
2	3	1	9	7	8	6	4	5
9	5	6	3	2	4	8	7	1
7	9	5	2	1	3	4	8	6
3	2	4	8	6	9	1	5	7
6	1	8	7	4	5	9	3	2

Sudoku 14

5	2	9	4	3	7	1	6	8
4	8	3	2	1	6	5	9	7
6	7	1	9	5	8	4	3	2
9	1	6	7	8	2	3	4	5
7	5	2	3	6	4	9	8	1
8	3	4	1	9	5	2	7	6
3	4	5	8	7	1	6	2	9
1	9	8	6	2	3	7	5	4
2	6	7	5	4	9	8	1	3

Sudoku 15

4	9	1	3	8	6	2	5	7
5	7	6	4	1	2	9	8	3
3	2	8	5	7	9	4	1	6
8	4	9	1	3	7	5	6	2
1	5	2	9	6	4	3	7	8
7	6	3	2	5	8	1	4	9
2	8	4	6	9	1	7	3	5
6	1	5	7	2	3	8	9	4
9	3	7	8	4	5	6	2	1

Sudoku 16

3	7	4	1	2	6	5	9	8
9	5	2	8	4	7	1	3	6
8	1	6	3	9	5	7	4	2
6	2	7	9	3	8	4	1	5
5	3	1	6	7	4	8	2	9
4	8	9	5	1	2	3	6	7
2	9	8	4	5	3	6	7	1
1	6	3	7	8	9	2	5	4
7	4	5	2	6	1	9	8	3

Chapter 13: Cryptoquotes

Cryptoquote 1

Farming looks mighty easy when your plow is a pencil and you're a thousand miles from the corn field.

—Dwight Eisenhower

Cryptoquote 2

Sometimes your joy is the source of your smile, but sometimes your smile can be the source of your joy.

—Thich Nhat Hanh

Cryptoquote 3

Most truths are so naked that people feel sorry for them and cover them up, at least a little bit.

Edward R. Murrow

Cryptoquote 4

If tyranny and oppression come to this land, it will be in the guise of fighting a foreign enemy.

—James Madison

Cryptoquote 5

A painter is a man who paints what he sells. An artist, however, is a man that sells what he paints.

—Pablo Picasso

Cryptoquote 6

The grand essentials of happiness are: something to do, something to love, and something to hope for.

—Allan K. Chalmers

Cryptoquote 7

My doctor told me to stop having intimate dinners for four. Unless there are three other people.

—Orson Welles

Cryptoquote 8

The test of literature is, I suppose, whether we ourselves live more intensely for the reading of it.

—Elizabeth Drew

Cryptoquote 9

A tyrant is always stirring up some war or other, in order that the people may require a leader.

—Plato

Cryptoquote 10

I don't want to achieve immortality through my work; I want to achieve immortality through not dying.

—Woody Allen

Cryptoquote 11

A shoe that fits one person pinches another; there is no recipe for living that suits all cases.

—Carl Jung

Cryptoquote 12

These days people seek knowledge, not wisdom. Knowledge is of the past, wisdom is of the future.

—Vernon Cooper

Cryptoquote 13

Be not afraid of life. Believe that life is worth living, and your belief will help create the fact.

—Henry James

Cryptoquote 14

How is it that little children are so intelligent and men so stupid? It must be education that does it.

—Alexandre Dumas

Cryptoquote 15

I do not want the peace that passeth understanding. I want the understanding which bringeth peace.

—Helen Keller

Cryptoquote 16

There are perhaps no days of our childhood we lived so fully as those we spent with a favorite book.

—Marcel Proust

Cryptoquote 17

If my doctor told me I had only six minutes to live, I wouldn't brood. I'd type a little faster.

—Isaac Asimov

Cryptoquote 18

Ultimately the bond of all companionship, whether in marriage or in friendship, is conversation.

—Oscar Wilde

Cryptoquote 19

I think it's the duty of the comedian to find out where the line is drawn and cross it deliberately.

—George Carlin

Cryptoquote 20

The man who reads nothing at all is better educated than the man who reads nothing but newspapers.

—Thomas Jefferson

Cryptoquote 21

Nearly all men can stand adversity, but if you want to test a man's character, give him power.

—Abraham Lincoln

Cryptoquote 22

I have found the paradox that if I love until it hurts, then there is no hurt, but only more love.

—Mother Teresa

Cryptoquote 23

There are two kinds of failures: those who thought and never did, and those who did and never thought.

—Laurence Peter

Cryptoquote 24

No tears in the writer, no tears in the reader. No surprise in the writer, no surprise in the reader.

—Robert Frost

Cryptoquote 25

Do not dwell in the past, do not dream of the future, concentrate the mind on the present moment.

—Buddha

Cryptoquote 26

Kindness is more important than wisdom, and the recognition of this is the beginning of wisdom.

—Theodore Rubin

Cryptoquote 27

Creativity is a type of learning process where the teacher and pupil are located in the same individual.

—Arthur Koestler

Cryptoquote 28

Decision by democratic majority vote is a fine form of government, but it's a stinking way to create.

—Lillian Hellman

Cryptoquote 29

True religion is real living; living with all one's soul, with all one's goodness and righteousness.

—Albert Einstein

Cryptoquote 30

Men are born with two eyes, but only one tongue, in order that they should see twice as much as they say.

—Charles Caleb Colton

Cryptoquote 31

If you want others to be happy, practice compassion. If you want to be happy, practice compassion.

—Dalai Lama

Cryptoquote 32

One of the advantages of being disorderly is that one is constantly making exciting discoveries.

—A. A. Milne

Cryptoquote 33

When you have only two pennies left in the world, buy a loaf of bread with one, and a lily with the other.

—Chinese proverb

Cryptoquote 34

I'm all in favor of keeping dangerous weapons out of the hands of fools. Let's start with typewriters.

—Frank Lloyd Wright

Cryptoquote 35

I have learned silence from the talkative, tolerance from the intolerant and kindness from the unkind.

—Kahlil Gibran

Cryptoquote 36

Life does not cease to be funny when people die any more than it ceases to be serious when people laugh.

—George Bernard Shaw

Printed in the United States
by Baker & Taylor Publisher Services